PC-KIMMO:
A Two-level Processor for
Morphological Analysis

by   Evan L. Antworth

Summer Institute of Linguistics

Occasional Publications in Academic Computing
Number 16

Occasional Publications in Academic Computing is a series devoted to publishing computer software and documentation deemed useful to those carrying out field projects in linguistics, literacy, anthropology, and translation.

Series Editor Gary F. Simons   *Assistant Editors* Linda L. Simons
Priscilla M. Kew

PC-KIMMO:
A Two-level Processor for
Morphological Analysis

by   Evan L. Antworth

Summer Institute of Linguistics
Dallas, Texas

ISBN: 0-88312-639-7

ISSN: 1041-1054

Editorial correspondence: Academic Computing Department
                               Summer Institute of Linguistics
                               7500 W. Camp Wisdom Road
                               Dallas, TX 75236 USA

Distributed by: International Academic Bookstore
                               Summer Institute of Linguistics
                               7500 W. Camp Wisdom Road
                               Dallas, TX 75236 USA
                               214/709-2404

CONTENTS

FIGURES

ACKNOWLEDGEMENTS

Despite the fact that this book appears with a single author's name on it, the PC-KIMMO project has involved a number of individuals. In 1985, after learning about Koskenniemi's two-level processor, Gary Simons envisioned a project that would implement a version of it on personal computers, thus making it available to field linguists. The coding of the original version of PC-KIMMO was done by David Smith under Simons's direction. In the fall of 1986, Simons taught a conference course on computational morphology at the University of Texas at Arlington for Dan Boerger and Greg Lyons. A similar course was held in the spring of 1988 for Steve Echerd and Evan Antworth. As these students used PC-KIMMO in their term projects, it was debugged and enhanced in response to their suggestions. In 1989, Stephen McConnel took Smith's original program and extensively revised it, changing the user interface and adding many new features.

In 1989, Antworth started work on this book with input from Simons, Echerd, Smith, and McConnel. Some of the material in chapters 1 and 3 was drawn from course notes prepared by Simons, who also edited the entire book. Chapters 2, 4, and 5 incorporate material originally developed by Echerd. Dave Smith wrote a reference manual for the original version of the program, but due to massive changes in the program, the manual was rewritten by Antworth and now appears as chapter 7. The sample language descriptions on the release diskette are due to Antworth, with help from Echerd on the English description. Special thanks go to Jonathan Kew and Steve McConnel, who made typesetting this book in TEX possible.

Chapter

1

INTRODUCTION

1.1 What is PC-KIMMO?

PC-KIMMO is a computer program that uses a linguist's description of the phonology and morphology of a natural language to recognize and generate words in that language. It is a new implementation for microcomputers of a program dubbed KIMMO after its inventor Kimmo Koskenniemi, a Finnish computational linguist. PC-KIMMO is especially aimed at the field linguist who wants to develop and test a morphological description of the language he is studying. The purpose of this book is to show how this can be done.

PC-KIMMO provides a general computational machine that executes a language description written by the user. The structure of the language-specific description is based on the linguistic distinction between *phonology,* the study of sound structure, and *morphology,* the study of word structure. (It should be noted that the term "morphological" as it is used in the title of this book and occasionally in the text is intended in a general sense to include both phonology and morphology as they have just been defined.) Phonological analysis of a language identifies the set of significant speech sounds, called *phonemes,* and specifies rules governing alternations between phonemes in certain contexts (often called *morphophonemic* alternation). For the purposes of practical natural language processing, the same techniques apply to the analysis of words written in a language's standard *orthography* or writing system, where instead of phonemes and phonological rules we speak of characters and spelling rules. Morphological analysis identifies the set of minimal meaningful units, called *morphemes,* that compose words, and specifies constraints on the relative order of morphemes in a word (such constraints are called *morphotactic* constraints or rules). A PC-KIMMO description of a language consists of two files provided by the user:

- a *rules* file, which specifies the alphabet and the phonological (or spelling) rules, and
- a *lexicon* file, which lists lexical items (words and morphemes) and their glosses, and encodes morphotactic constraints.

The theoretical model of phonology embodied in PC-KIMMO is called *two-level* phonology. In the two-level approach, phonology is treated as the correspondence between the *lexical level* of underlying representation of words and their realization on the *surface level.* The two functional components of PC-KIMMO are the *generator* and the *recognizer.* The generator accepts as input a lexical form, applies the phonological rules, and returns the corresponding surface form. It does not use the lexicon. The recognizer accepts as input a surface form, applies the phonological

Default file names and extensions

rules file:	RULES.RUL
	*.RUL
lexicon file:	LEXICON.LEX
	*.LEX
generation comparison file:	DATA.GEN
	*.GEN
recognition comparison file:	DATA.REC
	*.REC
pairs comparison file:	DATA.PAI
	*.PAI
take file:	PCKIMMO.TAK
	*.TAK
log file:	PCKIMMO.LOG

Semantics of two-level rules

L:S ⇒ E   "Only but not always."

L is realized as S only in E.
L realized as S is not allowed in ~E.
If L:S, then it must be in E.
Implies L:~S in E is permitted.

L:S ⇐ E   "Always but not only."

L is always realized as S in E.
L realized as ~S is not allowed in E.
If L is in E, then it must be L:S.
Implies L:S may occur elsewhere.

L:S ⇔ E   "Always and only."

L is realized as S only and always in E.
Both L:S ⇒ E and L:S ⇐ E.
Implies L:S is obligatory in E and occurs nowhere else.

L:S /⇐ E   "Never."

L is never realized as S in E.
L realized as S is not allowed in E.
If L is in E, then it must be L:~S.

Truth tables for two-level rules

There is an L.		Is the rule satisfied?			
Is it realized as S?	Is it in E?	L:S ⇒ E	L:S ⇐ E	L:S ⇔ E	L:S /⇐ E
T	T	T	T	T	F
T	F	F	T	F	T
F	T	T	F	F	T
F	F	T	T	T	T

PC-KIMMO Quick Help

Command line format: pckimmo [-c *char*] [-r *rulefile*] [-l *lexfile*] [-t *cmdfile*]

PC-KIMMO commands

Square brackets indicate optional elements.
{ x | y } indicates either x or y.
Elements in italics are replaced with instances of that type.
Command keywords are not case sensitive and can be shortened to any unambiguous form.

?	display list of commands
Help [*command-name*]	display description of command
New	erase all currently loaded rules or lexicon
Load Rules [*filename*]	load a new rules file
Load Lexicon [*filename*]	load a new lexicon file
Generate [*lexical-form*]	process lexical form to produce surface form
Recognize [*surface-form*]	process surface form to produce lexical form
[File] Compare Generate [*filename*]	generate and compare surface forms from a file
[File] Compare Recognize [*filename*]	recognize and compare lexical forms from a file
[File] Compare Pairs [*filename*]	analyze and compare both surface and lexical forms from a file
File Generate filename1 [*filename2*]	read lexical forms from a file, generate surface forms
File Recognize filename1 [*filename2*]	read surface forms from a file, recognize lexical forms
Set Rules {on	off} {all	*numbers*}	turn selected rules on/off
Set Comment *char*	set comment delimiter character
Set Limit {on	off}	turn limit output mode on/off
Set Timing {on	off}	turn timing mode on/off
Set Tracing {on	off	0	1	2	3}	turn tracing mode on/off, set level
Set Verbose {on	off}	turn verbose comparison mode on/off
List Pairs	display list of feasible pairs
List Rules	display rule names, on/off status
List Lexicon	display sublexicon names
Show Rule [*number*]	display a rule's column headers and feasible pairs
Show Lexicon [*name*]	display contents of a sublexicon
[Show] Status	display filenames and system flags
Log [*filename*]	open a log file
Close	close the current log file
Take *filename*	read PC-KIMMO commands from a file
Edit *filename*	edit a file
System [*command*]	execute an operating system command (synonym: !)
Exit	exit PC-KIMMO (same as Quit)
Quit	exit PC-KIMMO (same as Exit)

rules, consults the lexicon, and returns the corresponding lexical form with its gloss. Figure 1.1 shows the main components of the PC-KIMMO system.

Figure 1.1 Main components of PC-KIMMO

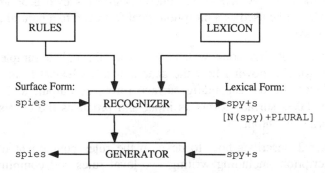

Around the components of PC-KIMMO shown in figure 1.1 is an interactive shell program that serves as a user interface. When the PC-KIMMO shell is run, a command-line prompt appears on the screen. The user types in commands which PC-KIMMO executes. The shell is designed to provide an environment for developing, testing, and debugging two-level descriptions. Among the features available in the user shell are:

- on-line help;
- commands for loading the rules and lexicon files;
- ability to generate and recognize forms entered interactively from the keyboard;
- a mechanism for reading input forms from a test list on a disk file and comparing the output of the processor to the correct results supplied in the test list;
- provision for logging user sessions to disk files;
- a facility to trace execution of the processor in order to debug the rules and lexicon;
- other debugging facilities including the ability to turn off selected rules, show the internal representation of rules, and show the contents of selected parts of the lexicon; and
- a batch processing mode that allows the shell to read and execute commands from a disk file.

Because the PC-KIMMO user shell is intended to facilitate development of a description, its data-processing capabilities are limited. This is in keeping with our focus on doing field analysis with PC-KIMMO. However, PC-KIMMO can also be put to practical use by those engaged in natural language processing. The PC-KIMMO functions are available as a source code library that can be included in another program. This means that the user can develop and debug a two-level description using the PC-KIMMO shell and then link PC-KIMMO's functions into his own program. Thus PC-KIMMO can be used as a morphological front end to a natural language processing system.

Chapter 2 of this book walks the reader through a sample session with PC-KIMMO, showing how the generator takes lexical forms as input and produces the corresponding surface forms as output, and how the recognizer takes surface forms as input and produces the corresponding lexical forms as output.

Chapter 3 describes how to develop the rules component of a two-level description, including writing two-level rules and compiling them into state tables. We recommend writing the rules file first because it can be developed and tested before the lexicon file is created. Chapter 4 then describes how to develop the lexical component.

Chapter 5 covers strategies for testing and debugging a two-level description. It explains how to use PC-KIMMO's debugging facilities such as tracing.

Chapter 6 focuses on phonology and illustrates how two-level rules are written and compiled into state tables for common processes like vowel harmony, reciprocal assimilation, coalescence, nasalization, deletion, insertion, stress placement, tonal change, and even nonconcatenative processes such as gemination, degemination, metathesis, infixation, and reduplication.

Chapter 7 is a reference manual for the PC-KIMMO program. It documents the user interface, the commands, input file formats, trace formats, and error messages. It also describes the underlying algorithms used by the generator and recognizer functions.

As an extended example of how to write a PC-KIMMO description, appendix A incrementally develops a description of English spelling. To illustrate that the two-level model is more of a general-purpose tool than a linguistic theory, appendix B shows how PC-KIMMO's two-level processor can be applied to other two-level problems such as phonotactic analysis, historical sound change, and solving a logic problem. Finally, appendix C documents PC-KIMMO's source code function library and shows how to include the PC-KIMMO functions in another program.

The PC-KIMMO release diskette contains the executable PC-KIMMO program, the function library, and examples of PC-KIMMO descriptions for various languages, including English, Finnish, Japanese, Hebrew, Kasem, Tagalog, and Turkish. These are not comprehensive linguistic descriptions, rather they cover only a selected set of data.

The rest of this chapter distinguishes KIMMO, the general processor specified in Koskenniemi 1983a and Karttunen 1983, from PC-KIMMO, our implementation for personal computers. Section 1.2 traces the history of KIMMO, culminating with a description of how PC-KIMMO was developed. Section 1.3 discusses the significance of KIMMO for linguistic theory and the field of natural language processing. These sections are not crucial to understanding and using the rest of the book. Readers may find they make more sense after working through the tutorial material in chapters 2 through 6.

1.2   The history of PC-KIMMO

The natural language processing branch of artificial intelligence and computational linguistics has traditionally concerned itself with syntax to the virtual exclusion of morphology. The basic reason for this is a pragmatic one—the economically dominant languages of the world (for which the vast majority of computational linguistics research is funded) have relatively simple morphologies. Implementors of natural language processing systems for these languages have been able to handle the morphology by storing all inflected forms in the lexicon, or by using pattern-matching techniques to strip off common affixes. Morphophonemic alternation, if addressed at all, has typically been taken care of by *ad hoc* procedures coded directly in the computer programming language. These methods were designed to work only for the language of interest—the investigators made no claims of general theoretical interest about their methods.

Computational morphology began to emerge as a discipline in its own right about ten years ago with two projects that sought to build production-quality morphological processors for agglutinative non-Indo-European languages. The first project, developed by David Weber and William Mann, was designed to translate texts in one dialect of the Quechua language family of Peru into other dialects of the same family—a method they called computer-assisted dialect adaptation or CADA (Weber and Mann 1979). Since the bulk of Quechua grammar is in the morphology, the heart of their system was a processor that analyzes and synthesizes Quechua words. A production version for field use on personal computers was then developed (Kasper and Weber 1986a, 1986b). From these early versions, which had much language-specific knowledge hardcoded into the programs, the team headed by Weber has now developed a fully generalized system for personal computers in which all the language-specific information is contained in rule and lexicon files provided by the user. The system has two main components: AMPLE, a morphological parser (Weber and others 1988), and STAMP, the synthesis and transfer component (Weber and others 1990).

The other major project in computational morphology came from Finland, a country that combines (perhaps uniquely) an advanced academic and technological society with a language that has complex morphology. Being of the Finno-Ugric language family, Finnish has a far more complex morphological system than its Indo-European neighbors—a noun can have some 2,000 inflected forms, and a verb can have over 12,000 (Koskenniemi 1985a:20). Natural language processing systems for Finnish could get nowhere without first accounting for its morphology. Over the past decade, the Finnish National Fund for Research and Development (SITRA) has sponsored several projects to develop computational models for the interpretation and generation of written Finnish. Several generalized models for computational morphology have resulted, for instance Jäppinen's associative model (Jäppinen and Ylilammi 1986).

However, the model that has attracted the most attention in academic circles has been Kimmo Koskenniemi's two-level model. The two-level model implements phonological rules as *finite state transducers*. Johnson (1972) observed that a set of simultaneous phonological rules (as opposed to sequentially ordered rules) could be represented as a finite state transducer. In an unpublished conference paper, Ronald Kaplan and Martin Kay (1981) suggested that the ordered rules of generative phonology could be implemented computationally as a cascading sequence of finite state transducers. (Kay 1983, pages 100–104, is the only published account of these ideas.) It is a well-known result of automata theory that such a sequence of automata can always be combined into a single (typically very large) automaton with the same output. They went on to observe that a system of ordered rules could be reduced to a single automaton that would produce surface output very efficiently, specifically, in time linearly proportional to the length of the input string.

In trying to apply this idea to the development of a working system, Koskenniemi found that the combined automaton got prohibitively large. He decided instead to model the phonological rules as a bank of automata running in parallel. This had an important effect on the nature of the rules. No longer could there be intermediate levels of representation as in generative phonology. Instead, there could be only two levels; all rules had to map directly from the underlying level to the surface level. In this respect Koskenniemi developed a model that was in tune with theories like natural phonology, which rejected the arbitrariness and unconstrained power of ordered rules and intermediate levels. Koskenniemi described his two-level model in a series of publications (Koskenniemi 1983a, 1983b, 1984, 1985a, 1985b, and Karlsson and Koskenniemi 1985).

Koskenniemi's original work sparked a lot of follow-up work. Volume 22 of the *Texas Linguistic Forum* is a collection of papers on the two-level model. It includes an introduction to the two-level model, a description (including source code) of a LISP implementation, and two-level descriptions of English, Rumanian, French, and Japanese. Karttunen called this implementation KIMMO; the name has stuck ever since. Bear 1986 proposes some enhancements to the model. Barton and others 1987 shows that the original claim of Koskenniemi—that the two-level processor runs in linear time—is mistaken; in fact KIMMO uses an exponential algorithm, since at each point in a parse (or a generation) there are as many paths to explore as there are alternations involving the current surface (or lexical) symbol. Koskenniemi and Church 1988 responds to this. Dalrymple and others 1987 describes DKIMMO/TWOL, which is implemented in the INTERLISP/D environment on Xerox workstations. The key innovation of this implementation is that it accepts two-level rules written in linguistic notation and automatically compiles them into finite state transducers. The documentation describes the algorithm for converting rules into regular expressions. A prepackaged regular expression compiler does the final conversion to finite state machines.

Work on the implementation described in this book, called PC-KIMMO, was begun in 1985. It follows the specifications of the LISP implementation in Karttunen 1983. The aim was to develop a version of KIMMO for field linguists that would run on an IBM PC-compatible computer and that would include an environment for testing and debugging a linguistic description. The PC-KIMMO program is actually a shell program that serves as an interactive user interface to the PC-KIMMO generation and recognition functions. These functions are available as a source code library that can be included in a program written by the user (see appendix C). The coding has been done in the C language by David Smith and Stephen McConnel under the direction of Gary Simons and under the auspices of the Summer Institute of Linguistics. For technical information on PC-KIMMO, see section 7.1.

1.3 The significance of PC-KIMMO

The preceding section on the history of KIMMO shows that it was developed primarily as a tool for natural language processing, not as a linguistic theory of phonology and morphology (for a discussion of tools versus theories, see Shieber 1986, page 38). Unlike a phonological theory, KIMMO makes no attempt to characterize the class of possible natural-language phonological phenomena, nor does it provide a means to evaluate competing descriptions. Rather, KIMMO is an abstract computing machine that can be used for a variety of purposes, including of course phonological description. However, unlike some computational approaches to phonology and morphology, KIMMO was deliberately constructed to reflect the most generally accepted aspects of phonology, namely: (1) there are two levels of phonological representation, an underlying level and a surface level, and (2) the two levels are related to each other by rules. Though KIMMO was developed as a tool, it puts constraints on the kinds of phonological theories that can be modeled with it. The model of two-level phonology that emerges from the finite-state approach to phonology turns out to be significantly different from standard generative phonology. In this respect KIMMO makes theoretical claims about the nature of phonology that challenge the prevailing paradigm of generative phonology.

1.3.1 The two-level model versus generative phonology

In generative phonology, the application of sequential rules creates intermediate levels of representation. Standard generative phonology has also claimed that rule ordering is necessary to provide expressive power adequate to describe natural-language phonological processes. In KIMMO, rules are neither ordered nor sequential; they apply in parallel, that is, simultaneously. This means that no intermediate levels are created as an artifact of rule application; thus the name two-level rules. While parallel two-level rules are in principle less powerful than sequentially ordered rules, they gain power by virtue of how they use environments. In generative rules, only the immediate, local environment at each stage of the derivation is available, while two-level rules allow reference to both lexical (underlying or phonemic) and surface (phonetic) environments. Generative rules cannot "look back" at underlying environments or "look ahead" to surface environments. In contrast, the environments of two-level rules are stated as lexical-to-surface correspondences. For example, a two-level rule can easily refer to an underlying *a* which corresponds to a surface *b* or a surface *b* which corresponds to an underlying *a*. Whether two-level rules are adequate to handle all attested natural-language phonological phenomena is an empirical question. The descriptive examples in this book support the contention that they are indeed comparable in expressive power to generative rules.

Another theoretical claim that KIMMO makes has to do with the nature of the relationship between the two levels of phonological representation. In generative phonology, the surface level is derived from the underlying level by means of rules that transform or rewrite symbols. For instance, a rule of the form $a \longrightarrow b / x\_\_\_$ means that the underlying symbol a is rewritten as the surface symbol b in the environment following x. There are two important consequences of this type of rule. First, after underlying a is written as surface b, a is no longer available for use in any other rules—it no longer "exists." Second, generative rules can only apply in one direction, from underlying representation to surface representation. The rules cannot be reversed to go from surface to underlying representation. In linguistic theory generative rules are known as process rules. Process rules attempt to characterize the relationship between levels of representation by specifying how to transform representations from one level into representations on the other. In contrast, two-level rules express the relationship between the lexical and surface levels as a static correspondence. Rather than rewriting a as b, a two-level rule states that a lexical a corresponds to a surface b in the environment following x (where x is also a lexical-to-surface correspondence). The two-level rule does not change a into b, so a is available to other rules.

An important consequence of the static nature of two-level rules is that they apply in both directions, lexical to surface and surface to lexical. In linguistic terms, two-level rules are not process rules but more like the realization rules of stratificational linguistics (see Lamb 1964). The linguistic opposition between dynamic, process rules and static, realization rules is mirrored in computer science in the opposition between procedural and declarative programming. A procedural program is an ordered collection of operations to perform on some data objects; a declarative program merely states the relationships among the data objects. Many real-world phenomena can be understood better when described declaratively rather than procedurally. KIMMO, then, makes the claim that phonological rules should be implemented declaratively, as static, two-level rules, rather than procedurally, as process rules. An important consequence of using declarative rules is that a computational implementation of the two-level model such as PC-KIMMO can both generate and recognize words.

1.3.2 Levels of adequacy

Linguistic descriptions or grammars are evaluated in terms of three levels of adequacy (Chomsky 1964:28–29). A grammar is *observationally* adequate if it "presents the observed primary data correctly" (Chomsky 1964:28). A grammar is *descriptively* adequate if it "gives a correct account of the linguistic intuition of the native speaker, and specifies the observed data (in particular) in terms of significant generalizations that express underlying regularities in the language" (Chomsky 1964:28). Whereas observational and descriptive adequacy are applied primarily to grammars (descriptions) and only secondarily to general theories, *explanatory* adequacy applies only to general theories. It is achieved when a linguistic theory provides a means to choose one grammar that achieves descriptive adequacy over others. KIMMO, as a tool rather than a theory, is limited to observational and descriptive adequacy. Proponents of theories such as generative phonology claim greater degrees of adequacy than this, and thus tend to belittle descriptive formalisms that cannot attain the explanatory adequacy of a fully developed theory. Unfortunately, descriptions using generative phonology, though notationally explicit, have not proved to lend themselves easily to verification by machine. Thus, while debating the relative explanatory merits of various theories, linguistic theorists have tended to ignore the empirical question of the relative observational and descriptive adequacy of competing descriptions as applied to a large corpus of data.

From the viewpoint of natural language processing, a linguistic formalism must be evaluated not only in terms of levels of adequacy, but also according to whether it can be implemented computationally, and whether such an implementation is computationally tractable and effective. KIMMO, which implements phonological rules as finite state transducers, has proved to be computationally both tractable and effective. In addition (and in contrast to generative phonology), KIMMO's rules can be used for both generation and recognition, a capability important to natural language processing.

The result of using a formalism that can be computationally implemented is a new era in descriptive accountability. It is humanly difficult if not impossible to scan a set of phonological rules and determine if they actually do what the analyst claims they do. It is even more difficult to determine whether the set of rules works over a full corpus and not just the examples that the linguist has handpicked. But with KIMMO a phonological description can be tested mechanically by applying it to the data that it is intended to account for. Any errors or inconsistencies in the analysis will quickly be exposed. Thus, while a tool like KIMMO falls short of a theory in not being able to make claims about its explanatory adequacy, it goes beyond most theories in being able to mechanically verify the observational and descriptive adequacy of a description.

1.3.3 Limitations of PC-KIMMO

PC-KIMMO is not without its weaknesses and limitations. Some of these could be fixed fairly easily by improving the implementation, while others are inherent in the notion of finite state morphology itself. This section discusses areas where PC-KIMMO could be improved.

Notational felicity

Perhaps the most obvious weakness is in the matter of notation. In this book we first develop the model of two-level phonology using a rule notation that is similar to generative phonology. While it could be further enriched, it is easy to learn, and lends itself to felicitous description. Unfortunately, the PC-KIMMO program does not use this notation; rather, the user must translate, by hand, each two-level rule into a table of state transitions. These state tables directly represent the finite state transducers that actually do the work in PC-KIMMO. State tables are obviously not a felicitous notation for phonological rules. Chapter 3 of this book is mainly devoted to teaching the user how to translate two-level rules into state tables. This obstacle to using PC-KIMMO could be removed by the addition of a rule compiler—a program that takes two-level rules written in linguistic notation and converts them into state tables. A rule compiler would effectively hide the inner workings of PC-KIMMO's finite state machinery from the user, making PC-KIMMO more attractive to a wider circle of linguists. Such a rule compiler has been built for a large computer (see Dalrymple and others 1987). It remains to be seen if such a project is feasible for small computers.

Nonconcatenative morphology

A more serious objection to PC-KIMMO is whether the finite state approach to morphology is capable of handling complex types of morphology, particularly nonconcatenative morphology such as gemination, metathesis, infixation, and reduplication. Typical non-finite state solutions to problems like these involve variables that can copy (in generation) or match (in recognition) an element specified by a corresponding variable. Finite state machinery has no such mechanism for matching variables. However, the same effect can be achieved by enumerating all the possible phonological segments that result from the application of the processes. For example, if a language has a rule that geminates (doubles) any consonant that occurs in a certain environment, a finite state table that expresses the rule must include a column for every consonant and have enough states to enumerate the sequential pairing of each consonant only with itself. This is necessary because a finite state table cannot refer to the entire set of consonants with a variable name such as C and test for identity.

Chapter 6 of this book contains examples of how to write state tables for various nonconcatenative processes. While the state table notation is clumsy, these examples demonstrate that finite state machines are mathematically adequate to handle nonconcatenative processes; that is, the tables produce the correct results. Unfortunately, such tables often get very large and run slowly. Thus the finite state approach to nonconcatenative morphology suffers both in notational felicity and in computational efficiency. At present we offer no immediate solution to this problem, but future research may produce improvements in the way finite state morphology handles nonconcatenative processes. We should point out, however, that nonconcatenative morphology has been a perennial problem both for linguistic theory and for other approaches to natural language processing.

Nonlinear representations

Another limitation of PC-KIMMO is that its phonological representations are strictly unilinear; that is, all phonological elements must be represented as a single linear string of symbols. Suprasegmental elements such as stress, length, and tone must be represented as symbols interspersed with segmental elements at the same level. In recent years, linguists have developed nonlinear types of phonology, such as autosegmental phonology (see Goldsmith 1976), where suprasegmental elements are represented on one or more levels or tiers independent of the segmental level. Suprasegmental elements are mapped onto the segmental elements, providing a more felicitous formalism for phonological description. PC-KIMMO does not support nonlinear representation, and it is not clear how finite state phonology could be modified to do so. Thus PC-KIMMO suffers from the same limitations as other linear types of phonology, but in this respect is at least no worse off than, say, classical generative phonology.

Morphotactics

PC-KIMMO has both a phonological component, which applies phonological rules, and a lexical or morphological component, which stores lexical items and enforces morphotactic constraints. Together, the two components enable PC-KIMMO to generate and recognize words that are both phonologically and morphologically well-formed. However, PC-KIMMO's phonological component is better developed and more powerful than its lexical component. In other words, PC-KIMMO is much better at phonology than it is at morphology. PC-KIMMO's lexical component is weak in two main areas.

First, the lexical component encodes morphotactic information by specifying for each lexical item the class of items that can follow it. This simple approach seriously breaks down when there are cooccurrence restrictions among morphemes that are not contiguous to each other, since whole sublexicons must be duplicated in order to represent different morphotactic sequences. For example, consider how a description of English should allow the words *enrich* and *enrichment* but prohibit the nonword *richment.* Clearly the suffix *+ment* follows verbs such as *enrich* and not adjectives such as *rich.* In PC-KIMMO this can be expressed only indirectly by allowing a path through the lexicon where the morpheme sequence *en+* followed by a member of a class of adjectives can be followed by *+ment* while also providing another path where word-initial adjective roots cannot be followed by *+ment.* This means that the class of adjective roots must be duplicated in the lexicon, at a great cost in storage resources. The source of this problem lies in the fact that PC-KIMMO encodes morphotactic information directly in the lexical entries themselves. A better approach would be to state morphotactic constraints in rules that are separate from the listing of lexical entries.

Another problem with a word such as *enrichment* is that PC-KIMMO cannot determine the lexical class (part of speech) of the whole word. This is because the gloss of a recognized form is merely a concatenated string of the glosses of the morphemes that comprise the form. For example, the gloss of *enrichment* would be something like *VR+ADJ(rich)+NR* (that is, verbalizer, adjective root, nominalizer). But is it a verb, an adjective, or a noun? Because the gloss is a flat sequence of labels, it does not express the internal bracketed structure of the word, as would

$$[[en+ [rich]_{adj}]_{verb} +ment]_{noun}$$

The latter representation shows that at its outermost layer it is a noun. One solution to this problem is to get away from simply labeling morphemes and install a feature-based lexicon that builds up structures by means of unification. These feature-attribute structures can be effectively manipulated by a syntactic parser. Such a lexicon is described in Dalrymple and others 1987.

With respect to PC-KIMMO's relative strengths and weaknesses in the areas of phonology and morphology, it is revealing to compare PC-KIMMO with another approach to computational morphology that is easily accessible to the personal computer user, namely the AMPLE and STAMP system (Weber and others 1988, 1990) mentioned above in section 1.2. Whereas PC-KIMMO is strong in phonology and relatively weak in morphology, AMPLE and STAMP are strong in morphology and relatively weak in phonology. AMPLE and STAMP allow the user to encode a much more fine-grained morphotactic analysis than does PC-KIMMO. While PC-KIMMO allows one to state only what can follow a morpheme, AMPLE and STAMP have several mechanisms for encoding morphotactic constraints. On the phonology side, however, AMPLE and STAMP differ from PC-KIMMO in that they have no lexical level; that is, they make no use of underlying lexical representations of morphemes. Instead, all the alternants (allomorphs) of a morpheme must be explicitly listed in the lexicon, rather than listing only its underlying form and accounting for its alternants by general phonological rules, as PC-KIMMO does. (For a review of AMPLE from a linguistic point of view, see Simons 1989.)

1.3.4 Who is PC-KIMMO for?

Despite its limitations, PC-KIMMO is a significant development for the field of applied natural language processing. Up until now, implementations of the two-level model have been available only on large computers housed at academic or industrial research centers. As an implementation of the two-level model, PC-KIMMO is important because it makes the two-level processor available to individuals using personal computers. Computational linguists can use PC-KIMMO to investigate for themselves the properties of the two-level processor. Theoretical linguists can explore the implications of two-level phonology, while descriptive linguists can use PC-KIMMO as a field tool for developing and testing their phonological and morphological descriptions. Finally, because the source code for the PC-KIMMO's generator and recognizer functions is being made available, those developing natural language processing applications can use PC-KIMMO as a morphological front end to their own programs.

2

A SAMPLE USER SESSION WITH PC-KIMMO

In order to give a better feel for what the PC-KIMMO program does, we now demonstrate the process of using PC-KIMMO on a description of English. The English example we have constructed is based on standard orthography rather than actual phonological transcriptions. Its purpose is to account for alternate spellings of certain morphemes in specific environments. For example, the plural suffix for nouns has the alternants *s* and *es* as in *cats* versus *foxes*. To account for this, the lexicon contains a lexical entry for the plural suffix that has the form *+s* (where *+* symbolizes a morpheme boundary) and the rules component includes a rule that inserts an *e* in the environment after a stem-final *s*, *x*, *z*, *sh*, or *ch* and before the plural suffix *+s* (precisely, between the *+* and the *s*). Thus the lexical form *fox+s* will produce the surface form *foxes*. Notice that the rules required for describing orthographic alternations do not differ in kind from phonological rules.

But before exploring how PC-KIMMO handles English morphology, we must first attend to installing PC-KIMMO on your computer. (For more detailed information on installing, starting, and interacting with PC-KIMMO, see sections 7.2 through 7.4.)

2.1 Installing PC-KIMMO

Our focus in this book is on doing linguistics, not on how to use a computer. We thus assume a basic knowledge of the IBM PC computer (or compatible), the MS-DOS operating system commands, and how to use a text editor. If the instructions that follow here or elsewhere in the book are overwhelming to you, look in the documentation that came with your computer for definitions of computer terms and for instructions about how to use your operating system to do the necessary operations. When all else fails, ask someone for help!

To run the PC-KIMMO program, you need a computer that has at least 256K of memory and uses the MS-DOS or PC-DOS operating system, version 2.0 or higher. Any computer that is compatible with the IBM PC will run PC-KIMMO. (See section 7.1 regarding running PC-KIMMO under other operating systems.)

If your computer has floppy disks only, make a working copy of the PC-KIMMO diskette that came with this book. Store the original in a safe place. Insert your working copy of the PC-KIMMO release diskette in drive A of your machine.

If your computer has a hard disk, use the INSTALL.BAT procedure on the PC-KIMMO diskette to install the system on your hard disk. To do this, insert the PC-KIMMO diskette in one of your disk drives. Type *A:* (or whatever the name of the drive is) in order to log control to that disk. Now type *install* followed by the name of the hard disk drive on which you want to install PC-KIMMO. For instance, to install PC-KIMMO on drive C with the release diskette in drive A, type the following. (In this chapter, views of the computer screen are enclosed in boxes with material displayed on the screen printed in typewriter style.)

```
A:\install c:
```

This will create a subdirectory called PCKIMMO on your hard disk and copy the contents of the release diskette (with all its subdirectories) into it.

Whether you are using a floppy or hard disk system, the operating system's PATH variable must be set to include the directory where the PC-KIMMO program is found. The AUTOEXEC.BAT file on your boot disk should contain a path statement that specifies all the disks and directories that contain programs. On a floppy disk system, the path statement should include as a minimum the root directory of drive A, for instance, PATH=A:\. On a hard disk system, add ;C:\PCKIMMO to the end of the path statement. For the path statement to become effective, you must reboot the computer. (If you want to change the path variable without changing the AUTOEXEC.BAT file and rebooting, enter a path command directly at the operating system prompt. For information on how to enable the *edit* command, see section 7.2.)

2.2 Starting PC-KIMMO

Be sure that DOS is logged onto the drive where PC-KIMMO is located. To change to the subdirectory that contains the English example, enter *cd \english* on a floppy disk system, or *cd \pckimmo\english* on a hard disk system. Now type *pckimmo*. When PC-KIMMO has successfully started up, you will see a version message and the PC-KIMMO command line prompt:

```
PC-KIMMO TWO-LEVEL PROCESSOR
Version 1.0 (6 February 1990), Copyright 1990 SIL
Type ? for help
PC-KIMMO>
```

The user interacts with PC-KIMMO by entering commands at the prompt, in much the same way that one enters commands at the operating system prompt. To get a complete list of the possible commands, type *?*.

```
Command, one of the following:
close           compare         edit            exit
file            generate        help            list
load            log             new             quit
recognize       set             show            status
system          take
Type HELP for more help
```

To get a one-line summary of what each of these commands does, type *help*.

```
CLOSE       close the current log file
COMPARE     compare prepared data to results of processing data
EDIT        edit a file
EXIT        exit PC-KIMMO (same as QUIT)
...
For more information, type HELP with a specific command name.
```

To get the specific syntax for a command, type *help* plus a specific command name; for instance,

```
PC-KIMMO>help load
LOAD RULES [<file>]     loads a new rules file
LOAD LEXICON [<file>]   loads a new lexicon file
```

Case is ignored for all command keywords. Keywords can be shortened to any unambiguous form. For instance, *load rules*, *load rul*, *load r*, and *loa r* are all acceptable. Typing just *l* is ambiguous for the commands *load*, *log*, and *list*. However, because *load* is such a frequently used command, it takes special precedence over the other commands beginning with *l*, which means that typing just *l* will execute only the *load* command.

We will use the *load* command now to load the English rules and lexicon. First, type *load rules english.rul*; after the rules have been loaded, type *load lexicon english.lex*. (The *load* command also recognizes default file names and extensions; see section 7.7.8.) The screen should appear as it does below. Once the rules and lexicon are loaded, the generator and recognizer are ready to use.

```
PC-KIMMO>load rules english.rul
Rules being loaded from english.rul
PC-KIMMO>load lexicon english.lex
Lexicon being loaded from english.lex
PC-KIMMO>
```

2.3   Using the generator function

The generator accepts as input the lexical form of a word and returns all the possible corresponding surface forms. Figure 2.1 is a list of some of the morphemes that are defined in the sample lexicon for English.

The *generate* command is issued by typing *generate* plus a lexical form. The keyword *generate* can be shortened to *gen* or even just *g*. When typing actual words (as opposed to command keywords), lowercase and uppercase are distinguished. Be sure to put a plus (+) sign between morphemes and to include the stress mark (grave accent or back quote key) on the roots and the apostrophe (single quote key) with the possessive suffix. Now type in some combinations of morphemes and see what the generator does with them.

```
PC-KIMMO>generate 'fox+s
  foxes

PC-KIMMO>generate 'fox+s+'s
  foxes'

PC-KIMMO>gen 'try+s
  tries

PC-KIMMO>g 'try+ed
  tried
```

If you want to run the *generate* command a number of times in succession, a special generator prompt is available. At the PC-KIMMO prompt type *generate* (or a shortened form) followed by the *Enter* key, that is, with no word. You will see the generator prompt. At this prompt lexical forms can be entered directly without any command keyword. No

Figure 2.1 Some English morphemes

PREFIXES:

dis+	un+	re-+

SUFFIXES:

+able	+er	+ing	+s	+ish	+ness
+ed	+est	+ly	+'s	+y	

NOUNS:

'baby	'cacti	'fox	'kiss	'mouse	'ski
'beer	'cactus	'grouch	'lash	'race	'spot
'boy	'church	'ice	'milk	'rally	'spy
'cat	'day	'industry	'mice	refer'ee	'toe

ADJECTIVES:

'big	'clear	'cool	'happy	'real	'red

VERBS:

a'gree	'carry	'gone	'notice	'slept	under'stood
'am	'did	'had	oc'cur	'slip	'was
'are	'die	'has	'pay	'spy	'went
'argue	'differ	'have	'race	'sue	'were
at'tack	'do	'hoe	re'fer	'tie	
'be	'does	'is	refer'ee	'tiptoe	
be'lieve	'done	'kill	re'ly	'trace	
'bit	'dye	'kiss	re'peat	'travel	
'bite	'go	'manage	'ski	'try	
'bitten	'goes	'move	'sleep	under'stand	

commands can be issued from this prompt. To return to the PC-KIMMO command prompt, just enter a blank line (that is, press *Enter* with nothing on the line). (In the following screen display, <Enter> means press the *Enter* key.)

```
PC-KIMMO>generate<Enter>
generator>>'big+er
  bigger

generator>>'cool+er
  cooler

generator>><Enter>
PC-KIMMO>
```

In addition, try some ungrammatical combinations of morphemes to see what happens. Because the generator does not consult the lexicon, it will give you an answer even though the input is an illegal sequence of morphemes. The generator merely applies phonological rules.

2.4 Using the recognizer function

The recognizer accepts as input a surface form and returns all of the possible lexical forms of that word, with each morpheme glossed. The *recognize* command is issued by typing *recognize* plus a surface form. As with other command keywords, the keyword *recognize* can be shortened to *rec* or even just *r*. Type in some surface forms using the list of roots and affixes in figure 2.1 and see what the recognizer does with them. (The sample English lexicon does not handle the entire range of English derivational morphology. Even using only the roots and affixes listed in figure 2.1 you may find PC-KIMMO does not recognize certain words. After working through the tutorial in this book you may want to exercise your new skills by extending the English lexicon to cover more data.)

```
PC-KIMMO>recognize tries
  'try+s      [ V(try)+3sg.PRES ]

PC-KIMMO>rec tried
  'try+ed     [ V(try)+PAST.PRTC ]
  'try+ed     [ V(try)+PAST ]
```

Like the generator, the recognizer has its own prompt. For instance,

```
PC-KIMMO>recognize<Enter>
recognizer>>bigger
  'big+er

recognizer>>cooler
  'cool+er

generator>><Enter>
PC-KIMMO>
```

In addition, try some morphologically incorrect surface forms to see what happens. Because the recognizer uses the lexicon as well as the rules, only words that use morphemes listed in the lexicon and that use them in the correct order are accepted.

2.5 Using the file comparison functions

Thus far we have used PC-KIMMO's generator and recognizer interactively, that is, by directly entering words from the keyboard. PC-KIMMO can also apply the generator and recognizer functions to data that are read from a disk file. In this section we will use the file comparison functions.

The purpose of the comparison functions is to verify the correctness of a PC-KIMMO description, both the rules and the lexicon, on well-formed data provided by the analyst. There are three types of comparison files: generation comparison file, recognition comparison file, and pairs comparison file. Figure 2.2 shows part of the generation comparison file (ENGLISH.GEN) supplied for the English example. Each group of data has the lexical form of the word as its first line and one or more surface forms on successive lines (the leading spaces before surface forms are used only for readability). Multiple surface forms are usually due to optional rules, such as the use of a hyphen in the spelling of English words such as *re-trace*. When the comparison function runs, it prints :OK on the right side of the screen to signal that the generator successfully produced the same surface form as the one given in the file. If the generator fails to produce the surface form given or finds other surface forms, appropriate messages are displayed. To try out the generation comparison function, type *set verbose on* and then *file compare generate english.gen*. (The *file compare* commands also recognize default file names and extensions; see section 7.7.8.) You will see a display like this on your screen:

```
PC-KIMMO>set verbose on
PC-KIMMO>file compare generate english.gen
  1.
  2.
  3. 'cat
  4.   cat                    :OK
  5.
  6. 'cat+s
  7.   cats                   :OK
  8.
  9. 'cat+'s
 10.   cat's                  :OK
 11.
 12. 'cat+s+'s
 13.   cats'                  :OK
...
```

Figure 2.2 Generation comparison file for English

```
'cat
  cat

'cat+s
  cats

'cat+'s
  cat's

'cat+s+'s
  cats'

'fox
  fox

'fox+s
  foxes

'fox+'s
  fox's

'fox+s+'s
  foxes'

re-+'trace
  re-trace
  retrace
```

Figure 2.3 Recognition comparison file for English

```
spy
   'spy            [ N(spy).SG ]
   'spy            [ V(spy).INF ]

spies
   'spy+s          [ N(spy)+PL ]
   'spy+s          [ V(spy)+3sg.PRES ]

spy's
   'spy+'s         [ N(spy).SG+GEN ]

spies'
   'spy+s+'s       [ N(spy)+PL+GEN ]

spied
   'spy+ed         [ V(spy)+PAST ]
   'spy+ed         [ V(spy)+PAST.PRTC ]
```

The recognition comparison file is just the converse of the generation comparison file. Figure 2.3 shows part of the recognition comparison file (ENGLISH.REC) supplied for the English example. Each group of data has the surface form of the word as its first line and one or more lexical forms on successive lines. Multiple surface forms may be due either to phonological rules that create surface homophony between distinct lexical forms or to ambiguity in the lexicon—such as the English word *spy*, which can be either a noun or verb. To try out the recognition comparison function, type *set verbose on* (if you have not already done so) and then *file compare recognize english.rec*. You will see on your screen a display like this:

```
PC-KIMMO>set verbose on
PC-KIMMO>file compare recognize english.rec
  1.
  2.
  3. spy
  4.    'spy            [ N(spy).SG ]              :OK
  5.    'spy            [ V(spy).INF ]             :OK
  6.
  7. spies
  8.    'spy+s          [ N(spy)+PL ]              :OK
  9.    'spy+s          [ V(spy)+3sg.PRES ]        :OK
...
```

Figure 2.4 Pairs comparison file for English

```
'fox
fox

'fox+s
foxes

'fox+'s
fox's

'fox+s+'s
foxes'

re-+'trace
re-trace

re-+'trace
retrace

'spy
spy

'spy+s
spies
```

The third type of comparison file is the pairs comparison file. It looks like the generation comparison file in that the first line of each group of data is a lexical form, but differs in that the lexical form can be followed by only one surface form. In other words, each group of data must be exactly one pair of lexical and surface forms. Figure 2.4 shows part of the pairs comparison file ENGLISH.PAI supplied for the English example. The pairs comparison function takes each pair of lexical and surface forms and applies both generation and recognition tests to see if the surface form can be generated from the lexical form and if the lexical form can be recognized from the surface form. It applies both the rules and the lexicon, though the lexical gloss is not included in the file. To try out the pairs comparison function, type *set verbose on* (if you have not already done so) and then *file compare pairs english.pai*. You will see on your screen a display like this:

```
PC-KIMMO>set verbose on
PC-KIMMO>file compare pairs english.pai
  1.
  2.
  3. 'fox              :OK
  4. fox              :OK
  5.
  6. 'fox+s            :OK
  7. foxes            :OK
  8.
  9. 'fox+'s           :OK
 10. fox's            :OK
 11.
 12. 'fox+s+'s         :OK
 13. foxes'           :OK
 14.
 15. re-+'trace        :OK
 16. re-trace         :OK
 17.
 18. re-+'trace        :OK
 19. retrace          :OK
 20.
 21. 'spy              :OK
 22. spy              Warning: 2 forms were recognized.
 23.
 24. 'spy+s            :OK
 25. spies            Warning: 2 forms were recognized.
...
```

This ends our brief tour of PC-KIMMO. When you are ready to return to the operating system, type *exit* to leave the program.

Chapter

3

DEVELOPING THE RULES COMPONENT

This chapter describes in detail the rules component of PC-KIMMO. Section 3.1 describes the formalism and meaning of two-level rules. Section 3.2 explains the relationship between two-level phonological rules and finite state transducers. Section 3.3 describes how to translate (or compile) two-level rules into the finite state transition tables that are used by PC-KIMMO. Section 3.4 provides specific information on the format of the rules file.

3.1 Understanding two-level rules

Section 3.1 describes the form and meaning of two-level rules: how they differ from the rules of generative phonology, their notation, the four types of two-level rules, and the concept of two-level environments.

3.1.1 Generative rules and two-level rules

Two-level rules are similar to the rules of standard generative phonology, but differ in several crucial ways. Rule 1 is an example of a generative rule.

R1 $t \longrightarrow c \: / \: \rule{1em}{0.4pt} \: i$

Rule 2 is the analogous two-level rule.

R2 $t{:}c \Rightarrow \rule{1em}{0.4pt} \: i$

The difference between the two rule formalisms is not just notational; rather their meanings are different.

Generative rules have three main characteristics. First, they are transformational rules—they transform or rewrite one symbol into another symbol. Rule 1 states that t becomes (is changed into) c when it precedes i. After rule 1 rewrites t as c, t no longer "exists." Second, sequentially applied generative rules convert underlying forms to surface forms via any number of intermediate levels of representation; that is, the application of each rule results in the creation of a new intermediate level of representation. Third, generative rules are unidirectional—they can only convert underlying form to surface form, not vice versa.

In contrast, two-level rules are declarative; they state that certain correspondences hold between a lexical (that is, underlying) form and its surface form. Rule 2 states that lexical t corresponds to surface c before i; it is not changed into c, and it still exists after the rule is applied. Because two-level rules express a correspondence rather than rewrite symbols, they apply in parallel rather than sequentially. Thus no intermediate levels of representation are created as artifacts of a rewriting process. Only the lexical and surface levels are allowed. It is this aspect of their nature that is emphasized by the name "two-level" rules. Furthermore, because the two-level model is defined as a set of correspondences between lexical and surface representation, two-level rules are bidirectional. Given a lexical form, PC-KIMMO will return the surface form. Given a surface form, PC-KIMMO will return the lexical form.

3.1.2   Correspondences and feasible pairs

Two-level rules treat each word as a correspondence between its lexical representation (LR) and its surface representation (SR). For example, consider the lexical form *tati* and its surface form *taci*:

LR: t   a   t   i
SR: t   a   c   i

Each pair of lexical and surface characters is a *correspondence pair* or simply correspondence. We write a correspondence with the notation *lexical-character:surface-character*, for instance *t:t*, *a:a*, and *t:c*. There must be an exact one-to-one correspondence between the characters of the lexical form and the characters of the surface form.

There are two types of correspondences exemplified in these forms: *default* correspondences such as *t:t* and *a:a*, and *special* correspondences such as *t:c*. The sum of the default and special correspondences makes up the set of *feasible pairs* sanctioned by the description. In other words, all feasible pairs must be explicitly declared in the description, either as default or as special correspondences.

3.1.3   Two-level rule notation

Looking again at rule 2 (from section 3.1.1), we see that a two-level rule is made up of three parts: the *correspondence*, the *rule operator*, and the *environment* or *context*. The first part of rule 2 is the correspondence *t:c*. It specifies a lexical *t* that corresponds to a surface *c*.

The second part of rule 2 is the rule operator ⇒. Although this operator is shaped like an arrow, its meaning is quite different from the rewriting arrow of generative rules (for instance, rule 1). The rule operator specifies the relationship between the correspondence and the environment in which it occurs. There are four operators: ⇒, ⇐, ⇔, and ⇍. The semantics of the rule operators are discussed in section 3.1.5 in detail, but briefly they mean the following:

⇒ the correspondence only occurs in the environment
⇐ the correspondence always occurs in the environment
⇔ the correspondence always and only occurs in the environment
⇍ the correspondence never occurs in the environment

The third part of rule 2 is the environment or context, written as ___ *i*. It specifies the phonological environment in which the correspondence is found. As in standard phonological notation, an underline, called an environment line, indicates the position of the correspondence in the environment.

The environment of rule 2 contains a notational shorthand. In its full form the rule is written this way:

R3   t:c ⇒ ___i:i

Rule 3 states that a lexical *t* corresponds to (or is realized as) a surface *c* only when it precedes a lexical *i* that corresponds to (or is realized as) a surface *i*. If the lexical and surface characters of a correspondence pair are identical, the correspondence can be written as a single character. Thus rule 2 is equivalent to rule 3.

Rule 3 illustrates that environments are also stated in terms of two-level correspondences. We cannot just say that *t* corresponds to *c* before *i*; we must specify whether it is a lexical or surface *i*. This means that a two-level rule has access to both the lexical and surface environments (see section 3.1.7 below on two-level environments). In contrast, rules in generative phonology can refer only to the environment of the local level of representation, which is often an intermediate level. To emphasize the two-level nature of rule 3, we can write it on multiple lines:

t   ___ i
    ⇒
c   ___ i

The environment of a rule can also make use of a special "wildcard" or ANY symbol (written here as @) that stands for any alphabetic character (as qualified below). For example,

R4   t:c ⇒ ___i:@

Rule 4 states that *t* corresponds to *c* before any feasible pair whose lexical character is *i* (that is, a lexical *i* regardless of how it is realized). In the example above, this could include both the default correspondence *i:i* and any special correspondences such as *i:y*. Note carefully that, when used in a rule, the ANY symbol does not really mean any alphabetic character, rather it means any alphabetic character that constitutes a feasible pair with the other character in the correspondence (see section 3.3.1). As a notational shorthand, a correspondence such as *i:@* is simplified to just the lexical character followed by a colon, that is, *i:*. The ANY symbol can also be used on the lexical side of a correspondence:

R5   t:c ⇒ ___ @:i

Rule 5 states that *t* corresponds to *c* before any feasible pair whose surface character is *i* (that is, a surface *i* regardless of what lexical character it realizes). This notation is simplified to just a colon followed by the surface character, that is, *:i*. It should be noted that the ANY symbol can only be used in the environment part of a rule, not in the correspondence part.

Another important characteristic of two-level rules is that they require a one-to-one correspondence between the characters of the lexical form and the characters of the surface form. That is, there must be an equal number of characters in both lexical and surface forms, and each lexical character must map to exactly one surface character, and vice versa. Phonological processes that delete or insert characters are expressed in the two-level model as correspondences with the NULL symbol, written here as 0 (zero). In the following forms, a lexical + (morpheme boundary) corresponds to a surface *0* (that is, it is deleted) and a surface ' (stress mark) corresponds to a lexical *0* (that is, it is inserted).

```
LR:  0  t  a  t  +  i
SR:  '  t  a  c  0  i
```

The NULL symbol is used only internally by the rules; it is not printed in output forms and does not need to be written in input forms. PC-KIMMO will accept the lexical input form *tat+i* and return the surface output form *'tati*. The NULL symbol can be used both in the environment and the correspondence parts of a rule.

Another special symbol is the BOUNDARY symbol, written here as #. It indicates a word boundary, either initial or final. It can be used only in the environment of a rule and can only correspond to another BOUNDARY symbol, that is, *#:#*.

3.1.4 Using character subsets in rules

In generative phonology, classes of characters are referred to using distinctive features; for example, vowels are referred to using the cluster of features [+syllabic, +sonorant, −consonantal]. PC-KIMMO does not support distinctive features. Instead, classes of characters are enumerated in lists that are given single-word names (one or more characters, no spaces). These character classes are defined in SUBSET statements in the rules file (see section 3.4.3). For example, the following declarations define *C* as the set of consonants, *V* as the set of vowels, *S* as the set of stops, and *NAS* as the set of nasals:

SUBSET C	p t k b d g m n ŋ s l r w y
SUBSET V	i e a o u
SUBSET S	p t k b d g
SUBSET NAS	m n ŋ

Suppose that after writing rule 2 above (section 3.1.1), further data show that all the alveolar obstruents are palatalized before high, front vowels. For example,

LR:	ati	ade	asi	aze
SR:	aci	aje	aši	aže

Rather than write a separate rule for each correspondence, we will define subset *D* for alveolar obstruents, subset *P* for their palatalized counterparts, and subset *Vhf* for the high, front vowels:

SUBSET D	t d s z
SUBSET P	c j š ž
SUBSET Vhf	i e

Rule 2 can now be generalized by writing it with subsets:

Palatalization
R6   D:P ⇒ ＿＿ Vhf

3.1.5 The four rule types

The rule operator specifies the logical relation between the correspondence and the environment of a two-level rule. The rule operators are roughly equivalent to the conditional or implicative operators of formal logic. Rule 7 (rule 2 above) is written with the rule operator ⇒.

R7   t:c ⇒ ＿＿ i

The ⇒ operator means "only but not always." Rule 7 states that lexical *t* corresponds to surface *c* only preceding *i*, but not necessarily always in that environment. Thus other realizations of lexical *t* may be found in that context, including *t:t*. In logical terms, the ⇒ operator means that the correspondence implies the context, but the context does not necessarily imply the correspondence. To state it negatively, rule 7 prohibits the occurrence of the correspondence *t:c* everywhere except preceding *i*.

The ⇒ rule is roughly equivalent to an optional rule in generative phonology, and is typically used in cases of so-called free variation. Rule 7 would be used if the occurrence of *t* and *c* freely varies before *i*. Given the lexical input form *tati* and rule 7, the PC-KIMMO generator will produce both surface forms *taci* and *tati*.

Rule 8 is the same as rule 7 except that it is written with the rule operator ⇐.

R8   t:c ⇐ ___i

The ⇐ operator means "always but not only." Rule 8 states that lexical *t* always (obligatorily) corresponds to surface *c* preceding *i*, but not necessarily only in that environment. Thus *t:c* is permitted to occur in other contexts. In logical terms, the ⇐ operator means that the context implies the correspondence, but the correspondence does not necessarily imply the context. To state it negatively, if *t:~c* (where *~c* means the logical negation of *c*) means the correspondence of lexical *t* to surface not-*c* (that is, anything except *c*), then rule 8 prohibits the occurrence of *t:~c* in the specified context.

The ⇐ rule is roughly equivalent to an obligatory rule in generative phonology. It is used in cases where a correspondence is obligatory in one environment but also occurs in some other environment as specified by another rule. Given the lexical input form *tati* and rule 8, the PC-KIMMO generator will produce both surface forms *taci* and *caci*, unless constrained by some other rule.

Rule 9 is again the same, except that it is written with the rule operator ⇔.

R9   t:c ⇔ ___i

The ⇔ operator is the combination of the operators ⇐ and ⇒ and means "always and only." Rule 9 states that lexical *t* corresponds to surface *c* always and only preceding *i*. The ⇔ rule is used when a correspondence obligatorily occurs in a given environment (compare the ⇐ operator) and in no other environment (compare the ⇒ operator). It is equivalent to the biconditional logical operator and means that the correspondence is allowed if and only if it is found in the specified context. Given the lexical form *tati* and rule 9, the PC-KIMMO generator will return only the surface form *taci*. Thus rule 9 is equivalent to the combination of rules 7 and 8. It is up to the analyst to choose between writing separate ⇐ and ⇒ rules or collapsing them into one ⇔ rule.

Rule 10 is written with the rule operator /⇐.

R10   t:c /⇐ ＿i:ə

The /⇐ operator means "never." It means that the correspondence specified by the rule is prohibited from occurring in the specified context. A /⇐ rule is usually used to cover "exceptions" to a more general rule. Rule 10 states that lexical *t* cannot correspond to surface *c* preceding *i:ə*. Given the lexical form *tati*, rule 10, and a rule sanctioning a *i:ə* correspondence, the PC-KIMMO generator will allow the surface forms *tatə* and *catə* but disallow *tacə* or *cacə*. As the operator symbol suggests, the /⇐ operator is similar to the ⇐ operator in that it does not prohibit the correspondence from occurring in other environments.

Figure 3.1 summarizes the diagnostic properties of rules 7 through 10. For more on the semantics of the four rule types, see section 3.3.3.

Figure 3.1 Diagnostic properties of the four rule types

Rules 7–10	Is *t:c* allowed preceding *i*?	Is preceding *i* the only environment in which *t:c* is allowed?	Must *t* always correspond to *c* before *i*?
t:c ⇒ ＿i	yes	yes	no
t:c ⇐ ＿i	yes	no	yes
t:c ⇔ ＿i	yes	yes	yes
t:c /⇐ ＿i	no	—	—

3.1.6 Expressing complex environments

Several notational conventions exist that can be used to build complex environment expressions. These involve optional elements, repeated elements, and alternative elements. As an example we will use a vowel reduction rule, which states that a vowel followed by some number of consonants followed by stress (indicated by ') is reduced to schwa (ə). For example,

LR: bab'a   bamb'a
SR: bəb'a   bəmb'a

Parentheses indicate an optional element. Rule 11 requires either one or two consonants.

R11   V:ə ⇔ ＿C(C)'

Rule 12 requires either zero, one, or two consonants.

R12   V:ə ⇔ ＿＿(C)(C)'

An asterisk indicates zero or more instances of an element. (The asterisk functions the same as a Kleene-star in regular expressions.) Rule 13 requires either zero, one, or more consonants.

R13   V:ə ⇔ ＿＿C*'

Rule 14 requires one or more consonants.

R14   V:ə ⇔ ＿＿CC*'

A correspondence may occur in more than one environment. Consider a rule of vowel lengthening whereby the correspondence *a:ā* (short and long *a*) occurs in two distinct environments: when it occurs in the syllable preceding stress (pretonic lengthening) and when it occurs in the stressed syllable (tonic lengthening). For example,

   LR: ladab'ar
   SR: ladāb'ār

Rule 15 expresses pretonic lengthening and rule 16 expresses tonic lengthening.

R15   a:ā ⇒ ＿＿C'

R16   a:ā ⇒ '＿＿

Note carefully that a description containing these two rules is self-contradictory. Both rules use the ⇒ operator, which permits the correspondence to occur only in the specified environment. Rule 15 says that *a:ā* occurs only in a pretonic syllable; rule 16 says that *a:ā* occurs only in a tonic syllable. Thus the two rules conflict with each other. This type of rule conflict is called an environment conflict (or a ⇒ conflict for short, since it involves ⇒ rules) and is discussed more fully in section 3.3.13. The conflict between rules 15 and 16 can be resolved by collapsing the two rules into one. In rule 17 the vertical bar indicates disjunction between expressions and the square brackets delimit the disjunctive expressions from the rest of the environment (which in this case is empty).

R17   a:ā ⇒ [＿＿C' | '＿＿]

Rule 17 now says, correctly, that the *a:ā* correspondence is allowed only in either pretonic or tonic position.

Now consider rules 18 and 19, which are the same as rules 15 and 16 except that they are written with the ⇐ operator.

R18   a:ā ⇐ ___C'

R19   a:ā ⇐ '___

The ⇐ operator means that the correspondence occurs always (obligatorily) in the environment but not only there. Rules 18 and 19 do not conflict with each other, and so do not have to be collapsed into a single rule. However, if the analyst so chooses, they can be collapsed into rule 20.

R20   a:ā ⇐ [___C' | '___]

Given the meanings of the rule types as explained in section 3.1.5, we have the following choices for writing rules for lengthening. If vowel lengthening occurs only but not always in the specified environments, we must use rule 17. If vowel lengthening occurs always but not only in the specified environments, we must use rule 20 (or rules 18 and 19). And if vowel lengthening occurs always and only in the specified environment, we must use both rules 17 and 20. If the last case is true, the analyst also has the option of collapsing rules 17 and 20 into one ⇔ rule, rule 21.

R21   a:ā ⇔ [___C' | '___]

Rule 21 is an example of inclusive disjunction; that is, the correspondence is found in either environment (or both) in the same input word. In standard generative phonology, the two subparts of a rule of this type must be implicitly ordered with the convention that if one of the subparts of the rule applies, the rest of the subparts are not skipped but also apply (this is called conjunctive ordering in Schane 1973:90). In the two-level model, rule ordering is both unavailable and unnecessary, since all rule environments are available simultaneously.

As an example of an exclusive disjunction, consider the situation where the vowel of the ultimate (final) syllable of a word is lengthened unless it is schwa, in which case the vowel of the penultimate (next to final) syllable is lengthened. For example,

LR: maman   mamanə
SR: mamān   mamānə

Assume these subsets, where *V* is the set of short vowels and *Vlng* is the set of their lengthened counterparts (but ə is not lengthened):

SUBSET V   i a u ə
SUBSET Vlng   ī ā ū

Rules 22 and 23 (where **#** represents word boundary) demonstrate a ⇒ conflict (see above and section 3.3.13 on rule conflicts) and must be collapsed.

R22   V:Vlng ⇒ ___ C*ə#

R23   V:Vlng ⇒ ___ C*#

In the example above on tonic and pretonic lengthening (rules 15 to 21), we collapsed the rules with the vertical bar notation, allowing lengthening to occur in either or both of the environments. This is what we wanted, since tonic lengthening and pretonic lengthening are separate phonological processes and both are possible in the same word. But in the present example we are dealing with just one lengthening process, though with two alternative environments. We want lengthening to occur in one or the other of the environments but not both in the same word. Rules 22 and 23 can then be collapsed as rule 24 by using the parenthesis notation.

R24   V:Vlng ⇒ ___ C*(ə)#

A word-final schwa will not be lengthened by this rule because, even though lexical schwa belongs to the *V* subset, no correspondence to a surface long schwa has been declared (see section 3.3.1 for details on subsets and declaring feasible pairs).

3.1.7 Understanding two-level environments

One of the defining features of two-level rules is that they can refer to both lexical and surface environments.[1] This makes it possible for a two-level description to handle many phenomena that would require sequentially ordered rules in standard generative phonology. For example, consider these two rules:

1. Nasal Assimilation: the nasal character *N* (unspecified for point of articulation) assimilates to the point of articulation of a following stop.

2. Stop Voicing: a voiceless stop is voiced after a nasal.

These rules relate the lexical sequences *Np*, *Nt*, and *Nk* to the surface sequences *mb*, *nd*, and *ŋg*, respectively. To account for these correspondences, generative phonology would require two rules (the following rules account only for labials):

---

[1]This section is based on Dalrymple and others 1987:19-22.

Nasal Assimilation

R25   N $\longrightarrow$ m / __p

Stop Voicing

R26   p $\longrightarrow$ b / m__

The rules must apply in this order, since if rule 26 were applied first it would destroy the environment needed for rule 25. The two-level versions of these rules do not need to be ordered; in effect they apply simultaneously:

Nasal Assimilation

R27   N:m $\Leftrightarrow$ __p:

Stop Voicing

R28   p:b $\Leftrightarrow$:m__

These rules work because of the careful specification of lexical and surface environments. Rule 27 says that a lexical N is realized as a surface m preceding a lexical p. In this context the notation p: (equivalent to p:@) stands for the correspondences p:p (by default) and p:b (from rule 28). Rule 28 says that a lexical p is realized as a surface b following a surface m. The notation :m (equivalent to @:m) stands for the correspondences m:m (by default) and N:m (from rule 27). Because the two-level model allows rule environments to have access to both the lexical and surface levels, rule ordering and intermediate levels are not needed.

A common error in writing two-level rule environments is to overspecify the environment. Consider this overspecified version of rule 27:

Overspecified version of Nasal Assimilation

R27a   N:m $\Leftrightarrow$ __p

Even though the symbol p seems simpler than p:, it actually is more specific, as it stands for the correspondence p:p only. Rule 27a is now in conflict with the voicing rule (28), which says that after a surface m only the correspondence p:b can occur. Conversely, the correspondence p:b of rule 28 is in conflict with rule 27a, which allows only p:p to occur after a surface m.

Now consider another incorrectly specified version of the Nasal Assimilation rule (27):

Overspecified version of Nasal Assimilation

R27b   N:m $\Leftrightarrow$ __p:b

At first this version seems correct, since it is precisely in the environment of p:b that we want the rule to apply. The problem is that rule 27b does not require *N* to be realized as *m* preceding a lexical *p* that is realized as anything other than surface *b*, and the Voicing rule (28) does not require *p* to be realized as *b* except when it follows a surface *m*. Assuming that otherwise lexical *N* corresponds to surface *n*, the lexical form *Np* will be realized as both *np* and *mb*. Thus overspecification does not always result in a rule conflict; it may also result in overgeneration. (See also section 3.3.12 on two-level environments.)

3.2 Implementing two-level rules as finite state machines

Section 3.2 explains how two-level rules operate, how they can be implemented as finite state machines, and how the four types of two-level rules can be translated into finite state tables.

3.2.1 How two-level rules work

To understand how two-level rules work, consider again rule 2, repeated here as rule 29.

R29   t:c ⇒ __i

The operator ⇒ in this rule means that lexical *t* is realized as surface *c* only (but not always) in the environment preceding *i:i*.

The correspondence *t:c* declared in rule 29 is a special correspondence. A two-level description containing rule 29 must also contain a set of default correspondences, such as *t:t*, *i:i*, and so on. The sum of the special and default correspondences are the total set of valid correspondences or feasible pairs that can be used in the description.

If a two-level description containing rule 29 (and all the default correspondences also) is applied to the lexical form *tati*, the PC-KIMMO generator would proceed as follows to produce the corresponding surface form.

Beginning with the first character of the input form, it looks to see if there is a correspondence declared for it. Due to rule 29 it will find that lexical *t* can correspond to surface *c*, so it will begin by positing that correspondence.

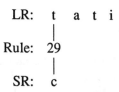

At this point the generator has entered rule 29. For the *t:c* correspondence to succeed, the generator must find an *i:i* correspondence next. When the generator moves on to the second character of the input word, it finds that it is a lexical *a*; thus rule 29 fails, and the generator must back up, undo what it has done so far, and try to find a different path to success. Backing up to the first character, lexical *t*, it tries the default correspondence *t:t*.

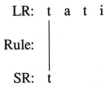

The generator now moves on to the second character. No correspondence for lexical *a* has been declared other than the default, so the generator posits a surface *a*.

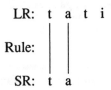

Moving on to the third character, the generator again finds a lexical *t*, so it enters rule 29 and posits a surface *c*.

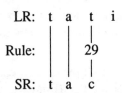

Now the generator looks at the fourth character, a lexical *i*. This satisfies the environment of rule 29, so it posits a surface *i*, and exits rule 29.

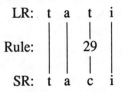

Since there are no more characters in the lexical form, the generator outputs the surface form *taci*. However, the generator is not done yet. It will continue backtracking, trying to find alternative realizations of the lexical form. First it will undo the *i:i* correspondence of the last character of the input word, then it will reconsider the third character, lexical *t*. Having already tried the correspondence *t:c*, it will try the default correspondence *t:t*.

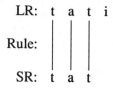

Now the generator will try the final correspondence *i:i* and succeed, since rule 29 does not prohibit *t:t* before *i* (rather it prohibits *t:c* in any environment except before *i*).

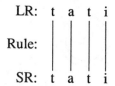

All other backtracking paths having failed, the generator quits and outputs the second surface form *tati*.

The procedure is essentially the same when two-level rules are used in recognition mode (where a surface form is input and the corresponding lexical forms are output).

3.2.2 How finite state machines work

The basically mechanical procedure for applying two-level rules makes it possible to implement the two-level model on a computer by using a formal language device called a *finite state machine*. The simplest finite state machine is a *finite state automaton* (FSA), which recognizes (or generates) the well-formed strings of a *regular language* (a certain type of formal language—see Chomsky 1965). While finite state machines are commonplace in computer science and formal language theory (see, for instance, Hopcroft and Ullman 1979), they may not be familiar to all linguists. They have, however, had their place in the linguistic literature. Most widely known would be chapter 3 of Chomsky's *Syntactic Structures* (1957) in which finite state grammars are dismissed as an inadequate model for describing natural language syntax. Other notable treatments of finite state automata in the linguistic literature are Chomsky 1965 and Langendoen 1975. A good introduction to finite state automata written for linguists is chapter 16 of Partee and others 1987.

An FSA is composed of states and directed transition arcs. There must minimally be an initial state, a final state, and an arc between them. A successful transition from one state to the next is possible when the next symbol of the input string matches the symbol on the arc connecting the states. For example, consider the regular language L1 consisting of the symbols *a* and *b* and the "grammar" $\{ab^na\}$ where $n \geq 0$. Well-formed strings or "sentences" in this language include *aa*, *aba*, *abba*, *abbba*, and so on. The language L1 is defined by the FSA in figure 3.2.

Figure 3.2 FSA for language L1

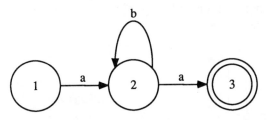

State 1 is the initial state and state 3 is the final state (signified by the double circle). States 1 and 2 are both nonfinal states (signified by the single circle). To recognize the string *abba*, proceed as follows:

1. Start at state 1.

2. Input the first symbol of the string and traverse the *a* arc to state 2.

3. Input the second symbol and traverse the *b* arc back to state 2.

4. Input the third symbol and again traverse the *b* arc back to state 2.

5. Input the last symbol and traverse the *a* arc to state 3, which is a final state.

Because the input string is exhausted and the machine is in a final state, we conclude that *abba* is a string in the language L1.

An FSA can also be represented as a *state transition table*. The FSA above is represented as this state table:

	a	b
1.	2	0
2.	3	2
3:	0	0

The rows of the table represent the three states of the FSA diagram, with the number of the final state marked with a colon and the numbers of the nonfinal states marked with periods. The columns represent the arcs from one state to another; the symbol labeling each arc in the FSA diagram is placed as a header to the column. The order of the columns in the table has no effect on the operation of the table, but is written to reflect the order of the FSA. Notice that the two *a* arcs in the FSA diagram are represented as a single column labeled *a*. The cells at the intersection of a row and a column indicate which state to make a transition to if the input symbol matches the column header. Zero in a cell indicates that there is no valid transition from that state for that input symbol; in the FSA diagram this is equivalent to having no arc labeled with that input symbol. The machine is said to fail when this happens, thus rejecting the input form. Note that the colon marks state 3 as the only final state. This means that if the machine is in any state but 3 when the input string is exhausted, the string is not accepted. The 0 transitions in state 3 say that once the machine gets to that state, the string is not accepted if there are remaining input symbols.

An FSA operates only on a single input string. A *finite state transducer* (FST) is like an FSA except that it simultaneously operates on two input strings. It recognizes whether the two strings are valid correspondences (or translations) of each other. For example, assume the first input string to an FST is from language L1 above, and the second input string is from language L2, which corresponds to L1 except that every second *b* is *c*. Here is an example correspondence of two strings:

L1:   abbbba
L2:   abcbca

Figure 3.3 shows the FST in diagram form. Note that the only differ- ence from an FSA is that the arcs are labeled with a correspondence pair consisting of a symbol from each of the input languages.

Figure 3.3 FST diagram for the correspondence between languages L1 and L2

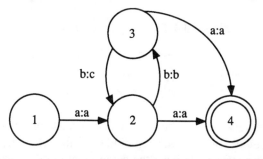

FSTs can also be represented as tables, the only difference being that the column headers are pairs of symbols, such as *a:a* and *b:c*. For example, the following table is equivalent to the FST diagram in figure 3.3.

	a	b	b
	a	b	c
1.	2	0	0
2.	4	3	0
3.	4	0	2
4:	0	0	0

3.2.3 A ⇒ rule as a finite state machine

The key insight of PC-KIMMO is that if phonological rules are written as two-level rules, they can be implemented as FSTs running in parallel. In the next four subsections we briefly show how each of the four rule types (see section 3.1.5) translates into an FST. Detailed procedures for compiling rules into state tables are found in section 3.3.

Consider rule 30.

R30   t:c ⇒ ___ i

In terms of FSTs, this rule defines two "languages" that are translations of each other. The "upper" or lexical language specifies the string *ti*; the "lower" or surface language says that *ci* may correspond to it. Note, however, that a two-level rule does not specify the grammar of a full language. Rather it deals with allowed substrings. A possible paraphrase of rule 30 is, "If ever the correspondence *t:c* occurs, it must be followed by *i:i*." In other words, if anything other than *t:c* occurs, this rule ignores it. This fact must be incorporated into our translation of a two-level rule into a transition diagram, shown in figure 3.4. In this FST, state 1 is both the initial and only final state. The *@:@* arc (where *@* is the ANY symbol, see section 3.1.3) allows any pairs to pass successfully through the FST except *t:c* and *i:i*.

Figure 3.4 FST diagram of a ⇒ rule

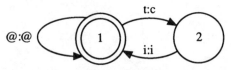

Rule 30, represented as the FST in 3.4, translates into the following state table, labeled T30. (In the remainder of this chapter, each rule and its corresponding state table have the same label number, for instance R30 and T30.) Notice that state 1, the initial state, is a kind of "default" state that ignores everything except the substring crucial to the rule.

Example of a ⇒ table

T30

	t	i	@
	c	i	@
1:	2	1	1
2.	0	1	0

A set of two-level rules is implemented as a system of parallel FSTs that specify all the feasible pairs and where they can occur. A state table is constructed such that the entire set of feasible pairs in the description is partitioned among the column headers with no overlap. That is, each and every feasible pair of the description must belong to one and only one column header. Table 30 specifies the special correspondence *t:c* and the environment in which it is allowed. The *@:@* column header in table 30 matches all the feasible pairs that are defined by all other FSTs of the system. Thus, with respect to table 30, *@:@* does not stand for all feasible pairs; rather it stands for all feasible pairs except *t:c* and *i:i*.

The default correspondences of the system must be declared in a trivial FST like table 31 (see section 3.3.2 (step 2) and section 3.4.4):

Table of default correspondences

T31

	p	t	k	a	i	u	@
	p	t	k	a	i	u	@
1:	1	1	1	1	1	1	1

Even this table of default correspondences must include *@:@* as a column header. Otherwise it would fail when it encountered a special correspondence such as *t:c*. This is due to the fact that all the rules in a two-level description apply in parallel, and for each character in an input string all the rules must succeed, even if vacuously. Now given the lexical form *tatik*, tables 30 and 31 will work together to generate the surface forms *tatik* and *tacik*.

To understand how to represent two-level rules as state tables, we must understand what the two-level rules really mean. (See section 3.1.5 above.) We tend to think of two-level rules positively, that is, as statements of where the correspondence succeeds. In fact, state tables are failure-driven; they specify where correspondences must fail. It is natural to think of rule 30 as saying that the correspondence *t:c* succeeds when it occurs preceding *i:i*. But state table 30 actually works because it fails when anything but *i:i* follows *t:c* (the zeros in state 2 indicate that the input has failed). This reorientation to thinking of phonological rules as failure-driven is one of the most difficult barriers to overcome in learning to write two-level rules and state tables, but it is the primary key to success with PC-KIMMO.

In summary, the rule type $L{:}S \Rightarrow E$ (where $L{:}S$ is a lexical:surface correspondence and E is an environment) positively says that L is realized as S only in E. Negatively it says that L realized as S is not allowed in an environment other than E. The state table for a $\Rightarrow$ rule must be written so that it forces $L{:}S$ to fail in any environment except E. In logical terms, the $\Rightarrow$ operator indicates conditionality, such that, if $L{:}S$ exists, then it must be in E.

3.2.4 A $\Leftarrow$ rule as a finite state machine

Rule 32 below is the same as rule 30 except that it is written with the $\Leftarrow$ operator.

R32   t:c $\Leftarrow$ ___i

This rule says that lexical t is always realized as surface c when it occurs before $i{:}i$, but not only before $i{:}i$. Thus the lexical form *tati* will successfully match the surface form *taci* but not *tati*. Note, however, that it would also match *caci* since it does not disallow $t{:}c$ in any environment. Rather, its function is to disallow $t{:}t$ in the environment of a following $i{:}i$. Remembering that state tables are failure-driven, the strategy of writing the state table for rule 32 is to force it to fail if it recognizes the sequence $t{:}t \; i{:}i$. This allows the correspondence $t{:}c$ to succeed elsewhere. The state table for rule 32 looks like this:

Example of a $\Leftarrow$ table

	t	t	i	@
	c	t	i	@
1:	1	2	1	1
2:	1	2	0	1

T32

In state 1 any occurrences of the pairs $t{:}c$, $i{:}i$, or any other feasible pairs are allowed without moving from state 1. It is only the correspondence $t{:}t$ that forces a transition to state 2, where all feasible pairs succeed except $i{:}i$ (the zero in the $i{:}i$ column indicates that the input has failed). Notice that state 2 must be a final state; this allows all the correspondences except $i{:}i$ to succeed and return to state 1. Also notice that in state 2 the cell under the $t{:}t$ column contains a two. This is necessary to allow for the possibility of a *tt* sequence in the input form; for instance, table 32 will apply to the lexical form *tatti* to produce the surface form *tatci*. This phenomenon is called backlooping and is treated in detail in section 3.3.4, part 2.

Actually, table 32 is potentially overspecified. It is not really the pair $t{:}t$ that is disallowed before i, but rather the pair $t{:}{\sim}c$; that is, lexical t and surface not-c (anything but c). Suppose our two-level description also contained a rule that defined a *t:n* correspondence. Like *t:t*, *t:n* should fail before *i:i*. Rather than add another column for *t:n* to table 32, we can replace the column header *t:t* with *t:@*. Given that the more specific correspondence *t:c* is also declared in the table, *t:@* will match all other valid surface correspondences to lexical *t*, such as *t:t*, *t:n*, and so on. Here is table 32 revised to use a *t:@* column header.

A ⇐ table

T32a	t	t	i	@
	c	@	i	@
1:	1	2	1	1
2:	1	2	0	1

In summary, the rule type *L:S* ⇐ *E* positively says that *L* is always realized as *S* in *E*. Negatively it says that *L* realized as any character but *S* is not allowed in *E*. The state table for a ⇐ rule must be written so that it forces all correspondences of *L* with anything but *S* to fail in *E*. Logically, the ⇐ operator indicates that if *L* is in *E*, then it must correspond to *S*.

3.2.5 A ⇔ rule as a finite state machine

Rule 33 uses the ⇔ operator and is equivalent to combining rules 32 and 30.

R33   t:c ⇔ ___i

The state table for a ⇔ rule is simply the combination of the ⇐ and the ⇒ tables. The state table for rule 33 is built by combining tables 32a and 30 to produce table 33 below. The column headers of table 33 are the same as table 32a. States 1 and 2 represent the ⇐ part of the table (corresponding to table 32a) while states 1 and 3 represent the ⇒ part (corresponding to table 30).

Example of a ⇔ table

T33	t	t	i	@
	c	@	i	@
1:	3	2	1	1
2:	3	2	0	1
3.	0	0	1	0

In summary, the rule type *L:S* ⇔ *E* says that *L* is always and only realized as *S* in *E*. It implies that *L:S* is obligatory in *E* and occurs nowhere else. The state table for a ⇔ rule must be written so that it forces all correspondences of *L* with anything but *S* to fail in *E*, and forces *L:S* to fail in any environment except *E*.

3.2.6 A ⊬ rule as a finite state machine

Rule 34 exemplifies the fourth type of rule, the ⊬ rule.

R34   t:c ⊬ ___ i:ə

This rule states that the correspondence *t:c* is disallowed when it precedes a lexical *i* that is realized as a surface *ə*. As the ⊬ operator suggests, this rule type shares properties of the ⇐ type rule. It states that the correspondence always fails in the specified environment, but allows it (does not prohibit it) in any other environment. The strategy for building a state table for the ⊬ rule is to recognize the correspondence in the specified environment and then fail. In table 34 the correspondence *t:c* forces a transition to state 2 where the table fails if it encounters the environment *i:ə*, but succeeds otherwise. Notice that like table 32 above for a ⇐ rule, state 2 is final.

Example of a ⊬ table

T34

	t	i	@
	c	ə	@
1:	2	1	1
2:	2	0	1

In summary, the rule type *L:S* ⊬ *E* positively says that *L* is never realized as *S* in *E*. Negatively it says that *L* realized as *S* is not allowed in *E*. Logically, the ⊬ operator indicates that if *L* is in *E*, then it must correspond to ~*S*.

3.3 Compiling two-level rules into state tables

Section 3.3.1 gives an overview of the structure of the rules component. Section 3.3.2 is a reference summary of the general procedure for compiling (translating) two-level rules into state transition tables. Detailed examples of how to apply the general procedure are found in sections 3.3.4 through 3.3.7. Sections 3.3.8 through 3.3.16 treat in detail various topics related to rule compilation, such as subsets, word boundary environments, complex environments, rule conflicts, and phonotactic constraints.

3.3.1 Overview of the rules component

This section discusses alphabetic characters, feasible pairs, using the ANY symbol and subset names, declaring default and special correspondences, mapping feasible pairs to column headers, and applying rules in parallel. Some of these topics, discussed here concisely, are covered in more detail in sections 3.3.4 through 3.3.16 and in section 3.4.

Alphabetic characters

All characters or symbols used in either lexical or surface forms in the description constitute the alphabet used by the rules. The NULL symbol and the BOUNDARY symbol are also considered alphabetic characters, though in the rules file they are declared separately from the rest of the alphabet (see section 3.4.1). The ANY symbol and subset names are not part of the alphabet.

Feasible pairs

A feasible pair is a specific correspondence between a lexical alphabetic character and a surface alphabetic character. The set of feasible pairs is the set of all such correspondences used in a description. Some of these correspondences are default correspondences, where the lexical and surface characters are identical (for instance *t:t* and *i:i*); others are special correspondences, where the surface character differs from the lexical character (for instance *t:c* and *i:ī*). Each feasible pair, whether a default or special correspondence, must be explicitly declared in a description. This is done by including each feasible pair as a column header in at least one state table. Only column headers consisting of alphabet characters, including the NULL symbol and the BOUNDARY symbol, are considered feasible pairs. Column headers containing the ANY symbol or subset names are ignored for the purpose of declaring feasible pairs.

When the user runs PC-KIMMO and loads a set of rules from a disk file, the column headers of every state table are scanned as they are read in and a list of feasible pairs is compiled. After the rules are loaded, the user can see the entire set of feasible pairs currently in use by the rules component by issuing the *list pairs* command (see section 7.5.5). It should also be remembered that the set of feasible pairs is revised each time one or more rules is turned on or off by means of the *set rules* [*on* | *off*] command (see section 7.5.6).

Using the ANY symbol and subset names in column headers

Although correspondences that contain the ANY symbol or subset names are not feasible pairs and cannot serve as the correspondence part of a rule, they do occur in the environment part of a rule and therefore appear as column headers in state tables. In order to write correct state tables, the analyst must understand exactly what set of pairs is specified by column headers that contain the ANY symbol or subset names. Although the ANY symbol is said to be a "wildcard" character that can stand for any alphabetic character, its effective meaning relative to a given set of rules is determined by the set of feasible pairs sanctioned by the rules.

For example, in a set of rules the correspondence *t:@* (where @ has been declared to be the ANY symbol) does *not* represent all possible correspondences that have *t* as their lexical character and any other member of the alphabet as their surface character; rather, it represents only the feasible pairs that match its pattern, for instance *t:t* and *t:c* if those correspondences are feasible pairs by virtue of appearing as column headers in one or more tables.

Similarly, a subset name is said to stand for a set of alphabetic characters; but its effective meaning relative to a given set of rules is determined by the set of feasible pairs sanctioned by the rules. For example, in a set of rules where the subset *S* has been declared to have the members *s*, *x*, and *z*, the correspondence *s:S* does *not* represent all possible correspondences that have *s* as their lexical character and one of the members of the subset *S* as their surface character; rather, it represents only the feasible pairs that match its pattern, for instance *s:s* and *s:z* if these are the only correspondences involving lexical *s* that have been used as column headers in one or more tables. This means that using the correspondence *s:S* as a column header in a rule does *not* implicitly declare as feasible pairs all correspondences that match it. That is, unless the correspondence *s:x* is explicitly declared as a feasible pair somewhere in the set of rules, it is not included in the set of feasible pairs represented by the correspondence *s:S*. (For more on using subsets, see section 3.3.8.)

Declaring default correspondences

The fact that each valid correspondence used in a description must be explicitly declared as a feasible pair in the rules has consequences for how default correspondences are declared. Since rules are written to express the conditions under which special correspondences occur, default correspondences are not normally included in each rule. Thus, in order to get every feasible pair into a column header of a state table, the rules component must contain a table strictly for the purpose of declaring the default correspondences (see sections 3.2.3 and 3.4.4). A table of default correspondences has only one state (which is a final state), and each transition is back to state 1. The column headers provide the list of default correspondences, with *@:@* (where @ is the ANY symbol) appended to the end of the list so as not to block the occurrence of special correspondences. It is impossible to include too many correspondences in this list. That is, it would be possible to make the list include every feasible pair and dispense with the final *@:@*. It is possible to underspecify, however. If a feasible pair is left out of the table of default correspondences and does not occur explicitly in any other table, then that correspondence will never be recognized as valid. For the sake of consistency, the table of default correspondences should even include pairs that also appear in the environments of other tables; the redundancy has no effect on the operation of the rules. (For more on writing tables of default correspondences, see section 3.4.4.)

Declaring special correspondences

Special correspondences do not need to be gathered into one table as is done with default correspondences since most special correspondences are used as column headers in the rules that apply to them. However, if a set of special correspondences is represented with subsets, it may be necessary to write a separate table declaring the special correspondences as feasible pairs. For example, consider a rule whose correspondence part is $D:P$, where D is a subset that contains the alveolar consonants t, d, and s and P is a subset that contains the palatalized consonants c, j, and $š$. The intention of the analyst is that the subset correspondence $D:P$ should stand for the feasible pairs $t:c$, $d:j$, and $s:š$. However, in the state table for this rule the column header $D:P$ will not match any feasible pairs except those that have been explicitly declared elsewhere. In this situation it is best to write a separate table where the feasible pairs intended to match the subset correspondence are explicitly used as column headers. For the sake of consistency this should be done even if the pairs do appear in tables elsewhere in the description; the possible redundancy has no effect on the operation of the rules. (For more on using subsets, see section 3.3.8.)

Mapping feasible pairs to column headers

As was described above, when a set of rules is loaded and the list of feasible pairs is compiled, the set of pairs that match each column header is determined. In the example above, the pairs $t:c$, $d:j$, and $s:š$ should match the column header $D:P$. In this instance the meaning of the column header $D:P$ is understood relative to the entire set of rules. However, relative to a single rule, a column header may actually specify only a subset of the pairs that it specifies relative to the entire rule set. This situation arises as follows.

Each state table must be constructed such that every feasible pair is represented by one of its column headers. That is, for each table in a rule set, the entire list of feasible pairs is partitioned among the column headers with no overlap. In a table, each feasible pair belongs to one and only one column header. After loading a set of rules and compiling the list of feasible pairs, PC-KIMMO goes through the set of rules again to interpret the column headers of each table. For each table it scans the list of all the feasible pairs and assigns each one to a column header. If a feasible pair matches more than one column header, it is assigned to the most specific one, where the specificity of a column header is defined as the number of feasible pairs that match it. For example, consider a table that contains both an *s:š* column header and a *D:P* column header, where the feasible pairs that match it include *t:c*, *d:j*, and *s:š*. When PC-KIMMO tries to assign the feasible pair *s:š* to a column header in this table, it finds that it matches both the *s:š* column and the *D:P* column. PC-KIMMO will assign it to the *s:š* column, since it is more specific than the *D:P* column (one versus three pairs that match). This means that, relative to this particular rule, the *D:P* column header represents only two feasible pairs, namely *t:c* and *d:j*. When running PC-KIMMO, the user can see exactly how feasible pairs are assigned to the column headers of a table by using the *show rule* command (see section 7.5.9).

It is possible to construct a state table in which a feasible pair matches multiple column headers that have the same specificity value, thus making it impossible to uniquely assign the pair to a column header. This constitutes an incorrectly written state table. When a rules file containing such a state table is loaded, a warning message is issued alerting the user that two columns have the same specificity. If the user proceeds to analyze forms with the incorrectly written table, the pair will be assigned (arbitrarily) to the leftmost column that it matches. Correct results cannot be assured. (For more on the problem of overlapping column headers, see section 3.3.9.)

In order to get every feasible pair in the column headers of a table without having to literally specify each pair, a column header of the form *@:@* (where *@* is the ANY symbol) is included in the table. This covers all pairs that are not part of the correspondence and environment of the rule.

Applying rules in parallel

To understand how the PC-KIMMO rules component works to generate and recognize forms, it must be kept in mind that two-level rules, represented as finite state tables, apply in parallel (or simultaneously). This means that for an input form to be successfully processed by PC-KIMMO, all of the rules must succeed. In other words, as each character of the input form is processed, it must pass successfully through every rule before the next character can be processed. It is precisely because of PC-KIMMO's parallel rule application that each state table must represent in its column headers the entire set of feasible pairs.

3.3.2 General procedure for compiling rules into tables

This section presents a step-by-step procedure for compiling rules into state tables. The following abbreviations are used in the discussion.

L a lexical character
S a surface character
~S any surface character but *S*
L:S the lexical-to-surface correspondence on left side of rule
E an environment
~E any environment but *E*
lc the left context in the environment
rc the right context in the environment
0 the NULL symbol
@ the ANY symbol
# the BOUNDARY symbol

1. Make a complete inventory of all the possible lexical-to-surface correspondences found in the data. From this, compile a list of all the symbols used as lexical and surface characters, including the NULL symbol and the BOUNDARY symbol. This full list is the alphabet used by the rules. The rules will also use the ANY symbol and subset names.

2. Declare all the default correspondences required by the description. This is done by writing one or more tables that contain only and all the default correspondences (see section 3.4.4).

3. For each special correspondence (*L:S*), write down your hypothesis about the environment (*E*) in which it occurs. (The environment may be disjunctive; that is, *E1* or *E2* or *E3*.) For each correspondence, answer the following two questions:

   a. Is *E* the only environment in which *L:S* is allowed?

   b. Must *L* always be realized as *S* in *E*?

   There are four possible outcomes. Depending on the outcome, do one of the following:

   a. If *a* is *yes* and *b* is *no*, posit the rule *L:S* $\Rightarrow$ *E* and proceed to step 4.

   b. If *a* is *no* and *b* is *yes*, posit the rule *L:S* $\Leftarrow$ *E* and proceed to step 5.

   c. If both *a* and *b* are *yes*, posit the rule *L:S* $\Leftrightarrow$ *E* and proceed to step 6.

d. If neither is *yes*, find the other environments in which *L:S* is allowed, combine these into a single disjunctive environment, and go through step 3 again.

It is also possible that it is easier to express the constraint on *L:S* in terms of the environment in which it is prohibited. In this case, posit the rule *L:S* ⇐ *E* and proceed to step 7.

If *L:S* contains subset names, it may be necessary to write a separate table to declare as feasible pairs the correspondences that *L:S* is intended to represent (see sections 3.3.8 and 3.4.4).

4. Compile each ⇒ rule. The rule *L:S* ⇒ *lc___rc* can be paraphrased as "the expression *lc L:S rc* is allowed, but *L:S* in any other context is not allowed." The strategy for compiling a ⇒ rule to a state table is to construct a table that recognizes the sequence *lc L:S rc*, forbids any other occurrence of *L:S*, and permits any other correspondences to occur anywhere. The steps in building the table are as follows:

   a. Make a list of column headers for the table by writing down all the correspondences used in the expression *lc L:S rc* (including correspondences with @ and subset names). Add @:@ to the end of the list.

   b. Beginning with state 1, add states (rows) and fill in the state transitions in the appropriate cells in the table to recognize the expression *lc L:S rc*. The final symbol in the expression normally should result in a transition back to state 1, except when backlooping is involved (see step 8 below).

   c. Use a colon to mark state 1 as a final state (that is, 1:). Mark every state that is traversed before *L:S* is reached as a final state. Mark the state in which *L:S* is recognized as a final state. Use a period to mark all states traversed after that point as nonfinal (for instance, 2.). That is, once *L:S* is encountered it is not in the correct environment unless the full right context is found; thus these states cannot be final.

   d. Since *L:S* in any other environment is not allowed, fill in the rest of the column for *L:S* with zeros. Furthermore, in any state traversed during the recognition of the right context, any correspondence encountered other than those provided for in *rc* means that *L:S* is in the wrong context. Thus, the rest of the cells for the states traversed in *rc* should be filled with zeros.

   e. All remaining cells in the transition table denote successful transitions as far as this rule is concerned. In most cases, these cells are filled with transitions back to the initial state (that is, 1), except where backlooping occurs (see step 8).

5. Compile each $\Leftarrow$ rule. The rule $L{:}S \Leftarrow lc\rule{1em}{0.4pt}rc$ can be paraphrased as "the expression lc $L{:}{\sim}S$ rc is not allowed." The strategy for compiling a $\Leftarrow$ rule to a state table is to construct a table that recognizes the sequence lc $L{:}{\sim}S$ rc and forbids it, while permitting any other correspondences to occur anywhere. (Note that the strategy for building the $\Leftarrow$ rule for an insertion, where L is 0 (the NULL symbol), is slightly different; see section 3.3.7.) The steps in building the table are as follows:

   a. Make a list of column headers for the table. First, put down $L{:}S$. Next, put down $L{:}@$, which now represents $L{:}{\sim}S$. Next, write down all the correspondences used in lc and rc (including correspondences with @ and subset names). Add $@{:}@$ to the end of the list.

   b. Beginning with state 1, add states (rows) and fill in the state transitions in the appropriate cells in the table to recognize the expression lc $L{:}@$ rc. The final symbol in the expression should result in failure (that is, the cell representing recognition of the final symbol should contain 0 (zero)).

   c. Use a colon to mark every state as a final state.

   d. All remaining cells in the transition table denote successful transitions as far as this rule is concerned. In most cases, these cells are filled with transitions back to the initial state (that is, 1), except where backlooping occurs (see step 8).

6. Compile each $\Leftrightarrow$ rule. The rule may be compiled as two separate state tables, one for the $\Leftarrow$ rule and the other for the $\Rightarrow$ rule. Or, the rule may be compiled as a single table that combines the $\Leftarrow$ and $\Rightarrow$ rules. In this case, construct the column headers as in 5a. Then perform steps 5b through 5d to encode the $\Leftarrow$ side of the rule. Finally, perform steps 4b through 4e to add the $\Rightarrow$ side of the rule. In 4b, add new states only as needed for the recognition of rc; the recognition of lc is the same. In 4c, mark as nonfinal the states added to recognize rc. (Alternatively, steps 4b to 4e can be done before steps 5b to 5d.)

7. Compile each $\nLeftarrow$ rule. The rule $L{:}S \nLeftarrow lc\rule{1em}{0.4pt}rc$ can be paraphrased as "the expression lc $L{:}S$ rc is not allowed." The strategy for compiling a $\nLeftarrow$ rule to a state table is to construct a table that recognizes the sequence lc $L{:}S$ rc and forbids it, while permitting any other

correspondences to occur anywhere. The steps in building the table are as follows:

    a. Make a list of column headers for the table by writing down all the correspondences used in the expression *lc L:S rc* (including correspondences with @ and subset names). Add *@:@* to the end of the list.

    b. Beginning with state 1, add states (rows) and fill in the state transitions in the appropriate cells in the table to recognize the expression *lc L:S rc*. The final symbol in the expression should result in failure (that is, the cell representing recognition of the final symbol should contain 0 (zero)).

    c. Use a colon to mark every state as a final state.

    d. All remaining cells in the transition table denote successful transitions as far as this rule is concerned. In most cases, these cells are filled with transitions back to the initial state (that is, 1), except where backlooping occurs (see step 8).

8. Check for backlooping. A *backloop* is a transition to a state that represents a previous point in the expression being recognized. The final step in compiling a rule (see steps 4e, 5d, and 7d) is to specify the transitions for all the remaining cells in the state table that are not part of the environment expression. Normally these are transitions back to state 1. However, backloops to states other than 1 must be specified if an input pair (or sequence of pairs) is recognized that matches the first symbol (or sequence of symbols) of the expression *lc L:S rc*. Transitions must be specified back to the states that represent the successful recognition of that symbol (or sequence of symbols). A detailed example of backlooping is given in part 2 of section 3.3.4.

3.3.3 Summary of two-level rule semantics

The semantics of the four kinds of two-level rules are now summarized in two ways. First, in table 3.5 a number of paraphrases are given for each rule type. Second, in table 3.6 truth tables (as in formal logic) are given. Note that the ⇐ and ⇒ rules have the familiar conditional pattern of formal logic. The ⇔ rule is the conventional biconditional.

3.3.4 Compiling rules with a right context

This section gives step-by-step examples of how to apply the general procedure given in section 3.3.2 for compiling rules into state tables to

Figure 3.5 Semantics of two-level rules

L:S ⇒ E   "Only but not always."
            L is realized as S only in E.
            L realized as S is not allowed in ~E.
            If L:S, then it must be in E.
            Implies L:~S in E is permitted.

L:S ⇐ E   "Always but not only."
            L is always realized as S in E.
            L realized as ~S is not allowed in E.
            If L is in E, then it must be L:S.
            Implies L:S may occur elsewhere.

L:S ⇔ E   "Always and only."
            L is realized as S only and always in E.
            Both L:S ⇒ E and L:S ⇐ E.
            Implies L:S is obligatory in E and occurs nowhere else.

L:S ⇍ E   "Never."
            L is never realized as S in E.
            L realized as S is not allowed in E.
            If L is in E, then it must be L:~S.

Figure 3.6 Truth tables for two-level rules

There is an L.		Is the rule satisfied?			
Is it realized as S?	Is it in E?	L:S ⇒ E	L:S ⇐ E	L:S ⇔ E	L:S ⇍ E
T	T	T	T	T	F
T	F	F	T	F	T
F	T	T	F	F	T
F	F	T	T	T	T

rules with only a right context. In the exposition of the following examples, phrases such as "part 4" or "step 4a" refer to the numbered subparts of section 3.3.2.

(1) Compiling a ⇒ rule with a right context

As an example, we will posit a *p:b* correspondence preceding *+m* (strictly, *+:0 m:m*), where the symbol + stands for a morpheme boundary. Assume that + is always deleted in surface forms and can thus be declared as the default correspondence *+:0*. Examples of the *p:b* correspondence are:

```
LR:   ap+ma   ap+ma   ap+ba
SR:   ab0ma   ap0ma   ap0ba
```

According to the diagnostic questions in part 3, these correspondences indicate that *p* is not always realized as *b* before *+m* (*p:p* also occurs before *+m*), but that *+m* is the only environment in which *p:b* is allowed. Therefore, posit a ⇒ rule:

R35   p:b ⇒ ___+:0 m

To compile rule 35 to a state table, follow the steps in part 4. First (step 4a), make a list of the column headers, consisting of all the correspondences used in rule 35 plus *@:@* :

```
p + m @
b 0 m @
```

The order of the columns of a state table do not affect its operation, but it is helpful to the reader to keep the columns in the same order as *lc L:S rc* so far as possible.

Next (step 4b), add rows (representing states) and fill in the cells with transitions to recognize the sequence *p:b +:0 m:m*. When the final symbol of the sequence (*m:m*) is reached, a transition is made back to state 1.

```
    |p + m @
    |b 0 m @
  ──┼──────────
  1 |2
  2 |  3
  3 |      1
```

Next (step 4c), mark state 1 as a final state (that is, 1:). This allows the table to succeed on any correspondence that does not occur in *L:S rc*. Step 4c says that every state traversed before and including the state where

L:S is recognized is marked as a final state. Since *p:b* is recognized in state 1, this is irrelevant. However, all states traversed after that point must be marked as nonfinal; that is, once *p:b* is recognized, it is not in the correct environment until the entire right context is found. Thus, states 2 and 3 cannot be final.

	p + m @		
	b 0 m @		
1:	2		
2.		3	
3.			1

Next (step 4d), fill in the rest of the column for *p:b* with zeros, since *p:b* in any other environment is not allowed. Also, for all the states traversed during the recognition of the right context, any correspondences other than those that are part of the right context mean that *p:b* is in the wrong context. Thus, the rest of the cells in rows 2 and 3 must be filled with zeros:

	p + m @			
	b 0 m @			
1:	2			
2.	0	3	0	0
3.	0	0	1	0

Finally (step 4e), all remaining cells are successful transitions for this rule and can be filled in with transitions back to the initial state (that is, state 1). Note that since the remaining empty cells are in state 1 and do not involve the first correspondence of *L:S rc*, backlooping (part 8) is not involved. Table 35 now gives the complete transition table for rule 35.

⇒ table with right context

T35

	p + m @			
	b 0 m @			
1:	2	1	1	1
2.	0	3	0	0
3.	0	0	1	0

(2) Compiling a ⇐ rule with a right context

Now suppose that the *p:b* correspondence is found in these forms (rather than the ones above):

LR: ap+ma   ap+ba   ap+ba
SR: ab0ma   ap0ba   ab0ba

According to the questions in part 3, these correspondences indicate that *p* is always realized as *b* before +*m*, but +*m* is not the only environment in which *p:b* is allowed (*p:b* also occurs before +*b*). Therefore, posit a ⇐ rule:

R36   p:b ⇐ ___+:0 m

To compile rule 36 to a state table, follow the steps in part 5. First (step 5a), make a list of the column headers, consisting of *p:b*, *p:@*, the correspondences used in the right context, and *@:@* :

$$
\begin{array}{ccccc}
p & p & + & m & @ \\
b & @ & 0 & m & @
\end{array}
$$

Due to the presence of *p:b*, *p:@* means all other feasible pairs with a lexical *p*. In other words, it represents *p:~b*.

Next (step 5b), add rows (states) and fill in the cells with transitions to recognize the sequence *p:@ +:0 m:m*. When the final symbol of the sequence is reached (*m:m*), the cell is filled with zero, indicating failure.

	p b	p @	+ 0	m m	@ @
1		2			
2			3		
3				0	

Next (step 5c), mark every state as final:

	p b	p @	+ 0	m m	@ @
1:		2			
2:			3		
3:				0	

Finally (step 5d), all remaining cells denote successful transitions back to the initial state and are filled in with ones, with the exception of cells where backlooping applies. To demonstrate backlooping, we will first ignore it and fill in the table with ones:

T36

	p b	p @	+ 0	m m	@ @
1:	1	2	1	1	1
2:	1	1	3	1	1
3:	1	1	1	0	1

There is a problem with this state table. As written, table 36 does not work correctly with more than one *p* in succession. For instance, given the lexical form *app+ma*, it will return *appma*, without voicing the second *p*. Step the example *app+ma* through table 36 to verify this. When the second *p:p* is encountered while in state 2, the FST will make a transition back to state 1, where *+:0* and *m:m* are recognized, leaving the FST in state 1. To remedy this, the FST must loop back to state 2 when it encounters *p:p*:

T36a

	p	p	+	m	@
	b	@	0	m	@
1:	1	2	1	1	1
2:	1	2	3	1	1
3:	1	1	1	0	1

But table 36a will still fail to recognize an input form such as *ap+p+ma*. This is because when the second *p:p* is encountered in state 3, the FST will make a transition back to state 1, again losing the fact that we are in the environment for the change. The table must be revised so that the FST will loop back to state 2 when a *p:p* is encountered in state 3 as well:

⇐ table with right context

T36b

	p	p	+	m	@
	b	@	0	m	@
1:	1	2	1	1	1
2:	1	2	3	1	1
3:	1	2	1	0	1

This is an example of the explanation given in part 8 of how to handle backlooping. Backlooping is a subtle but important point, and is the source of many errors in compiling tables. The name is intended to convey the idea that the FST must have transitions (loops) back to the states where symbols (or sequences of symbols) of the expression *lc L:S rc* have been recognized. The notion of backlooping transitions is clearer when the FST is represented as a diagram; see figure 3.7 (which is equivalent to table 36b, except that transitions back to state 1 are not drawn). There are two backloops in this FST: from state 2 there is an arc for *p:@* back to state 2, and from state 3 there is another arc for *p:@* back to state 2.

Why didn't we encounter backlooping while writing the state table for rule 35 above? With respect to backlooping, it may seem that table 35 should be written as follows (where states 2 and 3 have an arc back to state 2 if a *p:b* is recognized):

Figure 3.7 FST with backlooping

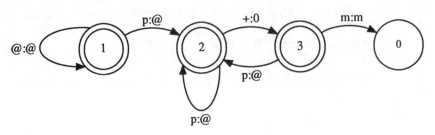

T35a

	p	+	m	@
	b	0	m	@
1:	2	1	1	1
2.	2	3	0	0
3.	2	0	1	0

The answer is that in this case step 4d overrides backlooping. Rule 35 is a ⇒ rule, which means that the correspondence *p:b* is disallowed in any environment other than preceding *+m*. Table 35a, however, would allow *p:b* to occur preceding another *p:b* or preceding the sequence *+:0 p:b*. To prevent this, step 4d requires the *p:b* column to contain zeros in states 2 and 3.

As a matter of practice in writing a state table, the analyst should carefully check the column that represents the first symbol of the expression *lc L:S rc* to see which state to loop back to in each state of the table.

Often it does not seem necessary in practice to account for backlooping because of language-specific phonotactic constraints. Taking the example word *app+ma* discussed above, suppose that the language being described does not have morphemes like *app*; that is, a phonotactic constraint prohibits the sequence *VCC*. In such a case, state table 36 (written without backloops) would always work correctly as long as it was given input conforming to the phonotactic constraints of the language. There are two reasons why we recommend that the user of PC-KIMMO write tables that account for backlooping even when it seems unnecessary.

First, if you are inductively developing a phonological analysis, you will not necessarily know all the phonotactic constraints until the entire analysis is completed. If rules are written with incorrect backloops, puzzling failures may occur when further data are collected that contain new phonotactic patterns.

Second, it is conceptually cleaner to keep phonotactic constraints separate from the general phonological rules. Rather than incorporating phonotactic constraints in tables that encode phonological rules, it is better to write tables so that they are minimally restrictive with respect to phonotactics. The analyst can encode phonotactic constraints in a set of rules (tables) dedicated specifically to that purpose. For more discussion on expressing phonotactic constraints, see section 3.3.16.

(3) Compiling a ⇔ rule with a right context

Now suppose that the *p:b* correspondence is found only in forms like these:

LR: ap+ma   ap+ba
SR: ab0ma   ap0ba

According to the questions in part 3, these correspondences indicate that *p* is always realized as *b* before *+m*, and that *+m* is the only environment in which *p:b* is allowed. Therefore, posit a ⇔ rule:

R37   p:b ⇔ ___+:0 m

As was explained in part 6 of section 3.3.2, a ⇔ rule can be compiled as two separate state tables, one for the ⇐ rule and one for the ⇒ rule. This is what has been done to produce state tables 35 and 36b above. Alternatively, a ⇔ rule can be compiled as a single table. To do this (see part 6), first construct the column headers by following the instructions in step 5a:

p p + m @
b @ 0 m @

Next perform steps 5b through 5d to construct the ⇐ part of the rule:

	p	p	+	m	@
	b	@	0	m	@
1:	2	1	1	1	
2:	2	3	1	1	
3:	2	1	0	1	

Now perform steps 4b through 4e to add the ⇒ part of the rule:

⇔ table with right context

T37

	p	p	+	m	@
	b	@	0	m	@
1:	4	2	1	1	1
2:	4	2	3	1	1
3:	4	2	1	0	1
4.	0	0	5	0	0
5.	0	0	0	1	0

Notice that to recognize *p:b* and the right context *+:0 m:m*, two states (4 and 5, corresponding to states 2 and 3 in table 35) must be added to the table. These states are nonfinal states.

Special attention must be paid to the transitions in states 2 and 3 of table 37. For the *p:@* column, states 2 and 3 must loop back to state 2, which is the state in the ⇐ part of the rule where *p:@*, the first symbol of the expression *lc L:S rc*, has been recognized. This is identical to table 36b. For the *p:b* column, states 2 and 3 must make a transition to state 4, which is the second state of the ⇒ part of the rule. This is the same transition as in state 1.

(4) Compiling a ⇍ rule with a right context

The fourth rule type, the ⇍ rule, disallows the correspondence in the specified environment. For example, rule 38 prohibits *p:b* before *+m*.

R38   p:b ⇍ ___ +:0 m

The state table that encodes rule 38 must recognize the sequence *p:b +:0 m:m* and then forbid it. As the left arrow of the ⇍ operator suggests, the semantics of this rule type is most similar to the ⇐ rule. Whereas rule 36 above (a ⇐ rule) states that *p* is always (obligatorily) realized as *b* before *+:0 m* but may also be realized as *b* in some other environment, rule 38 (a ⇍ rule) states that *p* is always (obligatorily) prohibited before *+:0 m:m*, but may be realized as *b* in some other environment.

To compile rule 38 to a state table, follow the steps in part 7. First (step 7a), make a list of the column headers needed to recognize *p:b* and the environment plus *@:@*:

p + m @
b 0 m @

Notice that unlike table 36b, which expresses a ⇐ rule, we do not need a *p:@* column header. This is because table 36b is built to prohibit the sequence *p:~b +:0 m:m*, but the table we are building for a /⇐ rule must prohibit *p:b +:0 m:m*.

Next (step 7b), add rows (states) and fill in the cells with transitions to recognize the sequence *p:b +:0 m:m*. When the final symbol of the sequence is reached (*m:m*), the cell is filled with zero, indicating failure.

	p + m @			
	b 0 m @			
1	2			
2		3		
3			0	

Next (step 7c), mark every state as final:

	p + m @			
	b 0 m @			
1:	2			
2:		3		
3:			0	

Finally (step 7d), all remaining cells denote successful transitions and are filled in with ones, with the exception of cells that meet the conditions of backlooping (part 8). Specifically, the cells in column *p:b* for states 2 and 3 must make a transition back to state 2, since state 2 represents the state where the first symbol (*p:b*) of the expression *lc L:S rc* has been recognized.

/⇐ table with right context

T38

	p + m @			
	b 0 m @			
1:	2	1	1	1
2:	2	3	1	1
3:	2	1	0	1

It is instructive to compare table 38 with both table 35 (for a ⇒ rule) and table 36b (for a ⇐ rule).

3.3.5 Compiling rules with a left context

This section gives step-by-step examples of how to apply the general procedure given in section 3.3.2 for compiling rules into state tables to rules with only a left context. In the exposition of the following examples, phrases such as "part 4" or "step 4a" refer to the numbered subparts of section 3.3.2.

(1) Compiling a ⇒ rule with a left context

In this section our example rule states that the correspondence *p:b* occurs following *m+*. For example,

```
LR:  am+pa   am+pa   ab+pa
SR:  am0ba   am0pa   ab0pa
```

According to the diagnostic questions in part 3, these correspondences indicate that *p* is not always realized as *b* after *m+* (*p:p* also occurs after *m+*), but that *m+* is the only environment in which *p:b* is allowed. Therefore posit a ⇒ rule:

R39   p:b ⇒ m +:0 ___

To compile rule 39, first (step 4a) make a list of the column headers:

$$m + p @$$
$$m \ 0 \ b @$$

Next (step 4b), add rows and fill in the cells to recognize the sequence *m:m +:0 p:b*:

	m	+	p	@
	m	0	b	@
1	2			
2		3		
3			1	

Next (step 4c), mark state 1 as a final state. Also, every state traversed up to and including the state where *p:b* is recognized is marked as a final state. Since there is no right context, there are no more states after that point.

	m	+	p	@
	m	0	b	@
1:	2			
2:		3		
3:			1	

Next (step 4d) fill in the rest of the *p:b* column with zeros, because the *p:b* correspondence cannot succeed until the entire left context has been recognized:

	m + p @
	m 0 b @
1:	2 0
2:	3 0
3:	1

Finally (step 4e), all remaining cells are successful transitions for this rule and can be filled in with transitions back to the initial state (state 1), with the exception of cells that meet the conditions of backlooping (part 8). Specifically, the cells in column *m:m* for states 2 and 3 must make a transition back to state 2, since state 2 represents the state where the first symbol (*m:m*) of the expression *lc L:S rc* has been recognized. Now table 39 will work correctly with input forms such as *amm+pa* and *am+m+pa*.

⇒ table with left context

T39

	m + p @
	m 0 b @
1:	2 1 0 1
2:	2 3 0 1
3:	2 1 1 1

(2) Compiling a ⇐ rule with a left context

Now suppose that the *p:b* correspondence is found in these forms:

LR: am+pa   ab+pa   ab+pa
SR: am0ba   ab0pa   ab0ba

According to the questions in part 3, these correspondences indicate that *p* is always realized as *b* after *m+*, but *m+* is not the only environment in which *p:b* is allowed (it also occurs after *b+*). Therefore, posit a ⇐ rule:

R40   p:b ⇐ m +:0____

To compile rule 40, first (step 4a) make a list of the column headers, including *p:@*:

m + p p @
m 0 b @ @

Due to the presence of *p:b*, *p:@* means all other feasible pairs with a lexical *p*. In other words, it represents *p:~b*.

Next (step 5b), add rows and fill in the cells to recognize the sequence *m:m +:0 p:@*. When the final symbol of the sequence is reached (*p:@*), the cell is filled with zero, indicating failure.

	m + p p @
	m 0 b @ @
1	2
2	3
3	0

Next (step 5c), mark every state as final:

	m + p p @
	m 0 b @ @
1:	2
2:	3
3:	0

Finally (step 5d), all remaining cells are successful transitions for this rule, and can be filled in with transitions back to the initial state (state 1), with the exception of cells that meet the conditions of backlooping (part 8). Specifically, the cells in column *m:m* for states 2 and 3 must make a transition back to state 2, since state 2 represents the state where the first symbol (*m:m*) of the expression *lc L:S rc* has been recognized. Now table 4 will work correctly with input forms such as *amm+pa* and *am+m+pa*.

⇐ table with left context

T40		m + p p @
		m 0 b @ @
	1:	2 1 1 1 1
	2:	2 3 1 1 1
	3:	2 1 1 0 1

(3) Compiling a ⇔ rule with a left context

Now suppose that the *p:b* correspondence is found only in forms like these:

LR: am+pa ab+pa
SR: am0ba ab0pa

According to the questions in part 3, these correspondences indicate that *p* is always realized as *b* after *m+*, and *m+* is the only environment in which *p:b* is allowed. Therefore, posit a ⇔ rule:

R41   p:b ⇔ m +:0___

As is explained in part 6 of section 3.3.2, a ⇔ rule can be compiled as two separate state tables, one for the ⇐ rule and one for the ⇒ rule. This is what has been done to produce state tables 39 and 40 above. Alternatively, a ⇔ rule can be compiled as a single table. To do this (see part 6), first construct the column headers following the instructions in step 5a:

m + p p @
m 0 b @ @

Next perform steps 5b through 5d to construct the ⇐ part of the rule:

	m + p p @	
	m 0 b @ @	
1:	2 1	1 1
2:	2 3	1 1
3:	2 1	0 1

Now perform steps 4b through 4e to add the ⇒ part of the rule. Since rule 41 has no right context, no new states need to be added. Simply fill in the column for *p:b*. Notice that in states 1 and 2 the *p:b* column must be filled with zeros just as it is in rule 39. If we encounter *p:@* in state 3, then we fail; if we encounter *p:b*, then we succeed.

⇔ table with left context

T41

	m + p p @
	m 0 b @ @
1:	2 1 0 1 1
2:	2 3 0 1 1
3:	1 1 1 0 1

(4) Compiling a ⇍ rule with a left context

The fourth rule type, the ⇍ rule, disallows the correspondence in the specified environment. For example, rule 42 prohibits *p:b m:m +:0*.

R42   p:b ⇍ m +:0____

To compile rule 42 to a state table, follow the steps in part 7. First (step 7a), make a list of the column headers needed to recognize *p:b* and the environment plus @:@ :

m + p @
m 0 b @

Next (step 7b), add rows (states) and fill in the cells with transitions to recognize the sequence *m:m +:0 p:b*. When the final symbol of the sequence is reached (*p:b*), the cell is filled with zero, indicating failure.

	m	+	p	@
	m	0	b	@
1	2			
2		3		
3			0	

Next (step 7c), mark every state as final:

	m	+	p	@
	m	0	b	@
1:	2			
2:		3		
3:			0	

Finally (step 7d), all remaining cells denote successful transitions and are filled in with ones with the exception of cells that meet the conditions of backlooping (part 8). Specifically, the cells in column *m:m* for states 2 and 3 must make a transition back to state 2, since state 2 represents the state where the first symbol (*m:m*) of the expression *lc L:S rc* has been recognized.

⇐ table with left context

T42

	m	+	p	@
	m	0	b	@
1:	2	1	1	1
2:	2	3	1	1
3:	2	1	0	1

3.3.6 Compiling rules with both left and right contexts

This section gives step-by-step examples of how to apply the general procedure given in section 3.3.2 for compiling rules into state tables to rules with both a left and right context. In the exposition of the following examples, phrases such as "part 4" or "step 4a" refer to the numbered subparts of section 3.3.2.

(1) Compiling a ⇒ rule with left and right contexts

The example rule used in this section states that the correspondence *s:z* occurs intervocalically. For example,

LR: sasa   sasa
SR: saza   sasa

According to the diagnostic questions in part 3, these correspondences indicate that *s* is not always realized as *z* between vowels (*s:s* also occurs between vowels), but that between vowels is the only environment in which *s:z* is allowed. Therefore, posit a ⇒ rule:

R43   s:z ⇒ V ___ V

To compile rule 43 to a state table, follow the steps in part 4:

T43   ⇒ table with left and right contexts

	V s @
	V z @
1:	2 0 1
2:	2 3 1
3.	2 0 0

While rule 43 contains the correspondence *V:V* twice, table 43 has only one *V:V* column header. The single *V:V* header serves for both instances of the correspondence in the environment. Having two identical column headers in a table will result in an error. (See also section 3.3.8 on using subsets in state tables.)

Notice that states 1 and 2 are final, while state 3 is nonfinal. Also note carefully that accounting for backlooping requires the transition in state 2 in the *V:V* column to remain in state 2. This is necessary to allow the correct recognition of words with consecutive vowels, for instance *saasa*. Less obvious is that when *V:V* is recognized in state 3 the FST must return to state 2 rather than the expected state 1. This is necessary to allow the rule to apply more than once in the same word where the environments overlap. For example, consider these forms:

LR: asasa
SR: azaza

In this example, the second *a* serves both as the right context of the first *s:z* correspondence and as the left context of the second *s:z* correspondence. Therefore, when it is first recognized in state 3 of the table, a transition must be made back to state 2 so that the rule can apply again.

(2) Compiling a ⇐ rule with left and right contexts

Now suppose that the *s:z* correspondence is found in these forms:

LR: sasa   sasa
SR: saza   zaza

According to the questions in part 3, these correspondences indicate that *s* is always realized as *z* between vowels, but between vowels is not the only environment in which *s:z* is allowed (it also occurs word-initially). Therefore, posit a ⇐ rule:

R44   s:z ⇐ V ___ V

To compile rule 44, follow the steps in part 5:

⇐ table with left and right contexts

T44		V	s	s	@
		V	z	@	@
	1:	2	1	1	1
	2:	2	1	3	1
	3:	0	1	1	1

To account for backlooping, state 2 must have a 2 in the *V:V* column, parallel to table 43. But unlike table 43, state 3 must have a 0 in the *V:V* column, not a 2. This is because rule 44 is a ⇐ rule and must disallow the sequence *V:V s:@ V:V*. However, table 44 still correctly handles lexical forms such as *asasa* because only states 1 and 2 are used.

(3) Compiling a ⇔ rule with left and right contexts

Now suppose that the *s:z* correspondence is found only in an intervocalic position and *s:s* never is:

LR: sasa
SR: saza

According to the questions in part 3, these correspondences indicate that *s* is always realized as *z* between vowels, and between vowels is the only environment in which *s:z* is allowed. Therefore, posit a ⇔ rule:

R45   s:z ⇔ V ___ V

To compile rule 45, follow the steps in part 6:

⇔ table with left and right contexts

T45		V	s	s	@
		V	z	@	@
	1:	2	0	1	1
	2:	2	4	3	1
	3:	0	1	1	1
	4.	2	0	0	0

Rows 1 through 3 constitute the ⇐ part of the rule (compare rule 44), and rows 1, 2, and 4 constitute the ⇒ part of the rule (compare rule 43).

(4) Compiling a $\Leftarrow$ rule with left and right contexts

The fourth rule type, the $\Leftarrow$ rule, disallows the correspondence in the specified environment. For example, rule 46 prohibits *V:V s:z V:V*.

R46   s:z $\Leftarrow$ V___V

To compile rule 46 to a state table, follow the steps in part 7:

$\Leftarrow$ table with left and right contexts

	V	s	@
	V	z	@
1:	2	1	1
2:	2	3	1
3:	0	1	1

T46

3.3.7 Compiling insertion rules

The procedure for compiling two-level rules into state tables is slightly different for rules that insert characters. Compiling a $\Rightarrow$ insertion rule is the same as described in the previous sections, but compiling a $\Leftarrow$ rule requires a different strategy. We will demonstrate the procedure for handling insertion rules with an example from the Hanunoo language of the Philippines. In Hanunoo, the consonant *h* is inserted to break up a vowel cluster. This occurs, for instance, when the suffix *i* is added to a root that ends with a consonant; compare the following forms (Schane 1973:54).

ROOT		ROOT+i	
ʔunum	'six'	ʔunumi	'make it six'
ʔusa	'one'	ʔusahi	'make it one'

In the following two-level representations, the inserted *h* is represented as corresponding to a lexical NULL symbol (zero):

LR: ʔunum+i   ʔusa+0i
SR: ʔunum0i   ʔusa0hi

The $\Rightarrow$ rule for *h*-insertion is written as expected:

h-insertion

R47   0:h $\Rightarrow$ V +:0___V

and is compiled into a state table in the usual way:

h-insertion

T47

	V + 0 @			
	V 0 h @			
1:	2	1	0	1
2:	2	3	0	1
3:	2	1	4	1
4.	2	0	0	0

Constructing the ⇐ table, however, is not as straightforward. Following the general procedure for compiling ⇐ rules to tables, we might expect to construct a the ⇐ table using the column headers *0:h* and *0:@*, where *0:@* is intended to specify *0:~h* (that is, a lexical *0* corresponding to anything except a surface *h*):

h-insertion

R48   0:h ⇐ V +:0 ___ V

h-insertion

T48

	V + 0 0 @				
	V 0 h @ @				
1:	2	1	1	1	1
2:	2	3	1	1	1
3:	2	1	1	4	1
4:	0	1	1	1	1

Unfortunately, if we submit the lexical input form *ʔusa+i* to rules 47 and 48, both the correct result *ʔusahi* and the incorrect result *ʔusai* will be returned. Why didn't rule 48, the ⇐ rule, force the insertion of *h* as expected? The answer is in the meaning of the column header *0:@*. What we really want the ⇐ rule to do is to recognize the absence of an inserted *h* in the specified environment and then to fail, that is, to prohibit the sequence *V +:0 V*. In effect this means that the table would have to recognize the correspondence *0:0* as an instance of the column header *0:@*. However, *0:0* is not a feasible pair (and indeed never could be); thus the column header *0:@* cannot specify *0:0*. As a matter of fact, if there are no other insertion correspondences in the description, PC-KIMMO will report an error when it tries to interpret table 48, since there would be no feasible pairs that would match the *0:@* column header.

The answer to writing a table that makes *h*-insertion obligatory (that is, the effect of a ⇐ rule) is that it is necessary only to disallow the sequence *V +:0 V*. This can be easily done with a ⇍ rule of this form:

h-insertion

R49   0:0 ⇍ V +:0 ___ V

This rule must be understood in a special way. Although it follows the general syntax of two-level rules (correspondence, operator, environment), it departs from the normal meaning of two-level rules in that its correspondence part, namely *0:0*, is not a feasible pair. However, its intended meaning is clear when it is compared to the corresponding ⇒ rule (see the rule in the header line in table 47). It simply means that something must be inserted where the environment line is located. The ⇒ rule provides the *h*, which is inserted at this point. The table that expresses rule 49 looks like this:

h-insertion

T49

	V	+	@
	V	0	@
1:	2	1	1
2:	2	3	1
3:	0	1	1

Now it is obvious that the two rules can be combined as a single ⇔ rule.

h-insertion

R50   0:h ⇔ V +:0 ___ V

h-insertion

T50

	V	+	0	@
	V	0	h	@
1:	2	1	0	1
2:	2	3	0	1
3:	0	1	4	1
4.	2	0	0	0

3.3.8 Using subsets in state tables

Section 3.1.4 introduced the use of subsets in two-level rules. This section discusses their use in state tables. Assume that a two-level description contains these subsets (see section 3.4.3 on subset declarations):

SUBSET D	t d s
SUBSET P	c j š
SUBSET Vhf	i e

In section 3.1.4 a rule using these subsets was introduced, repeated here as rule 51.

Palatalization

R51   D:P ⇒ ___ Vhf

Rule 51 states that the alveolar consonants in subset *D* may be realized as the palatalized consonants in subset *P* when they occur preceding the high, front vowels in subset *Vhf*. Specifically, we want the subset correspondence *D:P* to stand for the feasible pairs *t:c*, *d:j*, and *s:š*. Translating rule 51 into a state table is straightforward:

Palatalization

T51	D Vhf @		
	P Vhf @		
1:	2	1	1
2.	0	1	0

However, a two-level description containing table 51 will produce no correct results unless the feasible pairs *t:c*, *d:j*, and *s:š* are declared explicitly. The pairs must appear as column headers in a table somewhere in the description. This is typically done by constructing a table specifically for the purpose of declaring special correspondences. For example, the following table declares the feasible pairs that we want for the column header *D:P*:

Palatalization correspondences

T52	t d s @			
	c j š @			
1:	1	1	1	1

Now the *D:P* column header in table 51 will recognize all and only the pairs declared in table 52. Similarly, the feasible pairs that *Vhf:Vhf* stands for (that is, *i:i* and *e:e*) must be declared somewhere in the description. Since in this case the pairs are default correspondences, they will typically be included in the table with all the other default correspondences.

3.3.9 Overlapping column headers and specificity

Using subsets in rules often leads to a situation where a state table has column headers that potentially overlap. In such a case, unexpected results may occur. For example, consider this rule, which states that *t:c* occurs between any vowel and *i*:

R53   t:c ⇒ V___i

A first attempt at writing a state table for rule 53 might look like this:

T53	V t i @			
	V c i @			
1:	2	0	1	1
2:	2	3	1	1
3.	0	0	1	0

Given the lexical form *mati*, table 53 will correctly produce the surface form *maci*. But given the form *miti*, it will fail to produce the expected result *mici*. This is because of the interaction of the column headers *V:V* and *i:i*. Because the feasible pair *i:i* is an instance of *V:V*, we might expect that the first *i* in the input form *miti* would match the *V:V* column header and cause a successful transition to state 2. This is not the case. For each table in a PC-KIMMO description, the entire set of feasible pairs must be partitioned among the column headers with no overlap. Each feasible pair belongs to one and only one column header. When PC-KIMMO interprets the column headers of a table, it scans the list of all the feasible pairs and assigns each one to a column header. If a feasible pair matches more than one column header, it assigns it to the most specific one, where the specificity of a column header is defined as the number of feasible pairs that matches it. In order to see exactly how the feasible pairs are assigned to the column headers of a rule, use the *show rule* command (see section 7.5.9).

Thus in table 53 the feasible pair *i:i* potentially matches both the column headers *V:V* and *i:i*; but because *i:i* is more specific than *V:V*, the pair *i:i* is assigned to the column header *i:i*. This means that the column header *V:V* stands for all the feasible pairs of vowels except *i:i*. Thus the input pair *i:i* matches only the column header *i:i*. To work correctly, table 53 must allow *i:i* to be an instance of *V:V* in the left context by placing a 2 in states 1 and 2 under the *i:i* header. Note also that the order of the columns has no effect on which column header an input pair is matched to. Table 53a reflects these changes.

T53a

	V	t	i	@
	V	c	i	@
1:	2	0	2	1
2:	2	3	2	1
3.	0	0	1	0

Now consider a description that contains a subset *Vrd* for rounded vowels and a subset *Vhi* for high vowels:

SUBSET Vrd   o u
SUBSET Vhi   i e o u

Notice that the *Vhi* subset properly includes the *Vrd* subset. Assume that the description contains the following rule:

R54   t:c ⇒ Vrd___Vhi

We first write a state table for rule 54 like this:

T54

| | Vrd t Vhi @ |
	Vrd c Vhi @

1:	2	0	1	1
2:	2	3	1	1
3.	0	0	1	0

But the feasible pairs *o:o* and *u:u*, which match both the *Vrd:Vrd* and *Vhi:Vhi* column headers, must belong to the *Vrd:Vrd* column, since it is more specific. Thus the *Vhi* column represents only the pairs *i:i* and *e:e*. This means that a lexical input form such as *utu* will not produce the expected surface form *ucu*, because the second *u* will always match *Vrd*, not *Vhi*. This problem is fixed by including *u:u* and *o:o* as column headers in table 54a:

T54a

| | Vrd t Vhi u o @ |
	Vrd c Vhi u o @

1:	2	0	1	2	2	1
2:	2	3	1	2	2	1
3.	0	0	1	1	1	0

The solution, then, in cases of overlapping column headers is to explicitly include as headers in the table the feasible pairs that belong to both headers.

It is possible to construct a state table in which a feasible pair matches multiple column headers that have the same specificity value, making it impossible to uniquely assign the pair to a column. This constitutes an incorrectly written state table. When the rules file containing such a state table is loaded, a warning message is issued alerting the user that two columns have the same specificity. If the user proceeds to analyze forms with the incorrectly written table, a pair will be assigned (arbitrarily) to the leftmost column that it matches. Correct results cannot be assured.

3.3.10 Expressing word boundary environments

Consider a phonological rule that states that stops are devoiced when they occur in word-final position. For example,

LR: mabab
SR: mabap

Assume these subsets for voiced stops (*B*) and voiceless stops (*P*):

SUBSET B   b d g
SUBSET P   p t k

Two-level rules use the BOUNDARY symbol (#) to indicate word boundary:

Devoicing
R55   B:P ⇔ ___ #

The corresponding state table is written with *#:#* as the column header representing word boundary. Note that a boundary symbol used in a column header can only correspond to another boundary symbol; that is, correspondences such as *#:0* are illegal.

Devoicing

T55		B	B	#	@
		P	@	#	@
	1:	3	2	1	1
	2:	3	2	0	1
	3.	0	0	1	0

Rules and tables that refer to an initial word boundary are written in a similar way. Here is a rule for word-initial spirantization.

Spirantization
R56   p:f ⇔ # ___ V

Spirantization

T56		#	p	p	V	@
		#	f	@	V	@
	1:	2	0	1	1	1
	2:	1	4	3	1	1
	3:	1	0	1	0	1
	4.	0	0	0	1	0

(Notice that since the first symbol of *lc L:S rc* is initial word boundary, backlooping is irrelevant.)

3.3.11   Expressing complex environments in state tables

Section 3.1.6 discussed the notational conventions used to express complex environments in two-level rules. Those rules are repeated here with instructions on how to express them in state tables.

As an example we will use a vowel reduction rule. It states that a vowel followed by some number of consonants followed by stress (indicated by ') is reduced to schwa (ə). For example,

LR: bab'a   bamb'a
SR: bəb'a   bəmb'a

In rule 57 we treat the case where there is exactly one or two intervening consonants. Parentheses indicate that the second consonant is optional.

Vowel Reduction

R57   V:ə ⇒ ___ C(C)'

In table 57, the second, optional consonant is implemented in state 3. The table succeeds when it recognizes the stress, either in state 3 after finding one consonant, or in state 4 after finding another consonant.

Vowel Reduction

T57

	V	C	'	@
	ə	C	'	@
1:	2	1	1	1
2.	0	3	0	0
3.	0	4	1	0
4.	0	0	1	0

Rule and table 58 specify either zero, one, or two consonants.

Vowel Reduction

R58   V:ə ⇒ ___ (C)(C)'

Vowel Reduction

T58

	V	C	'	@
	ə	C	'	@
1:	2	1	1	1
2.	0	3	1	0
3.	0	4	1	0
4.	0	0	1	0

The only difference from table 57 is found in state 2 of table 58, where it is allowed to encounter the stress immediately after the V:ə correspondence.

In rule 59 the asterisk indicates zero or more instances of C.

Vowel Reduction

R59   V:ə ⇒ ___ C*'

Table 59 succeeds in state 2 either by immediately finding stress or by repeating state 2 to find consonants until stress is reached.

Vowel Reduction

T59

	V	C	'	@
	ə	C	'	@
1:	2	1	1	1
2.	0	2	1	0

Rule 60 specifies one or more consonants.

Vowel Reduction

R60   V:ə ⇒ ___ CC* '

Vowel Reduction

T60

	V	C	'	@
	ə	C	'	@
1:	2	1	1	1
2.	0	3	0	0
3.	0	3	1	0

Here state 2 requires that at least one consonant be found. Then state 3 functions like state 2 of the previous example to repeat consonants until stress is found.

Section 3.1.6 discussed multiple environments in two-level rules. In this section the state tables for those rules are provided. The example used here is a vowel lengthening rule. It states that the correspondence *a:ā* (short and long *a*) occurs in two distinct environments: when it is stressed (tonic lengthening) or when it occurs in the syllable preceding stress (pretonic lengthening). For example,

    LR: ladab'ar
    SR: ladāb'ār

First, the tonic and pretonic lengthening rules and tables are written as separate rules:

Pretonic Lengthening

R61   a:ā ⇒ ___ C '

Pretonic Lengthening

T61

	a	C	'	@
	ā	C	'	@
1:	2	1	1	1
2.	0	3	0	0
3.	0	0	1	0

Tonic Lengthening

R62   a:ā ⇒ ' ___

Tonic Lengthening

T62

	'	a	@
	'	ā	@
1:	2	0	1
2:	2	1	1

Note that in state 2 the 2 under the stress header is due to backlooping, even though we do not expect to have two stress marks in succession (see section 3.3.4).

As discussed in section 3.1.6, rules 61 and 62 are contradictory; they both claim to specify the only environment in which *a:ā* is allowed. They must be combined into a single rule, rule 63, which is expressed as state table 63.

Pretonic and Tonic Lengthening

R63   a:ā ⇒ [___ C' | ' ___]

Pretonic and Tonic Lengthening

T63

	a C ' @
	ā C ' @
1:	2 1 4 1
2.	0 3 0 0
3.	0 0 4 0
4:	1 1 4 1

There is one key difference between table 63 and tables 61 and 62. This is the change in state 3 where stress now makes a transition to state 4 rather than back to state 1. This is necessary because stress (which is in the right context of rule 61) is the first symbol of the left context of rule 62. (Note that in state 4 in the stress column the transition back to state 4 is due to backlooping.)

Rules 64 and 65 and tables 64 and 65 express the same lengthening rules, only using the ⇐ operator.

Pretonic Lengthening

R64   a:ā ⇐ ___ C'

Pretonic Lengthening

T64

	a a C ' @
	ā @ C ' @
1:	1 2 1 1 1
2:	1 2 3 1 1
3:	1 2 1 0 1

Tonic Lengthening

R65   a:ā ⇐ ' ___

Tonic Lengthening

T65

	' a a @
	' ā @ @
1:	2 1 1 1
2:	2 1 0 1

In table 64 under the *a:@* header, there are transitions back to state 2 in both state 2 and state 3. This is due to backlooping.

Rules 64 and 65, being ⇐ rules, do not conflict, since each allows the *a:ā* correspondence in environments other than its own. Nevertheless, if the analyst so chooses, they can be combined into one table:

Pretonic and Tonic Lengthening

R66   a:ā ⇐ [___ C' | ' ___]

Pretonic and Tonic Lengthening

T66

	a	a	C	'	@
	ā	@	C	'	@
1:	1	3	1	2	1
2:	1	0	1	2	1
3:	1	3	4	2	1
4:	1	3	1	0	1

3.3.12 Expressing two-level environments

Section 3.1.7 discussed the use of two-level environments in phonological rules. The two rules developed in that section to account for Nasal Assimilation and Stop Voicing are repeated here with their state tables (assume that a default *N:n* correspondence is declared elsewhere in the description):

Nasal Assimilation

R67   N:m ⇔ ___ p:

Nasal Assimilation

T67

	N	N	p	@
	m	@	@	@
1:	3	2	1	1
2:	3	2	0	1
3.	0	0	1	0

Stop Voicing

R68   p:b ⇔ :m ___

Stop Voicing

T68

	@	p	p	@
	m	b	@	@
1:	2	0	1	1
2:	1	1	0	1

These rules relate the lexical sequence *Np* to the surface sequence *mb*. Note carefully that the symbol *p:* in rule 67 is expressed as the column header p:@ in table 67, and the symbol $:m$ in rule 68 is expressed as the column header @:m in table 68. (See section 3.1.7 on overspecification in rules of this type.)

Now assume that the lexical sequence Nb is realized as the surface sequence mb (that is, both lexical Np and Nb are realized as surface mb). This shows that the N:m correspondence is found before a surface b that realizes either a lexical p or b. The distribution of the p:b correspondence is the same. Rule 67 then must be revised as follows:

Nasal Assimilation

R67a   N:m $\Leftrightarrow$ ___:b

Nasal Assimilation

T67a

	N	N	@	@
	m	@	b	@
1:	3	2	1	1
2:	3	1	0	1
3.	0	0	1	0

Unfortunately, if a description containing tables 67a and 68 is given the lexical input form $aNpa$, it produces not only the expected surface form $amba$ but also the incorrect form $anpa$. The reason for this failure is similar to the problem of overspecification discussed in section 3.1.7. Notice the symmetrical, interlocking relationship between 67a and 68. The environment of each rule is the surface character of the correspondence part of the other rule; that is, the environment of 67a is $:b$, which is the surface character of the p:b correspondence of rule 68, and the environment of 68 is $:m$, which is the surface character of the N:m correspondence of rule 67a. This means, with respect to the lexical form $aNpa$, that rule 67a does not require N to be realized as m before a p that is realized as anything other than b, and rule 68 does not require p to be realized as b after an N that is realized as anything other than m. Thus the form $aNpa$ can pass through the two rules vacuously. Assuming that the analyst is correct in positing surface environments for these two rules, the only way to fix the problem is to prohibit the sequence N:n p:p. This can be done either by adding the rule N:n $\nLeftarrow$ ___p, or by incorporating this prohibition into one of the existing tables. For example, we can revise table 67a as follows:

Nasal Assimilation

T67b

	N	N	@	p	@
	m	@	b	p	@
1:	3	2	1	1	1
2:	3	1	0	0	1
3.	0	0	1	0	0

By including the column header *p:p* (or perhaps *@:p*) in table 67b, we can recognize *N:@ p:p* and force failure. Now the lexical form *aNpa* will match only the surface form *amba*. (Alternatively, table 68 could be revised to include the column header *N:n* and fail when the sequence *N:n p:@* is recognized.)

3.3.13 Rule conflicts

The two main types of rule conflicts are the ⇒ (or *environment*) conflict and the ⇐ (or *realization*) conflict (Dalrymple and others 1987:25). The ⇒ conflict arises when two conditions are met: (1) two ⇒ rules have the same correspondence on the left side of the rule, but (2) they have different environments on the right side. (This type of conflict has already been discussed in section 3.1.6.) For example,

Intervocalic Voicing
R69   p:b ⇒ V ___ V

Voicing after nasal
R70   p:b ⇒ m ___

Since the rule operator ⇒ means that the correspondence can occur only in the specified environment, rules 69 and 70 contradict each other. The simplest resolution of the conflict is to combine the two rules into one rule with a disjunctive environment:

Voicing
R71   p:b ⇒ [V ___ V | m ___]

The state table for rule 71 looks like this:

Voicing

	V	m	p	@
	V	m	b	@
1:	2	4	0	1
2:	2	4	3	1
3.	2	0	0	0
4:	2	4	1	1

T71

where states 1, 2, and 3 correspond to the *V___ V* part of rule 71 and states 1 and 4 correspond to the *m ___* part.

Now assume that rules 69 and 70 have been initially written as ⇔ rules:

Intervocalic Voicing
R72   p:b ⇔ V ___ V

Voicing after nasal

R73   p:b ⇔ m ___

Their state tables look like this:

Intervocalic Voicing

T72

	V p p @			
	V b @ @			
1:	2	0	1	1
2:	2	4	3	1
3:	0	0	1	1
4.	2	0	0	0

Voicing after nasal

T73

	m p p @			
	m b @ @			
1:	2	0	1	1
2:	2	1	0	1

A description containing tables 72 and 73 will not work, because the ⇒ sides of the rules conflict, just like rules 69 and 70. There are two ways to resolve the conflict between 72 and 73. First, the rules can be separated into their ⇐ parts and ⇒ parts, and the ⇒ parts combined as above:

Intervocalic Voicing

R74   p:b ⇐ V ___ V

Voicing after nasal

R75   p:b ⇐ m ___

Voicing

R76   p:b ⇒ [V ___ V | m ___]

State tables are easily written for 74 and 75 (not included here), and table 71 encodes rule 76 (same as rule 71).

The second way to resolve the conflict between rules 72 and 73 is to modify the environment of each table to allow the environment of the other. Tables 72 and 73 are revised as 72a and 73a.

Intervocalic Voicing

T72a

	V p p m @				
	V b @ m @				
1:	2	0	1	5	1
2:	2	4	3	5	1
3:	0	0	1	5	1
4.	2	0	0	0	0
5:	2	1	1	5	1

Voicing after nasal

T73a	m	p	p	V	@
	m	b	@	V	@
1:	2	0	1	3	1
2:	2	1	0	3	1
3:	2	1	1	3	1

Table 72a contains the column header *m:m* from table 73, and table 73a contains the column header *V:V* from table 72. This enables the sequence *m:m p:b* to pass vacuously through table 72a and the sequence *V:V p:b V:V* to pass vacuously through table 73a.

It should also be noted that tables 72a and 73a can be combined into a single table that expresses the disjunctive rule *p:b* ⇔ *[V___ V | m___]*. This can be done by dispensing with table 73a and placing a zero in the cell at the intersection of row 5 and the *p:@* column of table 72a. However, when dealing with very complex rules with perhaps more than one conflict, it may be clearer to keep the rules separate as shown above.

The second type of rule conflict is the ⇐ (or realization) conflict. It arises when two conditions are met: (1) the correspondence parts of two ⇐ rules have the same lexical character but different surface realizations of it, and (2) the environment of one rule is subsumed by the environment of the other rule. For example, to account for the following correspondences, we posit rules 77 and 78 (where *ž* stands for a voiced alveopalatal grooved fricative):

LR: asa   isi
SR: aza   iži

Intervocalic Voicing
R77   s:z ⇐ V ___ V

Palatalization
R78   s:ž ⇐ i ___ i

These rules meet both conditions of a ⇐ conflict. First, the lexical characters of their correspondence parts are the same (namely *s*), while the surface characters are different (*z* and *ž*). Second, because *i* is a member of the subset *V*, the environment of rule 77 subsumes the environment of rule 78; that is, *i___ i* is a specific instance of the more general environment *V___ V*. The state tables for 77 and 78 are as follows:

Intervocalic Voicing

T77

	V	s	s	@
	V	z	@	@
1:	2	1	1	1
2:	2	1	3	1
3:	0	1	1	1

Palatalization

T78

	i	s	s	@
	i	ž	@	@
1:	2	1	1	1
2:	2	1	3	1
3:	0	1	1	1

Given the lexical input form *asa*, only rule 77 will apply and return the correct surface form *aza*. Given the lexical form *isi*, we want rule 78 to apply and produce the surface form *iži*, but in fact the rules fail to return any result. This is because rule 77 disallows *s:ž* between vowels (including *i*'s), while rule 78 disallows *s:z* between *i*'s. Also, the rules cannot produce the surface form *izi*, because this contradicts rule 78, which states that *s* must be realized as *ž*.

In generative phonology this type of conflict is resolved by ordering the specific rule before the general rule, in this case Palatalization before Voicing. Rule ordering is of course not available in the two-level model. To resolve a ⇐ conflict in a two-level description, the general rule must be altered to allow (but not require) the correspondence of the specific rule to occur in its environment. Table 77 must therefore be revised as 77a.

Intervocalic Voicing

T77a

	V	s	s	s	@
	V	z	@	ž	@
1:	2	1	1	1	1
2:	1	1	3	1	1
3:	0	1	1	1	1

In table 77 the column header *s:@* stands for the set of correspondences *s:s* and *s:ž*, but in table 77a the inclusion of the header *s:ž* restricts the meaning of *s:@* to only *s:s*. Thus the occurrence of *s:ž* is not restricted by table 77a. Now *s* will be realized as *ž* in the environment *i___i* because table 77a allows it and table 78 requires it.

3.3.14 Comments on the use of ⇒ rules

The two major rule types, the ⇐ rule and the ⇒ rule, have been described informally as the "obligatory" rule and the "optional" rule. The meaning and use of the obligatory $\Leftarrow$ rule are fairly straightforward, but the use of the optional $\Rightarrow$ rule in actual two-level descriptions deserves more comment. There are three ways in which $\Rightarrow$ rules are employed.

First, as the term optional suggests, a $\Rightarrow$ rule is used in cases where two surface characters are truly in free variation, regardless of morphological or lexical context. For example, in many dialects of American English *t* is in free variation with an alveolar flap *D* when it occurs after a vowel and before an unstressed vowel; for example, the word *writer* can be pronounced either [r'aytər] or [r'ayDər]. This is expressed by a $\Rightarrow$ rule such as rule 79 (where the absence of the stress symbol (') indicates no stress). Such rules of free variation are typically low-level phonetic rules.

> Flapping
> R79   t:D $\Rightarrow$ V __ V

Second, a $\Rightarrow$ rule may be used in cases where a correspondence is restricted to certain lexical items or classes of lexical items (for instance, nouns or verbs), or to certain morphological contexts (for instance, nominative case). For example, English needs a rule for the *f:v* correspondence in pairs of words such as *wife* and *wives, leaf* and *leaves.* But this rule is restricted to a very small and arbitrary number of lexical items (it does not apply to *fife, reef,* and so on). The simplest solution is to write the *f:v* rule as a $\Rightarrow$ rule and let it overgenerate and overrecognize. That is, it will generate and recognize nonwords such as *wifes* (the plural of *wife*) and *fives* (the plural of *fife*). For purposes of testing a two-level description, the files of test data should contain only well-formed words.

In generative phonology the solution to this problem is to mark the lexical entries of the words *wife, leaf,* and so on for a "positive rule exception," which says that only words so marked can undergo the *f:v* rule. The lexical component of PC-KIMMO does not allow lexical entries to be so marked for lexical features. However, the same effect can be produced by introducing a special character (often called a diacritic) in the lexical forms of exceptional words. This character serves as the "trigger" for certain rules to apply. Thus *wife* and *leaf* could be given the lexical forms *wayf** and *liyf** while *fife* and *reef* would have the lexical forms *fayf* and *riyf.* The *f:v* rule would then be written like this (where +z stands for the plural morpheme):

R80   f:v $\Leftrightarrow$ __ *:0 +:0 z

While this solution works, it has the undesirable effect of positing lexical representations that contain nonphonological elements. Many linguists would reject such representations on theoretical grounds. (A similar solution is to posit lexical forms such as *wayF* and *liyF* and a rule for *F:v*. The same linguistic objections apply.)

Third, a ⇒ rule is used to "clean up" ⇐ rules. This is a nonobvious but very important use of ⇒ rules. For example, assume that a two-level description contains two obligatory rules for lengthening, namely rules 64 and 65 in section 3.1.6 for pretonic and tonic lengthening. While these rules may express intuitively that lengthening applies obligatorily in the specified environments, running PC-KIMMO with just these two rules will result in overgeneration. Because ⇐ rules do not restrict the occurrence of the correspondence in other environments, rules 64 and 65 will produce forms with the *a:ā* correspondence in environments where they do not occur. For example, given the lexical input *labad'ar*, rules 64 and 65 will return both *labād'ār* (correct) and *lābād'ār* (incorrect). To prevent this type of overgeneration, ⇐ rules must be accompanied by analogous ⇒ rules. Thus when rule 63 is added to the description containing rules 64 and 65, only correct surface forms will be generated.

As a practical procedure in developing a two-level description, the user will typically write all the obligatory ⇐ rules for a given correspondence first. Then to correct the resulting overgeneration, the user must write a single ⇒ rule for the correspondence; it must contain as a multiple environment (to avoid ⇒ conflicts) all the contexts of the ⇐ rules for the correspondence.

As another example of the use of ⇒ rules as "clean-up" rules, consider again an example used in section 3.1.6 where the vowel of the ultimate syllable of a word is lengthened unless it is schwa, in which case the vowel of the penultimate syllable is lengthened (for example, *mamān* and *mamānə*).

Assume these subsets:

SUBSET V   i a u ə
SUBSET Vlng   ī ā ū

and these special correspondences:

Lengthening correspondences

$$
\begin{array}{c|cccc}
 & i & a & u & @ \\
 & ī & ā & ū & @ \\
\hline
1: & 1 & 1 & 1 & 1 \\
\end{array}
$$

Following the procedure described above, assume that this is an obligatory process. Here is the ⇐ rule and its state table:

Lengthening
R81   V:Vlng ⇐ ___ C(ə)#

Lengthening

T81

	V	V	C	ə	#	@
	Vlng	@	C	ə	#	@
1:	1	2	1	1	1	1
2:	1	2	3	1	1	1
3:	1	2	1	4	0	1
4:	1	2	1	1	0	1

Now to prevent the overgeneration of ill-formed surface forms such as *māmān* and *māmānə*, this "clean-up" ⇒ rule must be included:

Lengthening
R82   V:Vlng ⇒ ___ C(ə)#

Lengthening

T82

	V	C	ə	#	@
	Vlng	C	ə	#	@
1:	2	1	1	1	1
2.	0	3	0	0	0
3.	0	0	4	1	0
4.	0	0	0	1	0

3.3.15 Comments on the use of morpheme boundaries

In standard generative phonology, a phonological rule that applies to the segments XY also applies to X+Y, where + indicates a morpheme boundary (Chomsky and Halle 1968:364). In other words, a phonological rule that applies within a morpheme is assumed also to apply across morpheme boundaries. Thus it is not necessary to include optional morpheme boundaries in rules. Clearly two-level rules can also be written without optional morpheme boundaries; but state tables must explicitly include a morpheme boundary column even if they are optional at each point in the input string. To make a morpheme boundary completely optional in a table, simply loop back to the current state in each state of the table. For example, here is a rule and table for intervocalic voicing:

Intervocalic voicing
R83   s:z ⇔ V ___ V

T83

	V	s	s	+	@
	V	z	@	0	@
1:	2	0	1	1	1
2:	2	4	3	2	1
3:	0	0	1	3	1
4.	2	0	0	4	0

(Notice that rows 1–3 encode the ⇐ part of the rule and rows 1–2 and 4 encode the ⇒ part.) This table will allow a morpheme boundary at any point in the lexical form, for instance *sa+za* and *saz+a*.

It should be noted that generative descriptions do use explicit morpheme boundaries in rules; in such cases the rule only applies in the presence of the boundary. Often this is done to limit the rule's application to a specific morpheme by actually "spelling out" the morpheme in the rule's environment. This trick is necessary also in PC-KIMMO, since PC-KIMMO does not allow the application of rules to be limited to certain lexical items by means of lexical features. For example, the English prefix *in+* has the allomorphs *il+* and *ir+* in words such as *illegal* and *irregular* (compare *intolerable*). But we do not want to write a rule that changes *n* to *l* or *r* everywhere (compare *unlawful, inlet, enlarge, unreal*). Therefore we write the ⇒ rule and table for *n:l* to limit the application of the rule to the lexical form *in+*. (The rule could be made even more specific by requiring the prefix to be word-initial.)

R84   n:l ⇒ i___+l

T84

	i	n	+	l	@
	i	l	0	l	@
1:	2	1	1	1	1
2:	2	3	1	1	1
3.	0	0	4	0	0
5.	0	0	0	1	0

3.3.16 Expressing phonotactic constraints

In section 3.3.4 we recommended that tables should be written without incorporating phonotactic constraints in them. As a matter of practice, this approach may result in less time spent debugging a set of rules. But more importantly, a linguistic description should distinguish between phonological rules (correspondences between lexical and surface characters) and phonotactic constraints (restrictions on permitted sequences of characters). For instance, just as the phonological description of English includes allophonic rules stating the distribution of aspirated and unaspirated voiceless stops, it also includes phonotactic constraints such as restrictions on possible word-initial consonant clusters.

As an example of how to encode phonotactic constraints as state tables, consider a language that allows words of the phonological shape CV(C)CV(C). That is, a word minimally consists of two open (CV) syllables, each of which can optionally be closed by a consonant. Possible words are *baba*, *bamba*, *bambam*, and so on. The following state table restricts all words to this pattern:

CV(C)CV(C) pattern

T85	#	C	V	@
	#	@	@	@
1:	2	1	1	1
2.	0	3	0	2
3.	0	0	4	3
4.	0	5	0	4
5.	0	6	7	5
6.	0	0	7	6
7.	1	8	0	7
8.	1	0	0	8

By using the column headers *C:@* and *V:@* rather than *C:C* and *V:V*, table 85 is a statement of phonotactic constraints on lexical forms, not surface forms. Phonological rules such as deletions could result in surface forms that do not conform to the lexical-level phonotactic pattern. To allow for diacritics such as stress ('), the *@:@* column in table 85 ignores all symbols that are not either consonants or vowels. Thus a word such as *bab'a* is allowed by the table.

As another example, we will attempt to describe the constraints on initial consonant clusters in English. First we will define the following subsets for voiceless stops (*P*), liquids (*L*), and nasals (*N*):

SUBSET P   p t k c
SUBSET L   l r
SUBSET N   m n

We want to allow word-initial clusters of the following types: *sP*, *sL*, *sN*, *sPL*, and *PL*. These constraints on clusters at the lexical level are encoded in table 86.

Word-initial consonant cluster constraints

T86	#	s	P	L	N	V	C	@
	#	@	@	@	@	@	@	@
1:	2	1	1	1	1	1	1	1
2:	1	3	4	5	5	1	5	2
3.	0	0	4	5	5	1	0	3
4.	0	0	0	5	0	1	0	4
5.	0	0	0	0	0	1	0	5

Table 86 will allow the lexical forms of words such as *spit, slit, snip, prick, click, split, string,* and so on, but disallow *sbit, slpit, spmit, mlik,* and so on. Unfortunately, it will also allow nonoccurring words such as *srit, tlick,* and *sklit* (though *scl* does occur in words of Greek origin, for instance *sclera*). To disallow these, another table can encode refinements to the above table:

More initial consonant cluster constraints

T87	#	s	t	k	l	r	N	V	C	@
	#	@	@	@	@	@	@	@	@	@
1:	2	1	1	1	1	1	1	1	1	1
2:	1	3	4	1	1	1	1	1	1	2
3.	0	0	4	4	1	0	1	1	1	3
4.	0	0	0	0	0	1	0	1	0	4

(Note that tables 86 and 87 disallow the clusters *sph* and *sv*, which occur in words of foreign origin such as *sphere* and *svelte*.)

Another example of analyzing phonotactic structure with PC-KIMMO is found in appendix B, section B.1.

3.4 Writing the rules file

This section contains instructions on how to write the rules file for the PC-KIMMO program (a more detailed specification of the rules file is found in section 7.7.1). We will develop a sample rules file for a set of hypothetical data. In this section, examples of parts of the rules file are printed in typewriter style.

The general structure of the rules file is a list of declarations composed of a keyword followed by data. The set of valid keywords in a rules file includes ALPHABET, NULL, ANY, BOUNDARY, SUBSET, RULE, and END. Only the SUBSET and RULE keywords can appear more than once. The ALPHABET declaration must appear first in the file. The other declarations can appear in any order. The NULL, ANY, BOUNDARY, and SUBSET declarations can even be interspersed among the rules. However, these declarations must appear before any rule that uses them or an error will result.

To begin creating a rules file, use your text editor or word processing program to create a file with the extension .RUL (for example, SAM-PLE.RUL). When you save the file to disk, be sure to save it as plain text (ASCII). We also recommend that you use an editor that handles column blocks; this makes manipulating state tables much easier. Type the basic skeleton of a PC-KIMMO rules file as shown in figure 3.8 (a template of a rules file is also available in the file RULES.RUL on the PC-KIMMO release diskette):

Figure 3.8 The skeleton of a PC-KIMMO rules file

```
ALPHABET
NULL
ANY
BOUNDARY
SUBSET
RULE
END
```

Comments can be added to the rules file that are ignored by PC-KIMMO. The default comment delimiter character is semicolon (;). Anything on a line following a semicolon is considered a comment and is ignored. Extra spaces and blank lines are also ignored.

3.4.1 The ALPHABET

The rules file must first declare the alphabet. This is the entire set of characters, both lexical and surface, used by the rules and lexicon. The first keyword of the rules file must be the word ALPHABET. It is followed by any number of lines of characters, each separated by at least one space. For example,

```
ALPHABET
p t k b d g m n ñ ç j s S z Z h l r w y
i e a o u ï ë ä ö ü
+ '
```

The alphabet can consist of any alphanumeric characters, including those available in the extended character set on IBM PC-compatible computers. Uppercase and lowercase are considered distinct characters. Nonalphabetic characters such as $, &, !, ', #, and + may also be used. In the above alphabet, + indicates a morpheme boundary and ' indicates stress. In this section, the examples printed in typewriter style use only those characters available on IBM PC compatible computers. For instance, elsewhere in this chapter we have used characters such as *ā* and *š*, but in this section characters such as ä and S are used.

It should be noted that digraphs can be used in a PC-KIMMO description, though we recommend that they be avoided. For example, say we want to use the digraph *ng* to represent the velar nasal. *ng* cannot be included in the alphabet; rather both *n* and *g* must be included separately. Rules cannot refer to *ng* directly; *n* and *g* must be treated as if they were separate characters. For example, it is not possible to write a rule such as this:

N:ng ⇔ ___ k

This is because there must be a one-to-one relationship between lexical and surface characters. To produce the effect of such a rule, the rule must be written this way:

N:n ⇔ ___ 0:g k

That is, *N* is realized as *n* before a zero that is realized as *g* which is followed by *k*. This will account for correspondences such as *aN0ka:angka*. To avoid such complicated insertions and deletions, digraphs should not be used.

3.4.2 NULL, ANY, and BOUNDARY symbols

Next, the NULL (empty or zero) symbol is declared. Any character not already in the alphabet can be chosen, but for obvious reasons 0 (zero) is typically used. The NULL symbol is used for deletions, for instance *h:0*, and insertions, for instance *0:h*. The NULL symbol is declared by including this line:

```
NULL 0
```

Next, the ANY ("wildcard") symbol is declared. Again, any character not already in the alphabet can be chosen; in this book we use @ ("at" sign). The ANY symbol is declared by including this line:

```
ANY @
```

Next, the BOUNDARY (word boundary) symbol is declared. Again, any character not already in the alphabet can be chosen; in this book we use **#** (crosshatch or pound sign). The BOUNDARY symbol is declared by including this line:

```
BOUNDARY #
```

3.4.3 Subsets

Next in the rules file the subsets, if any, are declared. A subset declaration is composed of the keyword SUBSET followed by a subset name followed by a list of subset characters. A subset name can be any alphanumeric string (one or more characters, no spaces) so long as it is unique; that is, it cannot be a single character already declared in the alphabet. Uppercase characters are useful for subset names because they are usually distinct from their lowercase equivalents. All characters defined as belonging to a subset must also be in the complete alphabet. Subsets are declared by including lines such as these:

```
SUBSET C     p t k b d g m n ñ ç j s S z Z h l r w y
SUBSET V     i e a o u
SUBSET Vlng  ï ë ä ö ü
SUBSET Cvd   b d g m n ñ z l r w y
SUBSET Oalv  t d s z
SUBSET Opal  ç j S Z
SUBSET Ovd   b d g z
SUBSET Ovl   p t k s
```

3.4.4 Rules

The rest of the rules file consists of the rules. A rule declaration is composed of the keyword RULE followed by the rule name, number of states, number of columns, and the state table itself. The rule name is enclosed in a pair of identical delimiter characters such as double quotes. The rule name has no effect on the operation of the table. It actually can contain any information, but by convention we use it for the name and the two-level notation of the rule. It is also useful to include a sequence number for each rule, as rules are referred to by number in some of the diagnostic displays for rule debugging. Notice that the horizontal and vertical lines printed in the tables shown in this chapter are not present in an actual rules file.

By common convention, the first rules listed are the tables of default correspondences, though these correspondences can be listed anywhere in the file. For the sake of consistency, it is best to place all the default correspondences in these tables even if they also occur in other tables. The possible redundancy has no effect on the operation of the tables. Tables of default correspondences for the alphabet given in section 3.4.1 look like this:

```
RULE "1 Consonant defaults" 1 17
   p t k b d g m n ñ s z h l r w y @
   p t k b d g m n ñ s z h l r w y @
1: 1 1 1 1 1 1 1 1 1 1 1 1 1 1 1 1 1

RULE "2 Vowels and other defaults" 1 8
   i e a o u ' + @
   i e a o u ' 0 @
1: 1 1 1 1 1 1 1 1
```

The two tables could be combined into one; consonants and vowels have been separated here for increased readability. Notice that the morpheme boundary symbol (+) is deleted by default; that is, it has no surface realization other than 0.

After the tables of default correspondences come the rules for special correspondences. The rules developed below account for examples such as these:

```
LR:  s'ati   s'adi   bab'at   bab'ad
SR:  s'açi   s'äji   bab'at   bab'ät
```

These rules account for Palatalization:

```
RULE "3 Palatalization correspondences" 1 5
   t d s z @
   ç j S Z @
1: 1 1 1 1 1

RULE "4 Palatalization, Oalv:Opal <=> __i" 3 4
   Oalv Oalv i @
   Opal  @   i @
1:   3    2  1 1
2:   3    2  0 1
3.   0    0  1 0
```

Rule 4 is a palatalization rule that states that the alveolar consonants are realized as palatalized consonants before i. Because rule 4 uses subsets, the feasible pairs represented by the correspondence Oalv:Opal must be explicitly declared. Rule 3 contains these correspondences which are relevant only to rule 4. The special correspondences from all the rules in the description could be combined into one table (or they could even be combined with the tables of default correspondences). However, for readability and to make it easier to modify and debug the rules file, we recommend that a separate table of special correspondences be kept with each rule that uses subsets.

Rules 5 and 6 state that vowels are lengthened when they are stressed (that is, follow ') and precede a lexical voiced consonant (that is, a member of the subset Cvd).

```
RULE "5 Lengthening correspondences" 1 6
    a e i o u @
    ä ë ï ö ü @
1: 1 1 1 1 1 1

RULE "6 Vowel Lengthening, V:Vlng <=> '__Cvd:" 4 5
    '    V    V Cvd @
    ' Vlng  @  @  @
1: 2   0    1  1  1
2: 2   4    3  1  1
3: 2   1    1  0  1
4. 0   0    0  1  0
```

The environment of rule 6 contains the correspondence Cvd:@ rather than Cvd:Cvd because of rules 7 and 8, which devoice obstruents word finally.

```
RULE "7 Devoicing correspondences" 1 5
    b d g z @
    p t k s @
1: 1 1 1 1 1

RULE "8 Final Devoicing, Ovd:Ovl <=> __#" 3 4
    Ovd Ovd # @
    Ovl  @  # @
1: 3   2  1 1
2: 3   2  0 1
3. 0   0  1 0
```

The rules file optionally ends with a line containing only the word END. Any material in the file after this line is ignored by PC-KIMMO.

```
END
```

3.4.5 Example of a rules file

As a ready model for the format of a rules file, the example developed above is repeated in its entirety in figure 3.9. This file is found on the PC-KIMMO release diskette in the SAMPLE subdirectory.

Figure 3.9 Sample rules file

```
ALPHABET
  p t k b d g m n ñ ç j s S z Z h l r w y
  i e a o u ï ë ä ö ü
  + '
NULL 0
ANY @
BOUNDARY #
SUBSET C p t k b d g m n ñ ç j s S z Z h l r w y
SUBSET V i e a o u
SUBSET Vlng ï ë ä ö ü
SUBSET Cvd b d g m n ñ z l r w y
SUBSET Oalv t d s z
SUBSET Opal ç j S Z
SUBSET Ovd b d g z
SUBSET Ovl p t k s
END

RULE "1 Consonant defaults" 1 17
   p t k b d g m n ñ s z h l r w y @
   p t k b d g m n ñ s z h l r w y @
1: 1 1 1 1 1 1 1 1 1 1 1 1 1 1 1 1 1

RULE "2 Vowels and other defaults" 1 8
   i e a o u ' + @
   i e a o u ' 0 @
1: 1 1 1 1 1 1 1 1

RULE "3 Palatalization correspondences" 1 5
   t d s z @
   ç j S Z @
1: 1 1 1 1 1

RULE "4 Palatalization, Oalv:Opal <=> __i" 3 4
   Oalv Oalv i @
   Opal @    i @
1:   3    2   1 1
2:   3    2   0 1
3.   0    0   1 0
```

```
RULE "5 Lengthening correspondences" 1 6
   a  e  i  o  u  @
   ä  ë  ï  ö  ü  @
1: 1  1  1  1  1  1

RULE "6 Vowel Lengthening, V:Vlng <=> '__Cvd:" 4 5
   '    V    V  Cvd  @
   '  Vlng   @   @   @
1: 2    0    1   1   1
2: 2    4    3   1   1
3: 2    1    1   0   1
4. 0    0    0   1   0

RULE "7 Devoicing correspondences" 1 5
   b  d  g  z  @
   p  t  k  s  @
1: 1  1  1  1  1

RULE "8 Final Devoicing, Ovd:Ovl <=> __#" 3 4
   Ovd  Ovd  #  @
   Ovl   @   #  @
1:  3    2   1  1
2:  3    2   0  1
3.  0    0   1  0

END
```

4

DEVELOPING THE LEXICAL COMPONENT

This chapter describes the structure of PC-KIMMO's lexical component, how morphotactic constraints are encoded, and how to write a PC-KIMMO lexicon file.

4.1 Structure of the lexical component

PC-KIMMO's lexical component works together with its rules component (see chapter 3) to recognize words. PC-KIMMO's lexicon performs three functions:

- it cites the *lexical representation* of each lexical item;

- it specifies *morphotactic constraints* (that is, the allowed order of morphemes in a word); and

- it provides a *gloss* or parse of each lexical item.

PC-KIMMO's lexicon consists of a list of lexical entries for all the lexical items accounted for by the description. A lexical item can be either a single morpheme (such as a root, prefix, or suffix) or a morphologically complex word (root plus prefixes and suffixes). However, most complex words are not given lexical entries in the lexicon; rather their constituent morphemes are entered together with rules of combination (morphotactic rules). For instance, to account for the English words *happy*, *unhappy*, *happily*, and *unhappily*, the lexicon needs entries only for *un+*, *happy*, and *+ly*. Morphotactic rules state that *un+* can be followed by *happy*, which in turn can be followed by *+ly*.

The lexicon also contains lexical entries for alternants of lexical items that cannot be accounted for by phonological rules specified in the rules component. For example, the English word *went* could be given the lexical representation *go+ed*, but they could not be related by general phonological rules; thus the lexicon must contain entries for both *go* and *went*. All irregular and suppletive forms are handled in this way.

The lexicon is divided into sublexicons. Each sublexicon represents a class of lexical items that behave alike morphotactically. For instance, a description of English would have a large class of lexical items that fill the same position as *happy*; these can be placed in a sublexicon named ADJ_ROOT. While these sublexicons often reflect major word-classes such as Noun, Verb, and Adjective, their main function is to define morphotactic patterns (as will become clear in section 4.2). Grammatical properties of lexical items, such as word-class membership, are best recorded in the gloss part of the lexical entry (see below).

Each sublexicon contains lexical entries. A lexical entry consists of three parts:

- the *lexical item* (usually a single morpheme);
- its *continuation class*; and
- its *gloss*.

A lexical entry for *happy* might look like this:

happy   ADJ_SUFFIX   "Adj(happy)"

The first part of this lexical entry is the lexical item itself, *happy*. It is cited in its lexical (underlying) representation (the English example used in this chapter will use standard orthography). It is related to its surface realizations (allomorphs) by means of phonological rules of the kind described in chapter 3.

The second part of the entry specifies the continuation class of the lexical item—that is, the sublexicon that can follow the lexical item. Thus *happy* can be followed by a lexical item from the sublexicon called ADJ_SUFFIX. PC-KIMMO's lexical component uses continuation classes to encode morphotactic rules. Continuation classes have the inherent limitation that they can specify only what can follow a certain lexical item. In this example the continuation class specifies only one sublexicon. But often a lexical item can be followed by any of several different sublexicons. For example, the lexical item *happy* can be followed either by a sublexicon containing *+ness* or by a sublexicon containing *+er* and *+est*. In the PC-KIMMO lexicon an *alternation* is a list (possibly with only one member) of continuation classes (sublexicon names). In other words, an alternation defines the set of sublexicons that can follow a lexical item. Thus in the above lexical entry the label ADJ_SUFFIX could be redefined as an alternation that stands for the continuation classes (sublexicons) ADJ_SUFFIX1 and ADJ_SUFFIX2. (The term alternation is not well chosen, but is fixed in the literature on KIMMO. Its intended sense is closer to "alternative continuations.")

The third part of the above lexical entry, the gloss, contains any information about the lexical item the analyst wants to record. It typically gives the word-class and a gloss of the lexical item, but can be used to record any morphological, grammatical, lexical, or semantic properties of the lexical item. When a word is processed by the recognizer, the gloss of each constituent morpheme as it is recognized is appended to the result string.

4.2 Encoding morphotactics as a finite state machine

Section 3.2 introduced finite state machines and showed how PC-KIMMO implements phonological rules as finite state transducers (FSTs). The lexical component of PC-KIMMO also uses finite state machines. Morphotactic constraints are represented in the lexicon by structuring it as a finite state automaton (FSA). Whereas two-level phonological rules require an FST that can operate on two strings at once, the process of recognizing morpheme sequences in the lexical form of a word deals with only one level. Thus it uses the less complex formalism of the FSA, which operates on only a single string. The PC-KIMMO lexicon is an FSA in which (1) each alternation name is a state; (2) continuation classes are the arcs that point to the next state; and (3) sublexicons of lexical items are the labels on the arcs.

As an example of how to represent morphotactic rules as an FSA, we will construct a lexicon to account for the set of English adjectives found in figure 4.1. From this data we infer that adjectives are composed of an optional prefix *un+*, an adjective root, and an optional suffix taken from the set *+er*, *+est*, and *+ly*. In other words, the morphotactic structure of adjectives consists of three linear positions or slots, each of which is filled by a class of morphemes. This analysis is shown in chart form in figure 4.2.

Figure 4.1 English adjectives sample data

big, bigger, biggest
cool, cooler, coolest, coolly
red, redder, reddest
clear, clearer, clearest, clearly, unclear, unclearly
happy, happier, happiest, happily
unhappy, unhappier, unhappiest, unhappily
real, unreal, really

Figure 4.3 shows our analysis of the internal structure of English adjectives represented as an FSA. The FSA diagram is read as follows (see also section 3.2 on understanding finite state machines).

1. The initial state, labeled Begin, represents the beginning of the word. It has two arcs leading from it, an arc labeled ADJ_PREFIX and an arc labeled with a zero. The arcs leading from the Begin state indicate what can occur word-initially in an adjective. The ADJ_PREFIX arc stands for the prefix *un+*. A zero arc in an FSA means that the arc is traversed to the next state without consuming any input. In other

Figure 4.2 Positional analysis of English adjectives

± PREFIX	+ ROOT	± SUFFIX
	big	
	big	+er
	big	+est
	cool	
	cool	+er
	cool	+est
	cool	+ly
	red	
	red	+er
	red	+est
	clear	
	clear	+er
	clear	+est
	clear	+ly
un+	clear	
un+	clear	+ly
	happy	
	happy	+er
	happy	+est
	happy	+ly
un+	happy	
un+	happy	+er
un+	happy	+est
un+	happy	+ly
un+	happy	
	real	
	real	+ly
un+	real	

Figure 4.3 FSA diagram of English adjectives

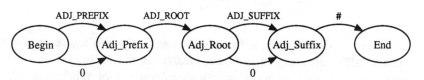

words, it is a free jump to the next state. In this FSA, the zero arc represents the absence of ADJ_PREFIX; that is, the ADJ_PREFIX slot is optional.

2. The second state, labeled Adj_Prefix, has only one arc leading from it, labeled ADJ_ROOT. This arc representing the class of adjective roots. The fact that there is no zero arc leading from this state indicates that the adjective root slot is obligatory.

3. The third state, labeled Adj_Root, has two arcs leading from it, one labeled ADJ_SUFFIX and the other a zero arc. The ADJ_SUFFIX arc stands for the class of suffixes that includes +er, +est, and +ly. The zero arc indicates that the adjective suffix slot is optional.

4. The fourth state, labeled Adj_Suffix, has only one arc leading from it, labeled with a # symbol. This arc indicates a final word boundary. It leads to the fifth and final state, labeled End, which represents the end of the input word.

This FSA will recognize all the adjectives listed in the chart in figure 4.2. Unfortunately, it will also recognize many forms not listed in the chart, for instance, *unbig, redly, unclearer,* and *realest.* Our initial analysis, based strictly on the identification of root and affix positions and their linear order, is not adequate to exclude these nonoccurring forms. To solve this problem, it is necessary to set up subclasses of lexical items in each positional slot and specify cooccurrence restrictions among them. For instance, to exclude *unbig,* adjective roots must be divided into two subclasses: ADJ_ROOT1 (including *clear, happy,* and *real*) which can cooccur with the prefix *un+,* and ADJ_ROOT2 (including *big, cool,* and *red*) which cannot cooccur with *un+.* The FSA for this analysis is shown in figure 4.4.

Figure 4.4 Another FSA diagram of English adjectives

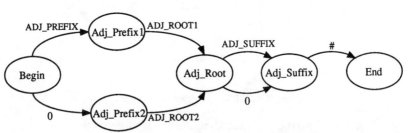

Now consider that the suffix *+ly* cooccurs only with adjectives from the ADJ_ROOT1 subclass; for instance, *clearly* but not *bigly.* The suffixes *+er* and *+est,* however, cooccur with both adjective root subclasses (*clearer, bigger*). Therefore, we need two ADJ_SUFFIX subclasses: ADJ_SUFFIX1, which includes *+ly*, and ADJ_SUFFIX2, which includes *+er* and *+est*. This analysis is shown in figure 4.5.

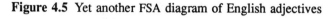

Figure 4.5 Yet another FSA diagram of English adjectives

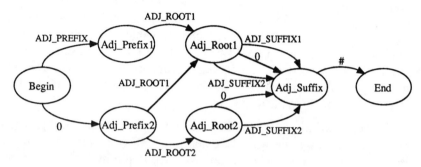

We have now assigned every morpheme in the original data to at least one subclass based on its relative position in the word and cooccurrence constraints with other morphemes. This is as far as we will take the analysis of the English adjectives data. It would be possible to make further subclasses in our analysis to restrict the cooccurrences of particular morphemes even more accurately. For instance, the FSA in figure 4.5 allows the dubious forms *realer* and *realest*. It is up to the analyst to decide where the boundaries are between actual words, potential but nonoccurring words, and impossible words.

Because each lexical item in a language has a complex network of relationships to other lexical items, an exhaustive analysis could end up with each morpheme in a separate subclass. As a matter of practice when analyzing language data and setting up a PC-KIMMO lexicon, it is advisable to start with a simple positional analysis of word structure and defer the problem of handling cooccurrence restrictions among lexical subclasses.

We should emphasize that PC-KIMMO does not itself perform morphotactic analysis; it only encodes and checks the analysis provided by the linguist. For languages with very complicated morphotactics, simple inspection and charting of data may be insufficient. A more formal approach may be necessary to discover affix positions and cooccurrence restrictions, such as the one described in Grimes 1983.

4.3 Writing the lexicon file

This section contains instructions on how to write the lexicon file for the PC-KIMMO program. A detailed specification of the lexicon file is found in section 7.7.2. In what follows here, examples of parts of the lexicon file are printed in typewriter style.

The general structure of the lexicon file is a list of declarations composed of a keyword followed by data. The set of valid keywords includes ALTERNATION, LEXICON, INCLUDE, and END. The declarations can appear in any order with the exception that a LEXICON declaration must appear after the ALTERNATION declaration that refers to it. The only required declaration is LEXICON INITIAL; that is, a lexicon file must minimally be composed of one sublexicon named INITIAL. The whole file is optionally terminated by the keyword END; any material in the file after it is ignored by PC-KIMMO.

To begin writing a lexicon file, use your text editor or word processing program to create a file with the extension .LEX (for example, ADJ.LEX). Be sure to save the file as plain text (ASCII). Begin by typing in the basic skeleton of a PC-KIMMO lexicon file as shown in figure 4.6 (a template of a lexicon file is also available in the file LEXICON.LEX on the PC-KIMMO release diskette).

Figure 4.6 The skeleton of a PC-KIMMO lexicon file

```
ALTERNATION End                    End
LEXICON INITIAL
    0                End                  "[ "
LEXICON End
    0                #                    " ]"
END
```

The following restrictions apply to the lexicon file.

- All names that are used in the continuation class field of a lexical entry must be declared previously in the file as alternations, even if the continuation class represents only one sublexicon.

- There must be a sublexicon named INITIAL (must be spelled with all uppercase letters). In a PC-KIMMO lexicon, the INITIAL sublexicon is equivalent to the initial state of the lexical FSA.

- The square brackets in the glosses of the lexical entries for zero in both the INITIAL and End sublexicons are optional. The brackets are included merely to visually set off the gloss from the lexical form in the result string returned by PC-KIMMO.

- The sublexicon named End is optional, but is included here to match the INITIAL sublexicon. Spell it "End" to avoid conflict with the reserved keyword END.

We begin to flesh out the skeleton of the PC-KIMMO lexicon file by entering a name for each sublexicon (lexical class) represented by a labeled arc in the diagram in figure 4.5, one line per name, as in figure 4.7. The keyword LEXICON is followed by a unique name for each lexical (sub)class. Use a word or a phrase that is meaningful to you when you name each of these lexical classes. Keep them short, but don't make them so short that they are cryptic. As a useful convention, we suggest that these names appear as all uppercase letters. No spaces are allowed in names, so if you want to use more than one word in a name, separate the words with an unobtrusive character, like underline (_), hyphen (-), or period (.).

Figure 4.7 LEXICON names for English adjectives

```
ALTERNATION ADJ_PREFIX          ADJ_PREFIX
LEXICON INITIAL
    0                   ADJ_PREFIX          "[ "
LEXICON ADJ_PREFIX
LEXICON ADJ_ROOT1
LEXICON ADJ_ROOT2
LEXICON ADJ_SUF1
LEXICON ADJ_SUF2
LEXICON End
    0                   #                   " ]"
END
```

Now list the lexical entries that are members of each sublexicon, one per line. Each line must contain three parts, in the order shown in figure 4.8: the lexical item, a continuation class, and a gloss, separated by one or more spaces.

Figure 4.8 Format of a lexical entry line

<lexical form>   {<alt. name> I <BOUNDARY symbol>}   <gloss>

The following restrictions apply to lexical entries.

- Each lexical item (typically a morpheme) should be written exactly as it was when you developed your phonological rules (see chapter 3). Whatever character(s) you used to represent a morpheme boundary in your phonological rules should be placed after all prefixes and before all suffixes, for instance *un+* and *+ly*.

- A lexical entry can have the NULL symbol (as defined in the rules file) as its lexical item. There are two reasons for using a null lexical entry. First, a null entry is used to make a sublexicon optional. In the analysis of English adjectives, the prefix position is optional; thus the prefix sublexicon will contain a null entry in addition to the prefix entries. If no prefix is found, the null entry allows the morphotactic machine to jump to the next sublexicon as specified in the continuation class of the null entry. Second, a null entry is used to express a zero morpheme. For example, since English nouns do not have any overt affix to signal singular number (as opposed to the *+s* suffix for plural number), one could place a null entry in the sublexicon containing the plural suffix that has +SINGULAR as its gloss. It should be noted that the use of zero morphemes in linguistic description is controversial.

- The symbol # in the lexical entry in the End sublexicon is the BOUNDARY symbol as declared in the rules file to indicate word boundary. When the boundary symbol occurs in the continuation class field, it indicates that no continuation is possible. In other words, the end of the input word must be encountered.

- The alternation name stands for a list of sublexicons out of which the next morpheme may come. If no further morphemes can follow, the BOUNDARY symbol must appear in this position.

- The gloss must be typed between two identical delimiter characters, like this: `"Adj(big)"`. Spaces can be used in a gloss. If you don't want a gloss to appear for a morpheme, you must enter two delimiters with nothing between (`""`).

Figure 4.9 is the lexicon file for the analysis of English adjectives represented by the FSA diagram in figure 4.5. Notice that several lexical items have more than one entry. For instance, in the ADJ_PREFIX sublexicon there are two null entries, one with the continuation class ADJ_ROOT1 and the other with the continuation class ADJ_ROOT2. In the ADJ_ROOT1 sublexicon each item has two entries, one with the continuation class ADJ_SUFFIX1 and the other with the continuation class ADJ_SUFFIX2. This redundancy can be eliminated by using alternations. (In the following text and examples, alternation names will be capitalized to distinguish

Figure 4.9 Lexicon file for English adjectives

```
ALTERNATION ADJ_PREFIX          ADJ_PREFIX
ALTERNATION ADJ_ROOT1           ADJ_ROOT1
ALTERNATION ADJ_ROOT2           ADJ_ROOT2
ALTERNATION ADJ_SUFFIX1         ADJ_SUFFIX1
ALTERNATION ADJ_SUFFIX2         ADJ_SUFFIX2
ALTERNATION End                 End
LEXICON INITIAL
    0                   ADJ_PREFIX          "[ "
LEXICON ADJ_PREFIX
    un+                 ADJ_ROOT1           "NEG+"
    0                   ADJ_ROOT1           ""
    0                   ADJ_ROOT2           ""
LEXICON ADJ_ROOT1
    clear               ADJ_SUFFIX1         "Adj(clear)"
    clear               ADJ_SUFFIX2         "Adj(clear)"
    happy               ADJ_SUFFIX1         "Adj(happy)"
    happy               ADJ_SUFFIX2         "Adj(happy)"
    real                ADJ_SUFFIX1         "Adj(real)"
    real                ADJ_SUFFIX2         "Adj(real)"
LEXICON ADJ_ROOT2
    big                 ADJ_SUFFIX2         "Adj(big)"
    cool                ADJ_SUFFIX2         "Adj(cool)"
    red                 ADJ_SUFFIX2         "Adj(red)"
LEXICON ADJ_SUFFIX1
    +ly                 End                 "+ADVBLZR"
    0                   End                 ""
LEXICON ADJ_SUFFIX2
    +er                 End                 "+COMP"
    +est                End                 "+SUPERL"
    0                   End                 ""
LEXICON End
    0                   #                   " ]"
END
```

them from sublexicon names, which are in all uppercase letters. For instance, Adj_Root is a alternation name and ADJ_ROOT is a sublexicon name.)

There are two "styles" for naming alternations. The first style chooses an alternation name that reflects the class of following sublexicon names. For the lexicon in figure 4.9 we could define an Adj_Root alternation for the set of sublexicons ADJ_ROOT1 and ADJ_ROOT2, and an Adj_Suffix alternation for the set of sublexicons ADJ_SUFFIX1 and ADJ_SUFFIX2. The disadvantage of this style is that if the class of possible following sublexicons is heterogeneous, no single name can easily refer to them. The second style chooses an alternation name that reflects the name of the current sublexicon. For the above example we could define an Adj_Prefix alternation for the set of sublexicons ADJ_ROOT1 and ADJ_ROOT2, and an Adj_Root alternation for the set of sublexicons ADJ_SUFFIX1 and ADJ_SUFFIX2. The advantage of this style is that the morphotactic combinations of a description can easily be read from the alternation statements of a lexicon file. For the present example, we will follow the second style. The lexicon files of the various descriptions found on the release diskette provide examples of both styles. Very simple lexicons tend to use the first style, lexicons with extensive morphotactics tend to use the second style.

As shown in figure 4.10, the format of an alternation declaration consists of an alternation name followed by one or more sublexicon names. The sublexicon names that are listed are the lexical classes that can legally follow a lexical item that names the alternation as its continuation class.

Figure 4.10 Format of an ALTERNATION declaration

ALTERNATION <alt. name>   <lex. name$_1$> <lex. name$_2$>... <lex. name$_n$>

The alternation declarations of the PC-KIMMO lexical file for the English adjectives is shown in figure 4.11. Note that we have added a Begin alternation; it defines the set of sublexicons that can begin a word. The INITIAL sublexicon contains only a null entry that has Begin as its continuation and an opening square bracket as its gloss. The End sublexicon also contains only a null entry; it has the BOUNDARY symbol as its continuation and a closing bracket as its gloss. The lexicon file from figure 4.9 is now revised as figure 4.12. Notice that it more closely reflects the FSA diagram in figure 4.5.

Figure 4.11 ALTERNATION declarations for English adjectives

```
ALTERNATION Begin        ADJ_PREFIX
ALTERNATION Adj_Prefix1  ADJ_ROOT1
ALTERNATION Adj_Prefix2  ADJ_ROOT1 ADJ_ROOT2
ALTERNATION Adj_Root1    ADJ_SUFFIX1 ADJ_SUFFIX2
ALTERNATION Adj_Root2    ADJ_SUFFIX2
ALTERNATION Adj_Suffix   End
```

Figure 4.12 Revised lexicon file for English adjectives

```
ALTERNATION Begin        ADJ_PREFIX
ALTERNATION Adj_Prefix1  ADJ_ROOT1
ALTERNATION Adj_Prefix2  ADJ_ROOT1 ADJ_ROOT2
ALTERNATION Adj_Root1    ADJ_SUFFIX1 ADJ_SUFFIX2
ALTERNATION Adj_Root2    ADJ_SUFFIX2
ALTERNATION Adj_Suffix   End
LEXICON INITIAL
 0              Begin           "[ "
LEXICON ADJ_PREFIX
  un+           Adj_Prefix1     "NEG+"
  0             Adj_Prefix2     ""
LEXICON ADJ_ROOT1
  clear         Adj_Root1       "Adj(clear)"
  happy         Adj_Root1       "Adj(happy)"
  real          Adj_Root1       "Adj(real)"
LEXICON ADJ_ROOT2
  big           Adj_Root2       "Adj(big)"
  cool          Adj_Root2       "Adj(cool)"
  red           Adj_Root2       "Adj(red)"
LEXICON ADJ_SUFFIX1
  +ly           Adj_Suffix      "+ADVBLZR"
LEXICON ADJ_SUFFIX2
  +er           Adj_Suffix      "+COMP"
  +est          Adj_Suffix      "+SUPERL"
  0             Adj_Suffix      ""
LEXICON End
  0             #               " ]"
END
```

Chapter

5

TESTING A TWO-LEVEL DESCRIPTION

This chapter describes some common errors in PC-KIMMO descriptions and demonstrates strategies for testing rules and the lexicon.

5.1 Types of errors in two-level descriptions

It is only natural to hope that the first time you test your two-level analysis, it will give you the correct results. However, because of the complexity of the human language you are attempting to analyze, and of the complexity of the rule formalism used in this model, it will be very rare for you to get everything correct on the first try. Two-level descriptions are susceptible to many types of errors, but in general they fall into two types: analysis errors, where you have incorrectly analyzed the data, and coding errors, where you have incorrectly coded your analysis in PC-KIMMO.

Analysis errors are beyond the scope of this book. PC-KIMMO is intended to be used by those already competent in linguistic analysis. It does not do phonological and morphological analysis for you. However, PC-KIMMO is a very powerful tool for helping the linguistic researcher test and refine his analysis. This is the function of PC-KIMMO that is in focus in this book. For information on computational approaches to linguistic analysis, we suggest the following sources: Simons 1988 describes methods for studying morphophonemic alternations based on a corpus of annotated (glossed) interlinear text; and Grimes 1983 presents a computer program for discovering affix positions and cooccurrence restrictions.

Coding errors fall into two general subtypes, syntactic errors and semantic errors (these terms are used here as they apply to a computational formalism, not natural language). Syntactic errors are mistakes in the format of the rules file and the lexicon file and their constituent parts. These errors will cause PC-KIMMO to report an error message that will inform the user of what went wrong (see section 7.10 for a complete list of error messages with explanations). Typical syntactic errors include missing or incorrectly spelled keywords, incorrect number of rows or columns in a table, and incomplete lexical entries. Semantic errors are mistakes in what the rules or lexicon mean; that is, even though your analysis may be correct and the rule may be written syntactically correct, it produces the wrong results because the translation into an FST contains an error. Semantic errors do not necessarily result in error messages, rather in incorrect output. Incorrect output is of four types:

No Result PC-KIMMO returns the message *** NONE *** to tell you that it processed your input form completely through the rules but that there was no resultant surface form permitted by your rules. If this was because of syntactic mistakes in your rules or lexicon file or in the input form, an error message is produced; otherwise the source of the problem is a semantic error in the coding of the rules or lexicon or an error in your analysis.

Overgeneration Your description is said to overgenerate (or overrecognize) if it gives more output words than desired. Some of the output forms may be wrong due to problems with the way you have set up your two-level analysis. Others may be "incorrect" because they are just potential but nonoccurring words in the language.

Undergeneration Your description is said to undergenerate (or underrecognize) when it gives fewer output forms than desired. In this case your analysis may be overconstrained, or there may be mistakes in your rules or lexicon file.

Wrong result The program gives you the desired number of output forms, but one or more of them is wrong in some way. This can be due to either semantic or syntactic errors in the rules or lexicon.

The rest of this chapter will focus primarily on debugging a PC-KIMMO description for semantic errors.

5.2 Strategies for debugging a two-level description

The two main parts of a two-level description are the rules component and the lexical component. The rules can be tested by both the generator and recognizer functions, but the lexicon can be tested only by the recognizer; that is, the lexicon is not used by the generator.

PC-KIMMO accepts input in two ways that are useful for testing a description: immediate mode and file comparison mode. In immediate mode the *generate* or *recognize* command is used to enter input forms directly from the keyboard and then see the results displayed immediately on the screen (see chapter 2 for a demonstration of using PC-KIMMO in immediate mode). Immediate mode is useful for quick, interactive testing of a description. Parts of words can be entered in order to isolate critical environments.

In file comparison mode PC-KIMMO reads disk files of lists of prepared test data. PC-KIMMO reads an input form from the test list, computes the corresponding results allowed by the rules and lexicon, and then checks them against the "right" answers given in the test list. The results are printed on the screen and all discrepancies are reported. File comparison mode is useful for debugging because it allows the analyst to incrementally build up test lists of data as he develops his analysis (see chapter 2 for a demonstration of using PC-KIMMO in file comparison mode). Retesting the test list every time the analysis is changed insures that the new analysis still accounts for everything it used to. Specifications for the format of file comparison lists are found in sections 7.7.3, 7.7.4, and 7.7.5.

PC-KIMMO provides several facilities useful for debugging: logging, selecting rules, showing rules and sublexicons, and tracing. They are described in the following subsections. The use of the debugging facilities will be demonstrated with an early version of the rules file for the English example (found in its final form in appendix A). This example file is shown in figure 5.1.

5.2.1 Using a log file

The simplest debugging aid is logging. When logging is turned on, all information displayed on the screen during the analysis of a form (including tracing, see below) is written to a disk file, where it can be examined or printed. Logging is especially useful in file comparison mode when much information passes by on the screen. By studying the log file, the user can identify which forms are being incorrectly analyzed. Logging is controlled by the *log* command, described in section 7.5.7.

5.2.2 Selecting rules

PC-KIMMO allows the user to turn off selected rules during analysis. By turning rules off and on one by one, it is possible to isolate which rule is not behaving as expected. Conflicts among rules (see section 3.3.13) can be discovered this way. As a simple example of turning off a rule to find an error, suppose that in rule 3 in figure 5.1 state 1 was marked with a period instead of a colon. Since the rule is constructed so that it will be in state 1 at the end of an input form, making state 1 nonfinal will cause all input forms to fail. Thus entering the form *fox+s* will result in the message *** NONE ***. To find the offending rule, take each rule in the file, turn it off, and try to generate a form. (Normally you would not turn off the default rules (rules 1 and 2 above) unless you suspect that they are the cause of a problem.) When rule 3 is turned off, input forms will once again be successfully analyzed, indicating that it is the source of the error.

Rules are turned on and off with the *set rule* command, described in section 7.5.6. The *list rules* command (see section 7.5.5) is used to display the rules currently in use in order to see which are on and which are off.

5.2.3 Showing rules and sublexicons

One of the most difficult aspects of writing state tables is handling overlap among column headers (see section 3.3.9 for a discussion of overlap). The *show rule* command is useful for discovering overlap errors.

Figure 5.1 Example rules file for English

```
ALPHABET
   a b c d e f g h i j k l m n o p q r s t u v w x y z ' - ' +
NULL 0
ANY @
BOUNDARY #
SUBSET C b c d f g h j k l m n p q r s t v w x y z   ; consonants
SUBSET V a e i o u   ; vowels
SUBSET S s x z   ; sibilants


RULE "1 Consonant defaults" 1 22
      b  c  d  f  g  h  j  k  l  m  n  p  q  r  s  t  v  w  x  y  z  @
      b  c  d  f  g  h  j  k  l  m  n  p  q  r  s  t  v  w  x  y  z  @
  1:  1  1  1  1  1  1  1  1  1  1  1  1  1  1  1  1  1  1  1  1  1  1


RULE "2 Vowels and other defaults" 1 12
      a  e  i  o  u  '  -  -  '  +  #  @
      a  e  i  o  u  '  -  0  0  0  #  @
  1:  1  1  1  1  1  1  1  1  1  1  1  1


RULE "3 Epenthesis, 0:e ⇒ [S|ch|sh] +:0 __ s#" 7 8
      c  h  s  S  +  0  #  @
      c  h  s  S  0  e  #  @
  1:  2  1  4  3  1  0  1  1
  2:  2  3  3  3  1  0  1  1
  3:  2  1  3  3  5  0  1  1
  4:  2  3  3  3  5  0  1  1
  5:  2  1  2  2  1  6  1  1
  6.  0  0  7  0  0  0  0  0
  7.  0  0  0  0  0  0  1  0


RULE "4 Epenthesis, 0:0 /⇐ [S|ch|sh] +:0 __ s#" 6 7
      c  h  s  S  +  #  @
      c  h  s  S  0  #  @
  1:  2  1  4  3  1  1  1
  2:  2  3  3  3  1  1  1
  3:  2  1  3  3  5  1  1
  4:  2  3  3  3  5  1  1
  5:  2  1  6  3  1  1  1
  6:  2  3  4  3  1  0  1


RULE "5 y:i-spelling, y:i ⇐ C __ +:0" 3 5
      C  y  y  +  @
      C  i  @  0  @
  1:  2  1  1  1  1
  2:  2  1  3  1  1
  3:  2  1  1  0  1


RULE "6 y:i-spelling, y:i ⇒ C __ +:0" 3 4
      C  y  +  @
      C  i  0  @
  1:  2  0  1  1
  2:  2  3  1  1
  3.  0  0  1  0


END
```

It displays the column headers of a rule with the set of feasible pairs that each column header actually represents. Consider the following incorrectly written Epenthesis rule, which is a simplification of table 3 in figure 5.1. The subset *S* contains *s*, *x*, and *z*.

```
RULE "3a Epenthesis, 0:e ⇒ S +:0 ___ s#" 5 6
    s S + 0 # @
    s S 0 e # @
1:  1 2 1 0 1 1
2:  1 2 3 0 1 1
3:  1 2 1 4 1 1
4.  5 0 0 0 0 0
5.  0 0 0 0 1 0
```

Given the lexical form *fox+s* this table correctly produces the surface form *foxes*; but given the lexical form *kiss+s*, it fails to produce the correct surface form *kisses*. Doing the *show rule* command for this rule gives the information shown in figure 5.2.

Figure 5.2 The *show rule* command

```
PC-KIMMO>show rule 3
   3 on  3a Epenthesis, 0:e => S +:0___s#
s:s  ( s:s )
S:S  ( x:x z:z )
+:0  ( +:0 )
0:e  ( 0:e )
#:#  ( #:# )
@:@  ( b:b d:d f:f g:g j:j k:k l:l m:m n:n p:p q:q r:r t:t
v:v w:w y:y a:a e:e i:i o:o u:u ':' -:- -:0
':0 )
```

From this display it is immediately obvious that the column header *S:S* does not contain the pair *s:s* as might be expected. This is because the column headers *s:s* and *S:S* overlap with respect to the pair *s:s*; that is, the pair *s:s* matches both column headers. The pair *s:s* is assigned to the *s:s* column header because the *s:s* column header is more specific than the *S:S* column header. That is, only one feasible pair matches the *s:s* header while three pairs match the *S:S* header. Thus the input form *kiss+s* fails the rule because the root-final *s* is matched to the *s:s* column header, leaving the table in state 1. The table must be revised so that for the first three states the *s:s* column has the same state transitions as the *S:S* column.

As an aid to debugging the lexical part of a description, PC-KIMMO offers the *show lexicon* command. This command displays on the screen the contents of a sublexicon. It shows each lexical item, its gloss, and its continuation class. If the continuation class specifies an alternation name, the command expands the alternation into a list of sublexicon names. This helps the user to discover incorrectly written lexical entries or alternation declarations.

5.2.4   Using the tracing facility

If simply reflecting on the nature of the wrong results does not lead you to pinpoint the problem, then the best way to discover just where your description is going astray is to have the computer show you precisely what it is doing. Such a display is called a trace. Simply issue the *set trace on* command; then every *generate* and *recognize* operation thereafter will display a trace of its activity on the screen. You can stop the screen from scrolling by pressing either *Ctrl-S* or the *Pause* key; any key will resume scrolling. The *set trace* command actually allows three levels of tracing differing in the amount of detail that they show. The example in this chapter uses the middle level. For more information on tracing and the *set trace* command, see section 7.8.

It is often more useful to have a trace display captured in a file where it can be inspected using your word processing program, or printed out on paper. To have PC-KIMMO save tracing information to a file, simply turn logging on with the *log* command. Everything that is displayed on the screen is also written to the log file. (Also, MS-DOS computers use *Ctrl-P* to toggle the printer on and off. Press *Ctrl-P* to cause all screen output to be echoed on a printer; press *Ctrl-P* again to stop echoing.)

The remainder of this section focuses on using tracing to debug rules in generation mode. In recognition mode, the trace displays show all that the generator traces do plus they show the activity of the lexicon as it moves from one sublexicon to another. This information is useful for debugging morphotactic constraints. See section 7.8 for more on recognizer traces.

How to interpret the trace produced by the generator

To demonstrate how to interpret a trace, we will look at an actual example using the rules file in figure 5.1. The generator produced the following output for the lexical form *'baby+s*:

```
PC-KIMMO>generate 'baby+s
  babis
```

Figure 5.3 shows the results of tracing this generation. The trace contains a lot of information in a compact form, but it is not hard to use when you understand how the information is presented. The line and column numbers are printed here for reference; they are not printed in an actual screen display.

- Line 1 gives the lexical input form.

- Column 1 shows the recursion level of the generator function. This corresponds to the character position in the input form. For more on how the generator algorithm works, see section 7.9. The symbol - after the level number means that the current pair is blocked by a rule; the symbol < means that the generator is backing up to the previous level.

- Column 2 shows the input pair that is currently being tried.

- In lines 2 and 16 the input pair in column 2 is the special BOUND-ARY correspondence #:# which represents the beginning and end of the input word.

- In columns 3 through 8, there is one column of numbers for each rule in the rules file. In this example there are six rules. Rule number 1 is the first one on the left. The numbers tell what state (row number in the state table) each rule is in at that point in the generation process.

- Column 9 shows the surface form that the generator has output up to this point in its left-to-right progression through the input lexical form.

- The BLOCKED BY RULE message in line 9 means that the input pair +:0 was blocked by rule 5. The previous line shows that rule 5 was in state 3 when the block occurred. Look at table 5 in figure 5.1 and you will see in state 3 a zero (indicating failure) in the cell under the +:0 column header.

- Line 19 reports that the rules have generated *ObabiOs* as a valid surface form.

- In lines 21 through 41 the generator backtracks, trying to find other possible surface forms.

- Line 42 gives the final output list of all resulting surface forms, in this instance only one.

Figure 5.3 Generator trace for *'baby+s*

	1	2	3	4	5	6	7	8	9
1	'baby+s								
2	0	#:#	1	1	1	1	1	1	
3	0	':0	1	1	1	1	1	1	
4	1	b:b	1	1	1	1	1	1	0
5	2	a:a	1	1	1	1	2	2	0b
6	3	b:b	1	1	1	1	1	1	0ba
7	4	y:y	1	1	1	1	2	2	0bab
8	5	+:0	1	1	1	1	3	2	0baby
9	5-		BLOCKED BY RULE 5: 5 y:i-spelling, y:i ⇐ C___+:0 [il']						
10	5	0:e	1	1	1	1	3	2	0baby
11	5-		BLOCKED BY RULE 3: 3 Epenthesis, 0:e ⇒ [S|ch|sh] +:0___s#						
12	4<		1	1	1	1	2	2	0bab
13	4	y:i	1	1	1	1	2	2	0bab
14	5	+:0	1	1	1	1	1	3	0babi
15	6	s:s	1	1	1	1	1	1	0babi0
16	7	#:#	1	1	4	4	2	2	0babi0s
17	7		1	1	1	1	1	1	0babi0s
18									
19	RESULT = 0babi0s								
20									
21	6<		1	1	1	1	1	1	0babi0
22	6	0:e	1	1	1	1	1	1	0babi0
23	6-		BLOCKED BY RULE 3: 3 Epenthesis, 0:e ⇒ [S|ch|sh] +:0___s#						
24	5<		1	1	1	1	1	3	0babi
25	5	0:e	1	1	1	1	1	3	0babi
26	5-		BLOCKED BY RULE 3: 3 Epenthesis, 0:e ⇒ [S|ch|sh] +:0___s#						
28	4	0:e	1	1	1	1	2	2	0bab
29	4-		BLOCKED BY RULE 3: 3 Epenthesis, 0:e ⇒ [S|ch|sh] +:0___s#						
30	3<		1	1	1	1	1	1	0ba
31	3	0:e	1	1	1	1	1	1	0ba
32	3-		BLOCKED BY RULE 3: 3 Epenthesis, 0:e ⇒ [S|ch|sh] +:0___s#						
33	2<		1	1	1	1	2	2	0b
34	2	0:e	1	1	1	1	2	2	0b
35	2-		BLOCKED BY RULE 3: 3 Epenthesis, 0:e ⇒ [S|ch|sh] +:0___s#						
36	1<		1	1	1	1	1	1	0
37	1	0:e	1	1	1	1	1	1	0
38	1-		BLOCKED BY RULE 3: 3 Epenthesis, 0:e ⇒ [S|ch|sh] +:0___s#						
39	0<		1	1	1	1	1	1	
40	0	0:e	1	1	1	1	1	1	
41	0-		BLOCKED BY RULE 3: 3 Epenthesis, 0:e ⇒ [S|ch|sh] +:0___s#						
42	babis								

Keep in mind that the correct lexical-to-surface mapping is this:

```
'  b  a  b  y  +  0  s
0  b  a  b  i  0  e  s
```

The trace given in figure 5.3 shows that we got this incorrect mapping:

```
'  b  a  b  y  +  s
0  b  a  b  i  0  s
```

Epenthesis of the *e* before the plural suffix did not occur as expected. Line 15 of the trace is where Epenthesis should have occurred: the result built up thus far is *Obabi0*. Notice that at this point all the rules are in state 1; looking at the rules shows that nothing prevents them from accepting the pair *s:s* followed by word boundary. After the generator prints the successful (though ill-formed) result *babis* on line 19, it begins backtracking to try to find other possible results. At line 22 the generator is back at the point where the result is *Obabi0* and this time it tries the pair we expect at that point, *0:e*. But line 23 tells us that the pair *0:e* was blocked by rule 3. Looking at line 22 we see that rule 3 was in state 1 when the pair was tried. Looking at the state table for rule 3 we see that in state 1 the cell under *0:e* contains a zero, indicating failure. This, then, is where the rules are going wrong. The Epenthesis rule does not include *y:i* from the *y:i*-spelling rule in its environment. The Epenthesis rule must be revised to include *y:i* together with the sibilants in its left environment.

Reducing the amount of information given by trace

The trace for *'baby+s*, with just seven recursion levels, produced over forty printed lines of information. Most of the phonological rules you will write will probably involve environments of five characters or fewer: one or two characters for a left context, plus the L:S pair, plus one or two characters of right context. For *'baby+s*, the problem that causes the incorrect output *Obabi0s* is most likely to come from a rule involving the lexical *y*, in the fifth character position. The conditioning environment for *y* probably does not involve the first few characters of the word, or the last few.

We can take advantage of the fact that the PC-KIMMO generator does not impose any lexical constraints. We can input any string of characters to the generator and get an output, just so long as the input uses characters defined in the alphabet for the rules. This means that we can input a partial word which contains just the necessary environments for troubleshooting a problem. The trace of a four to six character form will be shorter than the trace of the whole word, plus it doesn't give a lot of information that is extraneous to tracking down the problem.

As you begin troubleshooting, it is probably worth a few minutes to experiment with partial words, to try to reduce the amount of information reported in a trace. Begin by running PC-KIMMO, loading your rules, and selecting the generator function. For the moment, do not turn on the trace or logging functions. Type in the word which gives a wrong output, but leave off the first character:

```
PC-KIMMO>generate baby+s
  babis
```

In this example, omitting the initial stress mark did not change anything, so we can take off another character:

```
PC-KIMMO>generate aby+s
  abis
```

Still the problem occurs. Here are further experiments shortening both the preceding and following contexts.

```
generator>>by+s
  bis

generator>>y+s
  ys

generator>>by+
  bi

generator>>y+
  y
```

These tests indicate that *by+s* is the shortest partial word that we can use to troubleshoot the problem. With only four characters, it has half as many recursion levels as the whole word, and its trace will be shorter. This technique can make a significant difference for a trace of a long word, which would be printed out multiple times as you modify and test rules to eliminate problems.

One caution for using partial words as input: always reduce the input form one character at a time. This will make sure that the partial word does in fact give the same output as the whole word. Because of the interactions of the phonological rules, removing a character may have a "ripple" effect which changes the environment that is producing the problems you are trying to eliminate.

Chapter

6

A SAMPLER OF TWO-LEVEL RULES

This chapter gives examples of various phonological and morphological processes encoded as two-level rules and finite state tables. The examples are not intended to cover all attested linguistic phenomena; rather they focus on types of rules that are nontrivial for the two-level formalism. The rules developed in this chapter are available in the rules file located in the SAMPLER subdirectory on the PC-KIMMO release diskette.

The printed format of the state tables in this chapter conforms closely to the format used in the rules file on the diskette, with the exception that lines are printed here to visually set off the column headers and row numbers. Note that each table includes a header line, which typically contains the two-level rule that the table expresses, followed by the number of rows and columns in the table.

Many of the phonological processes discussed in this chapter are encoded as two rules, a ⇐ rule and a ⇒ rule, which in turn are expressed in two state tables. In all of these instances, the two tables could be combined into one ⇔ table. We have written separate tables whenever doing so makes it easier to read and understand the tables. Also note that in most cases the ⇐ rule is given first, followed by the ⇒ rule. This is because the meaning of the ⇐ rule typically expresses what the linguist thinks of as an obligatory rule, whereas the accompanying ⇒ rule often functions merely as a "clean-up" rule (see section 3.3.14). However, in practice most users of PC-KIMMO find it easier to write a ⇒ table first, since it is simpler to understand. This is perfectly acceptable, so long as the user understands that in most cases it is the ⇐ table that is more basic.

Finally, the example tables in this chapter have, in most cases, been written free of phonotactic constraints; that is, they are phonotactically as general as possible. This accords with the advice given in section 3.3.16. Also, following section 3.3.15, rules are allowed to apply freely across a morpheme boundary unless the morpheme boundary is a crucial element of the rule's environment.

6.1 Assimilation

Assimilation is a phonological process in which one sound segment influences another so that the sounds become more alike, or even identical. Assimilation can be categorized in terms of the direction in which it works. In regressive assimilation (or anticipation) a sound changes due to the influence of a following sound; that is, a sound becomes more like (or anticipates) a following sound. In progressive assimilation (or lag) a sound changes due to the influence of a preceding sound; that is, a sound becomes more like a preceding sound. In other words, in regressive assimilation the direction of influence is against the flow of speech, whereas in progressive assimilation the direction of influence is with the flow of speech. When expressed as two-level rules, progressive assimilation requires a rule with a left context while regressive assimilation requires a rule with a right context. A third type of assimilation, called reciprocal assimilation, results in a mutual or bidirectional influence of sounds with each other, such that both sounds change to become more like each other. This can result in a fusion or coalescence of the sounds into one sound. Coalescence is treated in section 6.1.3, part 3 and section 6.2.4.

Assimilation processes can also be classified according to whether the sound that changes is adjacent to the influencing sound or farther away. The most common situation, called contiguous assimilation, occurs when the sounds are adjacent. A typical example is palatalization, where certain consonants become palatalized when they occur contiguous to high front vowels (see the data and the Palatalization rule in section 3.4.4). It should be noted that when assimilation occurs across a morpheme boundary, it is still considered contiguous assimilation. It is a peculiarity of the way PC-KIMMO works that morpheme boundaries in state tables are treated as if they were phonological segments. Less common is noncontiguous assimilation, where other segments intervene between the sound that changes and the influencing sound. Examples of noncontiguous assimilation are vowel harmony (see section 6.1.1) and spreading nasalization (see section 6.1.3, part 4). A feature common to both vowel harmony and spreading nasalization is that more than one segment in a word undergoes change; that is, the phonetic influence of a sound spreads to several sounds in the word.

6.1.1 Vowel harmony

Vowel harmony is an assimilation process whereby a vowel in one part of a word causes other vowels in the word to match certain of its phonetic features. Vowel harmony typically has a spreading effect, such that all vowels in the word that precede or follow are influenced.

In Turkish, the vowels of a suffix agree in backness and rounding with the preceding vowel (data from Schane 1973:52 and Merrifield and others 1987, problem 98).

	Sing.	Plural		Sing.	Plural
'tooth'	diš	dišler	'my tooth'	dišim	dišlerim
'house'	ev	evler	'my house'	evim	evlerim
'day'	gün	günler	'my day'	günüm	günlerim
'eye'	göz	gözler	'my eye'	gözüm	gözlerim
'head'	baš	bašlar	'my head'	bašïm	bašlarïm
'girl'	kïz	kïzlar	'my daughter'	kïzïm	kïzlarïm
'arm'	kol	kollar	'my arm'	kolum	kollarïm
'candle'	mum	mumlar	'my candle'	mumum	mumlarïm

The plural suffix has the surface alternants *ler* and *lar*. We give it the lexical representation *lAr*, where *A* is an unspecified nonhigh, unrounded vowel. The first person singular possessive suffix has the surface alternants *im*, *um*, *ïm*, and *üm*. We give it the lexical representation *Hm*, where *H* is an unspecified high vowel. For example,

LR: ev+lAr   ev+lAr+Hm   mum+Hm   mum+lAr+Hm
SR: ev0ler   ev0ler0im   mum0um   mum0lar0ïm

These examples show that vowel harmony creates a kind of chain reaction in a word, such that each vowel that changes influences the next vowel. It is not the case that the vowel of a suffix agrees with the vowel of the root; rather, it agrees with the preceding vowel, whether it occurs in the root or a suffix. This is demonstrated in the data above by the suffix *+Hm*. In the lexical form *mum+Hm*, the suffix vowel *H* is realized as *u* in the surface form *mumum*, thus agreeing in backness and roundness with the preceding vowel which happens to be in the root. But in the lexical form *mum+lAr+Hm*, the suffix vowel *H* is realized as *ï*, thus agreeing not with the root vowel but with the unrounded vowel of the preceding suffix.

The Turkish vowel harmony rules developed below use the following vowel subsets. Note that the subset names have been constructed to look like distinctive feature labels.

SUBSET V	a e i o u	(vowels)
SUBSET V[−bk]	i e ü ö	(front)
SUBSET V[−bk−rd]	i e	(front, unrounded)
SUBSET V[−bk+rd]	ü ö	(front, rounded)
SUBSET V[+bk]	a ï u o	(back)
SUBSET V[+bk−rd]	a ï	(back, unrounded)
SUBSET V[+bk+rd]	u o	(back, rounded)

The following rules account for the correspondences involving lexical *A*:

Vowel Harmony

T88   "A:a ⇔ :V[+bk] C* (+:0) C*___" 2 6

	@	C	+	A	A	@
V[+bk]		C	0	a	@	@
1:	2	1	1	0	1	1
2:	2	2	2	2	0	1

Vowel Harmony

T89   "A:e ⇔ :V[−bk] C* (+:0) C*___" 2 6

	@	C	+	A	A	@
V[−bk]		C	0	e	@	@
1:	2	1	1	0	1	1
2:	2	2	2	2	0	1

The following rules account for the correspondences involving lexical H:

Vowel Harmony

T90   "H:u ⇔ :V[+bk+rd] C* (+:0) C*___" 2 6

	@	C	+	H	H	@
V[+bk+rd]		C	0	u	@	@
1:	2	1	1	0	1	1
2:	2	2	2	2	0	1

Vowel Harmony

T91   "H:ü ⇔ :V[−bk+rd] C* (+:0) C*___" 2 6

	@	C	+	H	H	@
V[−bk+rd]		C	0	ü	@	@
1:	2	1	1	0	1	1
2:	2	2	2	2	0	1

Vowel Harmony

T92   "H:i ⇔ :V[−bk−rd] C* (+:0) C*___" 2 6

	@	C	+	H	H	@
V[−bk−rd]		C	0	i	@	@
1:	2	1	1	0	1	1
2:	2	2	2	2	0	1

Vowel Harmony

T93   "H:ï ⇔ :V[+bk−rd] C* (+:0) C*___" 2 6

	@	C	+	H	H	@
V[+bk−rd]		C	0	ï	@	@
1:	2	1	1	0	1	1
2:	2	2	2	2	0	1

Note that in each of the above tables the column header that represents the influencing vowel is specified in terms of its surface realization. For instance, in table 93 the column header @:V[+bk–rd] specifies a surface vowel belonging to the subset V[+bk–rd] that corresponds to any lexical vowel (with which it constitutes a feasible pair). This formulation is necessary because of the fact discussed above that a vowel harmonizes with its immediately preceding vowel, not necessarily with the vowel of the root. The influencing vowel could correspond to a lexical H or A, which both occur in suffixes. Since these lexical vowels are partially specified and are not included in the subsets, the table must be written so that it is sensitive to the surface realization of the influencing vowel. Note also the careful handling of backlooping. In state 2 of each table, the cell in the column that represents the vowel that changes contains an arc back to state 2 (for instance, the H:ï column of table 93), since it must be available as the environment of a possible following vowel (see section 3.3.2, part 8 on backlooping).

6.1.2 Reciprocal assimilation

Reciprocal or bidirectional assimilation is a process whereby two sounds mutually influence each other—assimilation that is simultaneously regressive and progressive. Consider a hypothetical case where a nasal consonant and a following obstruent agree in point of articulation and voicing. In other words, a nasal assimilates regressively to the point of articulation of a following obstruent, and an obstruent assimilates progressively to the voicing of a preceding nasal. In the following analysis, the lexical character N stands for a nasal consonant unspecified for point of articulation. For example,

LR: aN+pa   aN+ba   aN+ta   aN+da   aN+ka   aN+ga
SR: am0ba   am0ba   an0da   an0da   aŋ0ga   aŋ0ga

Assume these subsets:

SUBSET P	p f	(voiceless labials)
SUBSET T	t s	(voiceless dentals)
SUBSET K	k x	(voiceless velars)
SUBSET B	b v	(voiced labials)
SUBSET D	d z	(voiced dentals)
SUBSET G	g γ	(voiced velars)

Since the state tables will be written with subsets, the special correspondences must be declared in a separate table (the default N:n correspondence is also included).

T94   "Obstruent voicing correspondences" 1 8

	p	f	t	s	k	x	N	@
	b	v	d	z	g	γ	n	@
1:	1	1	1	1	1	1	1	1

Assuming that this assimilation process is obligatory, we write two ⇔ rules—one for Nasal Assimilation and another for Voicing Assimilation. (In the notation of the two-level rules below, curly braces ({}) indicate sets of elements that match respectively; for instance, in rule 95 *m* matches *:B*, *n* matches *:D*, and *ŋ* matches *:G*.)

Nasal Assimilation

T95   "N:{m,n,ŋ} ⇔ ___(+:0) {:B,:D,:G}" 5 9

	N	N	N	N	+	@	@	@	@
	m	n	ŋ	@	0	B	D	G	@
1:	3	4	5	2	1	1	1	1	1
2:	1	1	1	2	2	0	0	0	1
3.	0	0	0	0	3	1	0	0	1
4.	0	0	0	0	4	0	1	0	1
5.	0	0	0	0	5	0	0	1	1

Voicing Assimilation

T96   "{P,T,K}:{B,D,G} ⇔ N: (+:0)___" 2 9

	N	+	P	T	K	P	T	K	@
	@	0	B	D	G	@	@	@	@
1:	2	1	0	0	0	1	1	1	1
2:	2	2	1	1	1	0	0	0	1

What allows these two rules to interact in a reciprocal fashion is that one specifies a surface environment while the other specifies a lexical environment. In table 95 the *N:m* correspondence, for instance, is found in the environment of a surface *B* (whose lexical source may be either *P* or *B*); this is encoded as the column header *@:B*. In table 96 the correspondence *P:B* is found in the environment of a lexical *N* (whose surface realization may be *n*, *m*, or *ŋ*); this is encoded as the column header *N:@*.

6.1.3 Nasalization

This section develops several rules of vowel nasalization. The data are hypothetical, but the phonological processes they represent are well-attested in natural languages.

(1) A vowel is nasalized when followed by a word-final nasal conso-nant. For example,

LR: bon
SR: bõn

Assume these subsets:

SUBSET Vo	a e i o u	(oral vowels)
SUBSET Vn	ã ẽ ĩ õ ũ	(nasal vowels)
SUBSET NAS	m n ŋ	(nasal consonants)

and these special correspondences between the subsets *Vo* and *Vn*:

T97   "Nasalization correspondences" 1 6

	a	e	i	o	u	@
	ã	ẽ	ĩ	õ	ũ	@
1:	1	1	1	1	1	1

The following tables use the special word boundary column header (assume that # has been declared as the BOUNDARY symbol, see section 3.3.10 on expressing word boundaries in state tables).

Nasalization

T98   "Vo:Vn ⇐ ___NAS #" 3 5

	Vo	Vo	NAS	#	@
	Vn	@	NAS	#	@
1:	1	2	1	1	1
2:	1	2	3	1	1
3:	1	2	1	0	1

Nasalization

T99   "Vo:Vn ⇒ ___NAS #" 3 4

	Vo	NAS	#	@
	Vn	NAS	#	@
1:	2	1	1	1
2.	0	3	0	0
3.	0	0	1	0

(2) A vowel is nasalized when followed by a nasal consonant plus another consonant. (Assume the same subsets as above.) For example,

LR: bamba
SR: bãmba

Nasalization

T100 "Vo:Vn ⇐ ___ NAS C" 3 5

	Vo	Vo	NAS	C	@
	Vn	@	NAS	C	@
1:	1	2	1	1	1
2:	1	2	3	1	1
3:	1	2	0	0	1

Nasalization

T101 "Vo:Vn ⇒ ___ NAS C" 3 4

	Vo	NAS	C	@
	Vn	NAS	C	@
1:	2	1	1	1
2.	0	3	0	0
3.	0	1	1	0

(3) The two nasalization processes described above (1 and 2) can be combined into one rule that states that vowels are nasalized preceding a nasal consonant that is followed by either a consonant or a word boundary. Tables 98 and 100 combine as table 102, and tables 99 and 101 combine as table 103.

Nasalization

T102 "Vo:Vn ⇐ ___ NAS [C | #]" 3 6

	Vo	Vo	NAS	C	#	@
	Vn	@	NAS	C	#	@
1:	1	2	1	1	1	1
2:	1	2	3	1	1	1
3:	1	2	0	0	0	1

Nasalization

T103 "Vo:Vn ⇒ ___ NAS [C | #]" 3 5

	Vo	NAS	C	#	@
	Vn	NAS	C	#	@
1:	2	1	1	1	1
2.	0	3	0	0	0
3.	0	1	1	1	0

(4) As in part 3 above, vowels are nasalized preceding a nasal consonant that is followed by either a consonant or a word boundary, but in addition the nasal consonant is deleted. This phenomenon can be viewed as the coalescence of a vowel and a following nasal consonant, for instance *on* → *õ*. However, a two-level solution cannot map two lexical

characters to only one surface character; each lexical character must correspond to its own surface character. Thus, coalescence must be treated as assimilation plus deletion. For example,

LR: bon   bamba
SR: bõ0   bã 0 ba

These are special nasal deletion correspondences:

T104   "Deletion correspondences" 1 4

	m	n	ŋ	@
	0	0	0	@
1:	1	1	1	1

We write two ⇐ rules, one for the *Vo:Vn* correspondence, and another for the *NAS:0* correspondence.

Nasalization
T105   "Vo:Vn ⇐ ___ NAS: [C | #]" 3 6

	Vo	Vo	NAS	C	#	@
	Vn	@	@	C	#	@
1:	1	2	1	1	1	1
2:	1	2	3	1	1	1
3:	1	2	0	0	0	1

Nasal Deletion
T106   "NAS:0 ⇐ :Vn ___ [C | #]" 3 6

	@	NAS	NAS	C	#	@
	Vn	0	@	C	#	@
1:	2	1	1	1	1	1
2:	2	1	3	1	1	1
3:	2	1	0	0	0	1

Notice that table 105 contains the column header *NAS:@* (where we might expect *NAS:0*) and table 106 contains *@:Vn* (where we might expect *Vo:Vn*). The reason is that using *NAS:0* and *Vo:Vn* would overspecify the environments resulting in overgeneration (see sections 3.1.7 and 3.3.12). Specifically, a lexical form such as *bon* would match both the correct surface form *bõ* and the incorrect surface form *bon*.

Tables 107 and 108 are the "clean-up" rules (see section 3.3.14) that disallow *Vo:Vn* and *NAS:0* in any other environments.

Nasalization

T107 "Vo:Vn ⇒ ___ NAS: [C | #]" 3 5

	Vo NAS C # @				
	Vn @ C # @				
1:	2	1	1	1	1
2.	0	3	0	0	0
3.	0	1	1	1	0

Nasal Deletion

T108 "NAS:0 ⇒ :Vn___ [C | #]" 3 5

	@ NAS C # @				
	Vn 0 C # @				
1:	2	0	1	1	1
2:	2	3	1	1	1
3.	0	0	1	1	0

(5) Vowels preceding a nasal consonant are nasalized. Nasalization spreads regressively (leftward) through all vowels up to the first consonant that is not a voiced stop (that is, nasalization passes through voiced stops). For example,

LR: saban sapan
SR: sãbãn sapãn

Assume these subsets:

SUBSET Vo   a e i o u   (oral vowels)
SUBSET Vn   ã ẽ ĩ õ ũ   (nasalized vowels)
SUBSET B   b d g   (voiced stops)
SUBSET NAS   m n ŋ   (nasals)

and these correspondences:

T109 "Nasalization correspondences" 1 6

	a e i o u @					
	ã ẽ ĩ õ ũ @					
1:	1	1	1	1	1	1

In the two-level rule as it is written in the header of table 110 below, the expression *[B:B Vo:Vn]** means zero or more instances of the sequence *B:B Vo:Vn*.

Spreading Regressive Nasalization

T110   "Vo:Vn ⇔ ___ [B:B Vo:Vn]* NAS:NAS" 3 5

| | Vo | Vo | NAS | B | @ |
	Vn	@	NAS	B	@
1:	3	2	1	1	1
2:	0	2	0	2	1
3.	3	0	1	3	0

6.1.4 Tonal assimilation

In Mende (a language of West Africa), a lexical low tone corresponds to a surface high tone after a lexical high or rising tone (Halle
and Clements 1983). In the following forms, ´ indicates high tone, ` in-
dicates low tone, and ˘ indicates rising tone (Mende also has ˆ for falling
tone). The tone mark is placed preceding the vowel it is associated with,
a concession to the linear nature of two-level representations.

LR: n`av´o+m`a   mb˘a+m`a
SR: n`av´o0m´a    mb`a0m´a

This is the rule for Low-to-high Assimilation:

Low-to-high Assimilation

T111   "`:´ ⇔ [´ | ˘]: V +:0 (C)___ " 5 8

| | ´ | ˘ | V | + | C | ` | ` | @ |
	@	@	V	0	C	´	@	@
1:	2	2	1	1	1	0	1	1
2:	2	2	3	1	1	0	1	1
3:	2	2	1	4	1	0	1	1
4:	2	2	1	1	5	1	0	1
5:	2	2	1	1	1	1	0	1

The second form in the data above also shows that a lexical rising tone
corresponds to a surface low tone before a surface high tone. These are
the rules for the Rising-to-low Assimilation:

Rising-to-low Assimilation

T112   "˘:` ⇐ ___V +:0 (C) :´" 5 7

| | ˘ | ˘ | V | + | C | @ | @ |
	`	@	V	0	C	´	@
1:	1	2	1	1	1	1	1
2:	1	2	3	1	1	1	1
3:	1	2	1	4	1	1	1
4:	1	2	1	1	5	0	1
5:	1	2	1	1	1	0	1

Rising-to-low Assimilation

T113   “ ˅ ˋ ⇒ ___ V +:0 (C) :´ ” 5 6

```
      | ˅  V  +  C  @  @
      | ˋ  V  0  C  ´  @
   ___|_____
   1: | 2  1  1  1  1  1
   2. | 0  3  0  0  0  0
   3. | 0  0  4  0  0  0
   4. | 0  0  0  5  1  0
   5. | 0  0  0  0  1  0
```

A more extensive description of Mende tone is located in the MENDE subdirectory on the PC-KIMMO release diskette.

6.2 Deletion

Since two-level rules require that each character of a lexical form map onto exactly one character of a corresponding surface form, the deletion of a lexical character must be represented as a correspondence to a surface NULL symbol. The following subsections give four examples that involve deletion.

6.2.1 Finnish consonant gradation

Although this example is perhaps best understood as an instance of assimilation, it is included here because of the way deletion is involved. Finnish has a phonological process called consonant gradation, where certain consonants are weakened in an intervocalic environment (see Dalrymple and others 1987:42–43). In the following data, the lexical voiceless stops p, t, and k correspond to the surface characters v, d, and 0, respectively:

LR: papun   sotan   sikan
SR: pavun   sodan   si0an

To describe these data, first declare two subsets, subset T for the voiceless stops and subset D for their weakened variants. Notice that since the NULL symbol is an alphabetic character, it can be included in a subset.

SUBSET T   p t k
SUBSET D   v d 0

Next declare these special correspondences:

T114   "Consonant Gradation correspondences" 1 4

	p	t	k	@
	v	d	0	@
1:	1	1	1	1

The following rules for Consonant Gradation specify that the correspondence *T:D* occurs following a vowel and preceding a vowel that is followed by a consonant that is in turn followed by either another consonant or word boundary. Notice that in table 115 state 6 is included to account for backlooping.

Consonant Gradation

T115   "T:D ⇐ V___VC[C | #]" 6 6

	T	T	V	C	#	@
	D	@	V	C	#	@
1:	1	1	2	1	1	1
2:	1	3	2	1	1	1
3:	1	1	4	1	1	1
4:	5	6	2	5	1	1
5:	0	0	2	0	0	1
6:	0	0	4	0	0	1

Consonant Gradation

T116   "T:D ⇒ V___VC[C | #]" 5 5

	T	V	C	#	@
	D	V	C	#	@
1:	0	2	1	1	1
2:	3	2	1	1	1
3.	0	4	0	0	0
4.	0	0	5	0	0
5.	0	0	1	1	0

These Finnish data illustrate a situation where the subset notation makes possible a neater solution than does distinctive feature notation. Distinctive features can easily specify the lexical voiceless stops, but they cannot specify the heterogeneous surface characters *v* and *d* without using extra features, and more significantly distinctive features cannot refer to a NULL at all. Using distinctive features, at least two rules would have to be written, one to rewrite *p* and *t* as *v* and *d* and another to delete *k*. Two-level rules, on the other hand, treat NULL as an alphabetic character and can thus use it in subsets.

An extended description of some Finnish data is located in the FINNISH subdirectory on the PC-KIMMO release diskette.

6.2.2   Consonant deletion in French

In French, a consonant is deleted when it is followed by a morpheme boundary (+) and a following consonant, or a word boundary (=) and a following consonant (Schane 1973:90). In this example we cannot use the BOUNDARY symbol declared in the rules file, since that symbol is used by PC-KIMMO to represent the beginning or the end of an input string. To analyze multiple word sequences we must define an alphabetic symbol to represent a word boundary occurring in the middle of an input string. For example,

LR: pətit=ami   pətit+z=ami   pətit=garsõ   pətit+z=garsõ
SR: pətit0ami   pəti00z0ami   pəti00garsõ   pəti0000garsõ

The last pair of forms above shows that deletion can occur more than once in a single input form; that is, *t* is deleted before *z* which is itself deleted. This indicates that the deletion rule must be stated in terms of lexical environments rather than surface environments. All consonants that can be deleted must be declared in a table like this:

T117   "Deletion correspondences" 1 8

	p	t	k	b	d	g	z	@
	0	0	0	0	0	0	0	@
1:	1	1	1	1	1	1	1	1

The Consonant Deletion rules are as follows. Note that in table 118, the column header *C:@* represents both *C:* in the environment and *C:~0*, the column header used in ⇐ tables.

Consonant Deletion

T118   "C:0 ⇐ ____ [+ | =] C:" 3 5

	C	+	=	C	@
	0	0	0	@	@
1:	1	1	1	2	1
2:	1	3	3	2	1
3:	0	1	1	0	1

Consonant Deletion

T119   "C:0 ⇒ ____ [+ | =] C:" 3 5

	C	+	=	C	@
	0	0	0	@	@
1:	2	1	1	1	1
2.	0	3	3	0	0
3.	2	0	0	1	0

Notice that in standard generative phonology, deletion before $+C$ must be ordered before $=C$ (described as *conjunctive ordering* in Schane 1973:90). Because two-level rules allow reference to both lexical and surface environments, ordering is not necessary.

6.2.3 Elision

Elision is a phonological process in which sounds are omitted in unstressed syllables. The following subsections illustrate elision in word-medial position, called *syncope*, and elision in word-final position, called *apocope*.

Syncope

In the historical development of Latin to French, the penultimate vowel was deleted in words with antepenultimate stress (Schane 1973:57). For example,

> LR: t'abula   p'opulum
> SR: t'abOla   p'opOlum

T120   "Deletion correspondences" 1 4

	a	i	u	@
	0	0	0	@
1:	1	1	1	1

Syncope of penultimate vowel

T121   "V:0 $\Leftarrow$ 'VC*___C*VC*#" 5 6

	'	V	C	V	#	@
	'	V	C	0	#	@
1:	2	1	1	1	1	1
2:	2	3	1	1	1	1
3:	2	4	3	1	1	1
4:	2	5	4	1	1	1
5:	2	1	5	1	0	1

In table 121, the column header *V:V* represents both the *V* in the environment and what would otherwise be the column header *V:@* (that is, *V:~0*). Also note that if the description contains table 122 below, which is a $\Rightarrow$ rule, table 121 can be simplified by deleting the *V:0* column. This change would make table 121 a $\Leftarrow$ rule.

Syncope of penultimate vowel

T122 "V:0 ⇒ 'VC*___C*VC*#" 5 6

	'	V	C	V	#	@
	'	V	C	0	#	@
1:	2	1	1	0	1	1
2:	2	3	1	0	1	1
3:	2	1	3	4	1	1
4.	0	5	4	0	0	0
5.	0	0	5	0	1	0

Apocope

In colloquial French, a word-final, unstressed, reduced vowel (a schwa) is deleted (Schane 1973:57-58). For example,

LR: egl'izə   t'ablə
SR: egl'iz0   t'abl0

Apocope

T123 "ə:0 ⇐ C___#" 3 5

	C	ə	ə	#	@
	C	0	@	#	@
1:	2	1	1	1	1
2:	2	1	3	1	1
3:	2	1	1	0	1

Apocope

T124 "ə:0 ⇒ C___#" 3 3

	C	ə	#	@
	C	0	#	@
1:	2	0	1	1
2:	2	3	1	1
3.	0	0	1	0

6.2.4 Coalescence

Coalescence is a phonological process in which two sounds are fused into one. However, two-level rules cannot map two lexical characters to only one surface character; each lexical character must correspond to its own surface character. Thus, coalescence must be treated as assimilation plus deletion. In Tagalog, the final nasal consonant N (unspecified for point of articulation) of the prefix maN+ coalesces with a following consonant; that is, N assimilates to the point of articulation of a following consonant, which itself is deleted. For example,

LR: maN+pili maN+tahi maN+kuha
SR: mam00ili man 00ahi maŋ 0 0uha

To account for these data, first define these subsets:

SUBSET P   p b   (labials)
SUBSET T   t d   (dentals)
SUBSET K   k g   (velars)
SUBSET NAS   m n ŋ   (nasals)

and declare these special correspondences:

T125   "Deletion correspondences" 1 7

	p	b	t	d	k	g	@
	0	0	0	0	0	0	@
1:	1	1	1	1	1	1	1

These are the rules for Nasal Assimilation and Deletion:

Nasal Assimilation

T126   "N:{m,n,ŋ} ⇔ ___(+:0) {P:,T:,K:}" 5 9

	N	N	N	N	+	P	T	K	@
	m	n	ŋ	@	0	@	@	@	@
1:	3	4	5	2	1	1	1	1	1
2:	1	1	1	2	2	0	0	0	1
3.	0	0	0	0	3	1	0	0	0
4.	0	0	0	0	4	0	1	0	0
5.	0	0	0	0	5	0	0	1	0

Deletion

T127   "{P,T,K}:0 ⇔ :NAS (+:0)___" 2 9

	@	+	P	T	K	P	T	K	@
	NAS	0	0	0	0	@	@	@	@
1:	2	1	0	0	0	1	1	1	1
2:	2	2	1	1	1	0	0	0	1

The reciprocal interaction between these two rules is made possible by writing table 126 so that it is sensitive to a lexical environment and writing table 127 so that it is sensitive to a surface environment. Notice the similarity to reciprocal assimilation (see section 6.1.2).

6.3 Insertion

Since two-level rules require that each character of a lexical form map onto exactly one character of a corresponding surface form, the insertion of a surface character must be represented as a correspondence to a lexical NULL symbol. The following subsections give five examples that involve insertion. The procedure for compiling insertion rules into state tables is slightly different from the general procedure described in section 3.3.2. See section 3.3.7 for a detailed description of how to compile insertion rules, using the Hanunoo example given in the first subsection below.

6.3.1 Consonant insertion

In Hanunoo of the Philippines, the consonant *h* is inserted to break up a vowel cluster. This occurs, for instance, in the last two forms below when the suffix *i* is added (Schane 1973:54).

ROOT		ROOT+*i*	
ʔupat	'four'	ʔupati	'make it four'
ʔunum	'six'	ʔunumi	'make it six'
ʔusa	'one'	ʔusahi	'make it one'
tulu	'three'	tuluhi	'make it three'

In the following two-level representations, the inserted *h* is represented as corresponding to a lexical NULL symbol.

LR: ʔunum+i ʔusa+0i
SR: ʔunum0i ʔusa0hi

This is the ⇒ rule for *h*-insertion:

h-insertion

T128   "0:h ⇒ V +:0___V" 4 4

	V	+	0	@
	V	0	h	@
1:	2	1	0	1
2:	2	3	0	1
3:	2	1	4	1
4.	2	0	0	0

The next rule makes *h*-insertion obligatory by prohibiting the sequence *V +:0 V*:

h-insertion

T129   "0:0 ⇐ V +:0___V" 3 3

	V	+	@
	V	0	@
1:	2	1	1
2:	2	3	1
3:	0	1	1

The two rules can be combined as a single ⟺ rule:

h-insertion
T130   "0:h ⟺ V +:0 ___ V" 4 4

	V	+	0	@
	V	0	h	@
1:	2	1	0	1
2:	2	3	0	1
3:	0	1	4	1
4.	2	0	0	0

6.3.2 Vowel insertion

In Hanunoo, when a word would otherwise begin with two consonants, the vowel *u* is inserted to break up the consonant cluster (Schane 1973:66). Since Schane gives no examples, consider what might happen if the English word *truck* were borrowed into Hanunoo; we might hypothesize that it would be pronounced *turak*. Here is a two-level representation of this word:

LR: t0rak
SR: turak

This is a ⟺ rule for *u*-insertion:

u-insertion
T131   "0:u ⟺ #C ___ C" 4 4

	#	C	0	@
	#	C	u	@
1:	2	1	0	1
2:	1	3	0	1
3:	1	0	4	1
4.	0	1	0	0

6.3.3 Word-final stress

Consider this hypothetical example in which stress always occurs on the final syllable of the word; that is, stress is inserted before the last vowel of the word. For example,

LR: bat0o   tam0is
SR: bat'o   tam'is

This is the ⟹ rule for stress insertion:

Stress

T132   "0:' ⇒ ___ VC*#" 3 5

	0 V C # @				
	' V C # @				
1:	2	1	1	1	1
2.	0	3	0	0	0
3.	0	0	3	1	0

The following ⇐ rule makes stress insertion obligatory by disallowing unstressed words:

Stress

T133   "0:0 ⇐ #[C*V*]* ___ VC*#" 2 4

	# V C @			
	# V C @			
1:	2	1	1	1
2:	0	2	2	1

Tables 132 and 133 can be combined as a ⇔ table:

Stress

T134   "0:' ⇔ #[C*V*]* ___ VC*#" 4 5

	0 V C # @				
	' V C # @				
1:	0	1	1	2	1
2:	3	2	2	0	1
3:	0	4	0	0	0
4:	0	0	4	1	0

6.3.4 Stress in French

In French, words are stressed on one of the last two syllables. If a word ends in schwa the stress is on the vowel preceding the schwa. Otherwise, the stress is on the final vowel of word (Schane 1973:64-65). Notice that this is a disjunctive environment; stress occurs in either environment, but not in both environments in the same word (see Schane 1973:89). For example,

LR: pət0itə   am0i
SR: pət'itə   am'i

First the ⇒ rule:

Stress

T135   "0:' ⇒ ___ VC*(ə)#" 4 6

| | 0 | V | C | ə | # | @ |
	'	V	C	ə	#	@
1:	2	1	1	1	1	1
2.	0	3	0	0	0	0
3.	0	0	3	4	1	0
4.	0	0	0	0	1	0

The following ⇐ rule makes stress insertion obligatory by disallowing unstressed words:

Stress

T136   "0:0 ⇐ #[C*V*]* ___ VC*(ə)#" 2 5

| | V | C | ə | # | @ |
	V	C	ə	#	@
1:	1	1	1	2	1
2:	2	2	0	0	1

Tables 135 and 136 can be combined as a ⇔ table:

Stress

T137   "0:0 ⇐ #[C*V*]* ___ VC*(ə)#" 3 6

| | 0 | V | C | ə | # | @ |
	'	V	C	ə	#	@
1:	0	1	1	1	2	1
2:	3	2	2	0	0	1
3.	0	4	0	0	0	0
4.	0	0	4	1	1	0

6.3.5 Stress shift

The following data, based on Tagalog, show a shift of stress one syllable to the right.

ROOT	ROOT+SUFFIX
d'alaw	dal'awin
t'awag	taw'agan

We will assume that stress shift occurs under the following conditions:

1. Lexical stress must be located in the penultimate syllable of the root or earlier; that is, stress on the ultimate syllable of the root does not shift.

2. Stress shift occurs only when a root is suffixed. For example, words of the pattern C'VCVCV do not undergo stress shift, but words of the pattern C'VCV+CV do.

The strategy for handling stress shift is to delete stress from the lexical form and insert it into the surface form; for example,

LR: d'al0aw+in   t'aw0ag+an
SR: d0al'aw0in   t0aw'ag0an

This is the ⇒ rule for Stress Shift:

Stress Shift

T138   "':0 ⇒ ___ VC* 0:' V*C* +:0 [V* C*]*#" 6 7

	'	V	C	0	+	#	@
	0	V	C	'	0	#	@
1:	2	1	1	0	1	1	1
2.	0	3	0	0	0	0	0
3.	0	0	3	4	0	0	0
4.	0	5	0	0	0	0	0
5.	0	5	5	0	6	0	0
6.	0	6	6	0	0	1	0

This ⇐ rule ensures that Stress Shift is obligatory by prohibiting an un-shifted stress (that is, ':') in an antepenultimate (or earlier) syllable in a suffixed word.

Stress Shift

T139   "':' ⇐ ___ VC*V[V* | C*]* +:0 [V* C*]*#" 5 6

	'	V	C	+	#	@
	'	V	C	0	#	@
1:	2	1	1	1	1	1
2:	2	3	1	1	1	1
3:	2	4	3	1	1	1
4:	2	4	4	5	1	1
5:	2	5	5	1	0	1

6.4 Nonconcatenative processes

The term *nonconcatenative processes* is used here to cover a spectrum of phonological and morphological phenomena that require special treatment, including infixation, reduplication, gemination, degemination, and metathesis. In the case of infixation, an infix is a morpheme similar to a prefix or suffix; it differs in that it is inserted into the middle of another morpheme rather than simply concatenated to the beginning or end. In the case of reduplication, part of the phonological material of a word is copied and attached to the word. The result may look like an affix (prefix or suffix) in that it is a chunk of phonological material that occurs in linear order with the other morphemes that compose a word, but unlike true affixes it has no constant lexical (phonological) form; rather, reduplication is best understood as a process. Gemination is the doubling of a phonological segment; like reduplication, it involves the process of copying. Degemination is the reduction of a sequence of two identical segments to a single segment; it requires a matching test between segments. Metathesis is a process that interchanges the linear sequence of two segments.

Handling all of these processes, all of which involve copying or matching, is a special challenge for a finite state processor like PC-KIMMO. Though they can all be described using finite state automata, the strategies for constructing state tables may not be obvious. This section gives examples of how to describe each type of process. The final examples demonstrate how to handle the situation where a number of these processes simultaneously interact with each other.

6.4.1 Degemination

In degemination a sequence of two identical segments (a geminate cluster) is reduced to a single segment (degeminates). In process terms, this is expressed by a rule of the form $C_i C_i \longrightarrow C_i$ (where subscript i indicates an identical segment); for example, $bb \longrightarrow b$, $dd \longrightarrow d$, and $gg \longrightarrow g$. In two-level rules, degemination must be represented as a deletion. In the following hypothetical examples, the second consonant of the cluster is deleted (deleting the first consonant would have the identical effect):

LR: ab+ba ad+da ag+ga
SR: ab00a ad00a ag00a

Degemination requires testing whether two consecutive segments are identical. To perform such a test using finite state tables, each possible pair of cooccurring segments must be enumerated in the state table. In the following rules, curly braces ({}) indicate sets of elements that match respectively. Thus table 140 collapses these three rules: $b{:}0 \Leftrightarrow b\,(+{:}0)$___, $d{:}0 \Leftrightarrow d\,(+{:}0)$___, and $g{:}0 \Leftrightarrow g\,(+{:}0)$___ .

Degemination

T140   "{b,d,g}:0 ⇒ {b,d,g} (+:0)____" 4 8

	b	d	g	+	b	d	g	@
	b	d	g	0	0	0	0	@
1:	2	3	4	1	0	0	0	1
2:	0	3	4	2	1	0	0	1
3:	2	0	4	3	0	1	0	1
4:	2	3	0	4	0	0	1	1

(Table 140 is written as a ⇒ rule. But if lexical *b*, *d*, and *g* have no surface realizations other than those declared in this table, then table 140 will in effect be equivalent to a ⇔ rule.)

6.4.2 Gemination

In Hebrew, the definite proclitic *ha-* doubles (geminates) the first consonant of the stem:

melek	'king'	hammelek	'the king'
davar	'word'	haddavar	'the word'

This can be handled by positing *haX+* as the lexical representation of the definite morpheme and writing a rule that matches the surface realization of *X* to the following consonant. For example,

LR: haX+melek   haX+davar
SR: ham0melek   had0davar

The following rules include only the consonants *b*, *d*, and *m*; other consonants can be added in the same way.

Gemination

T141   "X:{b,d,m} ⇒ ____(+:0) {b,d,m}" 4 8

	X	X	X	b	d	m	+	@
	b	d	m	b	d	m	0	@
1:	2	3	4	1	1	1	1	1
2.	0	0	0	1	0	0	2	0
3.	0	0	0	0	1	0	3	0
4.	0	0	0	0	0	1	4	0

(Table 141 is written as a ⇒ rule. But if lexical *X* has no other surface realization, then table 141 will in effect be equivalent to a ⇔ rule.)

Gemination can also be done with a true insertion, that is, a surface character in correspondence with a lexical NULL. In the Hebrew example, this solution would posit *ha+* as the lexical form of the proclitic and a rule that inserts a consonant that matches the following consonant. (A similar example of doing gemination this way is in the English description found in the ENGLISH subdirectory on the PC-KIMMO release diskette.)

6.4.3 Metathesis

In Hanunoo, the cluster glottal stop plus consonant metathesizes to consonant plus glottal stop when it is between vowels (Schane 1973:67). For example (Schane 1973:56),

?usa	'one'	kas?a	'once'
?upat	'four'	kap?at	'four times'
?unum	'six'	kan?um	'six times'
tulu	'three'	katlu	'three times'

These data are consistent with the Hanunoo vowel insertion rule (see section 6.3.2), where the vowel u is inserted in a word-initial consonant cluster; therefore the following two-level correspondences and rules assume that the vowel insertion rule is included in the description. Two-level rules handle the metathesis process in the above data by positing the correspondences *?:C* and *C:?* where *C* is identical. For example,

LR: t0lu   ka+tlu   ?0sa   ka+?sa
SR: tulu   ka0tlu   ?usa   ka0s?a

In order to test whether two consonants are identical, each glottal and consonant pair must be enumerated in the rules. The strategy for expressing the metathesis of, say, *?* and *s* is to write one rule for the *?:s* correspondence and another rule for the *s:?* correspondence.

Metathesis

T142   "?:s ⇐ V (+:0)＿＿ s:@ V" 4 6

	V +	?	?	s	@
	V 0	s	@	@	@
1:	3 1	1	1	1	1
2:	0 2	1	1	1	1
3:	3 3	1	4	1	1
4:	3 4	1	1	2	1

Metathesis

T143   "s:? ⇐ V (+:0) ?:@ ___ V" 4 6

V	+	?	s	s	@
V	0	@	?	@	@
1: 3	1	1	1	1	1
2: 0	2	1	1	1	1
3: 3	3	4	1	1	1
4: 3	4	1	1	2	1

Notice that the environment of table 142 contains the expression *s:@* (where we might expect *s:?*) and the environment of table 143 contains *?:@* (where we might expect *?:s*); this prevents overgeneration (see sections 3.1.7 and 3.3.12). Tables 142 and 143 can be collapsed into table 144.

Metathesis

T144   "?:s ⇐ V (+:0)___ s:? V" 5 7

V	+	?	?	s	s	@
V	0	s	@	?	@	@
1: 3	1	1	1	1	1	1
2: 0	2	1	1	1	1	1
3: 3	3	5	4	1	1	1
4: 3	4	1	1	2	2	1
5: 3	5	1	1	1	2	1

This is the ⇒ rule corresponding to table 144:

Metathesis

T145   "?:s ⇒ V (+:0)___ s:? V" 4 5

V	+	?	s	@
V	0	s	?	@
1: 3	1	0	0	1
2. 1	2	0	0	0
3: 3	3	4	0	1
4. 0	4	0	2	0

Tables 144a and 145a are expansions of tables 144 and 145 to include the consonants *s*, *p*, and *n*. Notice that in tables 142 through 145a the *V* at the end of the right context is recognized in state 2. Constructing the tables in this manner allows more states to be added to the end of the table (representing more consonants) without having to renumber the rows.

Metathesis

T144a   "?:{s,p,n} ⇐ V (+:0)___ {s,p,n}:? V" 7 13

	V	+	?	?	?	?	s	s	p	p	n	n	@
	V	0	s	p	n	@	?	@	?	@	?	@	@
1:	3	1	1	1	1	1	1	1	1	1	1	1	1
2:	0	2	1	1	1	1	1	1	1	1	1	1	1
3:	3	3	5	6	7	4	1	1	1	1	1	1	1
4:	3	4	1	1	1	1	2	2	2	2	2	2	1
5:	3	5	1	1	1	1	1	2	1	1	1	1	1
6:	3	6	1	1	1	1	1	1	1	2	1	1	1
7:	3	7	1	1	1	1	1	1	1	1	1	2	1

Metathesis

T145a   "?:{s,p,n} ⇒ V (+:0)___ {s,p,n}:? V" 6 9

	V	+	?	?	?	s	p	n	@
	V	0	s	p	n	?	?	?	@
1:	3	1	0	0	0	0	0	0	1
2.	1	2	0	0	0	0	0	0	0
3:	3	3	4	5	6	0	0	0	1
4.	0	4	0	0	0	2	0	0	0
5.	0	5	0	0	0	0	2	0	0
6.	0	6	0	0	0	0	0	2	0

6.4.4 Infixation

Tagalog has a verbalizing infix <*in*> that attaches between the first consonant and vowel of a base. For example,

ROOT	<*in*>+ROOT	
pili	pinili	'choose'
tahi	tinahi	'sew'
kuha	kinuha	'take'

We represent the infix lexically as a prefix *X+*. For recognition purposes, the form *X+* must be included as an entry in the lexicon, as it represents a morpheme. Rules insert <*in*> in the presence of *X+*, which is deleted. For example,

LR: X+p0 0ili   X+t0 0ahi   X+k0 0uha
SR: 00 p i nili   00 t i nahi   00 k i nuha

Infixation

T146 "X:0 ⇒ ___ +:0 C 0:i 0:n V" 6 7

X	+	C	0	0	V	@
0	0	C	i	n	V	@

	X	+	C	0	0	V	@
1:	2	1	1	0	0	1	1
2.	0	3	0	0	0	0	0
3.	0	0	4	0	0	0	0
4.	0	0	0	5	0	0	0
5.	0	0	0	0	6	0	0
6.	0	0	0	0	0	1	0

(Although table 146 is written as a ⇒ rule, if X has no other surface realization its effect is the same as a ⇔ rule.)

6.4.5 Reduplication

In Tagalog, one type of reduplication copies the first CV of a root. For example,

ROOT	CV+ROOT	
pili	pipili	'choose'
tahi	tatahi	'sew'
kuha	kukuha	'take'

We represent the reduplicated syllable as *RE+*. For recognition purposes, the form *RE+* must be included as an entry in the lexicon. Rules convert *RE* to match the first CV of the following root. For example,

LR: RE+pili   RE+tahi   RE+kuha
SR: p i 0pili   t a 0tahi   k u 0kuha

Since finite state tables cannot directly copy segments, table 147 matches R to the following consonant by means of enumerating each pair. The table only handles *p, t,* and *k,* but more consonants can be added to it in the same way.

C-Reduplication

T147   "R:{p,t,k} ⇒ ___E:V +:0 {p,t,k}" 10 9

	R	R	R	E	+	p	t	k	@
	p	t	k	V	0	p	t	k	@
1:	2	5	8	1	1	1	1	1	1
2.	0	0	0	3	0	0	0	0	0
3.	0	0	0	0	4	0	0	0	0
4.	0	0	0	0	0	1	0	0	0
5.	0	0	0	6	0	0	0	0	0
6.	0	0	0	0	7	0	0	0	0
7.	0	0	0	0	0	0	1	0	0
8.	0	0	0	9	0	0	0	0	0
9.	0	0	0	0	10	0	0	0	0
10.	0	0	0	0	0	0	0	1	0

Table 148 matches E to the following vowels a, i, and u. Other vowels can be added to the table in the same way.

V-Reduplication

T148   "E:{a,i,u} ⇒ R:C___+:0 C {a,i,u}" 11 10

	R	E	E	E	+	C	a	i	u	@
	C	a	i	u	0	C	a	i	u	@
1:	2	0	0	0	1	1	1	1	1	1
2:	1	3	6	9	1	1	1	1	1	1
3.	0	0	0	0	4	0	0	0	0	0
4.	0	0	0	0	0	5	0	0	0	0
5.	0	0	0	0	0	0	1	0	0	0
6.	0	0	0	0	7	0	0	0	0	0
7.	0	0	0	0	0	8	0	0	0	0
8.	0	0	0	0	0	0	0	1	0	0
9.	0	0	0	0	10	0	0	0	0	0
10.	0	0	0	0	0	11	0	0	0	0
11.	0	0	0	0	0	0	0	0	1	0

6.4.6 Reduplication with infixation

In Tagalog, both infixation and reduplication can occur in the same word:

ROOT	<in>+CV+ROOT	
pili	pinipili	'choose'
tahi	tinatahi	'sew'
kuha	kinukuha	'take'

Notice that the infix is placed in the reduplicated syllable, not in the root; that is, *kinukuha*, not *kukinuha*. Thus the lexical form is represented as *X+RE+kuha*. Here are some two-level correspondences:

LR: X+R00E+pili   X+R00E+tahi   X+R00E+kuha
SR: 00 p i n i 0pili   00 t i n a 0tahi   0 0k inu 0kuha

Table 146 from section 6.4.4 adequately handles infixation. The following tables are needed to handle reduplication. They differ from tables 147 and 148 only in allowing the infix *<in>* to pass through vacuously. Also note that *R* must be included in the *C* subset (for consonants) and *E* must be included in the *V* subset (for vowels).

C-Reduplication

T149   "R:{p,t,k} ⇒ ___ (0:i 0:n) E:V +:0 {p,t,k}" 10 11

	R	R	R	0	0	E	+	p	t	k	@
	p	t	k	i	n	V	0	p	t	k	@
1:	2	5	8	1	1	1	1	1	1	1	1
2.	0	0	0	2	2	3	0	0	0	0	0
3.	0	0	0	0	0	0	4	0	0	0	0
4.	0	0	0	0	0	0	0	1	0	0	0
5.	0	0	0	5	5	6	0	0	0	0	0
6.	0	0	0	0	0	0	7	0	0	0	0
7.	0	0	0	0	0	0	0	0	1	0	0
8.	0	0	0	8	8	9	0	0	0	0	0
9.	0	0	0	0	0	0	10	0	0	0	0
10.	0	0	0	0	0	0	0	0	0	1	0

V-Reduplication

T150   "E:{a,i,u} ⇒ R:C (0:i 0:n)___ +:0 C {a,i,u}" 11 12

	R	0	0	E	E	E	+	C	a	i	u	@
	C	i	n	a	i	u	0	C	a	i	u	@
1:	2	1	1	0	0	0	1	1	1	1	1	1
2.	1	2	2	3	6	9	1	1	1	1	1	1
3.	0	0	0	0	0	0	4	0	0	0	0	0
4.	0	0	0	0	0	0	0	5	0	0	0	0
5.	0	0	0	0	0	0	0	0	1	0	0	0
6.	0	0	0	0	0	0	7	0	0	0	0	0
7.	0	0	0	0	0	0	0	8	0	0	0	0
8.	0	0	0	0	0	0	0	0	0	1	0	0
9.	0	0	0	0	0	0	10	0	0	0	0	0
10.	0	0	0	0	0	0	0	11	0	0	0	0
11.	0	0	0	0	0	0	0	0	0	0	1	0

6.4.7 Reduplication with coalescence

Section 6.2.4 developed a nasal coalescence rule for Tagalog that applies to the prefix *maN+*. The following examples show how reduplication and coalescence interact:

ROOT	*maN+ROOT*	*maN+CV+ROOT*	
pili	mamili	mamimili	'choose'
tahi	manahi	mananahi	'sew'
kuha	maŋuha	maŋuŋuha	'take'

In process terms, coalescence precedes reduplication (the opposite order would result in the incorrect forms *mamipili, manatahi,* and *maŋukuha*). The coalescence rules developed above (section 6.2.4) were written to reflect the analysis that *N* assimilates to a following obstruent that is deleted (for example, *Nb:m0*). However, in order to combine coalescence with reduplication, the correspondences must be modified so that an obstruent corresponds to a homorganic nasal after an *N* that is deleted (for example, *Nb:0m*). The rule that reduplicates the first consonant of the root must then copy the surface realization of that consonant. For example,

LR: maN+p ili   maN+RE+p ili   maN+t ahi   maN+RE+t ahi
SR: ma0 0mili   ma0 0 mi 0mili   ma0 0nahi   ma0 0 n a 0nahi

Assume these subsets:

SUBSET P	p b	(labials)
SUBSET T	t d	(dentals)
SUBSET K	k g	(velars)
SUBSET NAS	m n ŋ	(nasals)

and these special correspondences:

T151   "Coalescence correspondences" 1 7

	p	b	t	d	k	g	@
	m	m	n	n	ŋ	ŋ	@
1:	1	1	1	1	1	1	1

These are the rules for Nasal Deletion and Assimilation to Nasal:

Nasal Deletion

T152   "N:0 ⇒ ___(+:0) (R:C E:V +:0) :NAS" 2 6

	N	+	R	E	@	@
	0	0	C	V	NAS	@
1:	2	1	1	1	1	1
2:	1	2	2	2	0	1

Assimilation to Nasal

T153   "{P,T,K}:{m,n,ŋ} ⇔ N: (+:0) (R:C E:V +:0)___ " 2 11

	N	+	R	E	P	T	K	P	T	K	@
	@	0	C	V	m	n	ŋ	@	@	@	@
1:	2	1	1	1	0	0	0	1	1	1	1
2:	2	2	2	2	1	1	1	0	0	0	1

(Table 152 is written as a ⇒ rule. But if lexical *N* has no other surface realization, then it will in effect be equivalent to a ⇔ rule.) The consonant reduplication rule (from table 147 above) must now be expanded to account for reduplication of consonants that have assimilated to a nasal. The following reduplication rule accounts only for the root-initial consonants *p*, *t*, and *k*.

C-Reduplication

T154   "R:{p,m,t,n,k,ŋ} ⇒ ___E:V +:0 {p,p,t,t,k,k}:{p,m,t,n,k,ŋ}" 19 15

	R	R	R	R	R	R	E	+	p	p	t	t	k	k	@
	p	m	t	n	k	ŋ	V	0	p	m	t	n	k	ŋ	@
1:	2	5	8	11	14	17	1	1	1	1	1	1	1	1	1
2.	0	0	0	0	0	0	3	0	0	0	0	0	0	0	0
3.	0	0	0	0	0	0	0	4	0	0	0	0	0	0	0
4.	0	0	0	0	0	0	0	0	1	0	0	0	0	0	0
5.	0	0	0	0	0	0	6	0	0	0	0	0	0	0	0
6.	0	0	0	0	0	0	0	7	0	0	0	0	0	0	0
7.	0	0	0	0	0	0	0	0	0	1	0	0	0	0	0
8.	0	0	0	0	0	0	9	0	0	0	0	0	0	0	0
9.	0	0	0	0	0	0	0	10	0	0	0	0	0	0	0
10.	0	0	0	0	0	0	0	0	0	0	1	0	0	0	0
11.	0	0	0	0	0	0	12	0	0	0	0	0	0	0	0
12.	0	0	0	0	0	0	0	13	0	0	0	0	0	0	0
13.	0	0	0	0	0	0	0	0	0	0	1	0	0	0	0
14.	0	0	0	0	0	0	15	0	0	0	0	0	0	0	0
15.	0	0	0	0	0	0	0	16	0	0	0	0	0	0	0
16.	0	0	0	0	0	0	0	0	0	0	0	1	0	0	0
17.	0	0	0	0	0	0	18	0	0	0	0	0	0	0	0
18.	0	0	0	0	0	0	0	19	0	0	0	0	0	0	0
19.	0	0	0	0	0	0	0	0	0	0	0	0	0	1	0

Table 148 above for vowel reduplication does not need to be modified to work with coalescence.

6.4.8 Reduplication with coalescence and infixation

The consonant reduplication rule can be extended further to interact correctly with both the coalescence rules (tables 152 and 153) and the infixation rule (table 146). The vowel reduplication rule in table 150 does not need to be further modified. Together these rules account for forms such as the following:

LR: maN+RE+pili X+R00E+pili maN+RE+tahi X+R00E+tahi
SR: ma00mi0mili 00pini0pili ma00na0nahi 00tina0tahi

Note that the tables developed here account only for the root-initial consonants *p*, *t*, and *k* and the vowels *a*, *i*, and *u*. The tables can be easily extended to include more consonants and vowels.

C-Reduplication

T155   "R:{p,m,t,n,k,ŋ} ___ (0:i 0:n) E:V +:0 {p,p,t,t,k,k}:{p,m,t,n,k,ŋ}" 19 17

	R	R	R	R	R	R	0	0	E	+	p	p	t	t	k	k	@
	p	m	t	n	k	ŋ	i	n	V	0	p	m	t	n	k	ŋ	@
1:	2	5	8	11	14	17	1	1	1	1	1	1	1	1	1	1	1
2.	0	0	0	0	0	0	2	2	3	0	0	0	0	0	0	0	0
3.	0	0	0	0	0	0	0	0	0	4	0	0	0	0	0	0	0
4.	0	0	0	0	0	0	0	0	0	0	1	0	0	0	0	0	0
5.	0	0	0	0	0	0	5	5	6	0	0	0	0	0	0	0	0
6.	0	0	0	0	0	0	0	0	0	7	0	0	0	0	0	0	0
7.	0	0	0	0	0	0	0	0	0	0	0	1	0	0	0	0	0
8.	0	0	0	0	0	0	8	8	9	0	0	0	0	0	0	0	0
9.	0	0	0	0	0	0	0	0	0	10	0	0	0	0	0	0	0
10.	0	0	0	0	0	0	0	0	0	0	0	0	1	0	0	0	0
11.	0	0	0	0	0	0	11	11	12	0	0	0	0	0	0	0	0
12.	0	0	0	0	0	0	0	0	0	13	0	0	0	0	0	0	0
13.	0	0	0	0	0	0	0	0	0	0	0	0	0	1	0	0	0
14.	0	0	0	0	0	0	14	14	15	0	0	0	0	0	0	0	0
15.	0	0	0	0	0	0	0	0	0	16	0	0	0	0	0	0	0
16.	0	0	0	0	0	0	0	0	0	0	0	0	0	0	1	0	0
17.	0	0	0	0	0	0	17	17	18	0	0	0	0	0	0	0	0
18.	0	0	0	0	0	0	0	0	0	19	0	0	0	0	0	0	0
19.	0	0	0	0	0	0	0	0	0	0	0	0	0	0	0	1	0

The rules developed in this chapter for infixation, reduplication, and coalescence in Tagalog are found in the file TAGALOG.RUL. Accompanying it is the lexicon file TAGALOG.LEX and the data comparison files TAGALOG.GEN, TAGALOG.REC, and TAGALOG.PAI. All of these files are located in the TAGALOG subdirectory on the PC-KIMMO release diskette.

REFERENCE MANUAL

7.1 Introduction and technical specifications

PC-KIMMO is a new implementation for microcomputers of a program dubbed KIMMO after its inventor Kimmo Koskenniemi. Koskenniemi's two-level model was designed to generate and recognize words (see Koskenniemi 1983a). Work on PC-KIMMO was begun in 1985, following the specifications of the LISP implementation of Koskenniemi's model described in Karttunen 1983. The aim was to develop a version of the two-level processor that would run on an IBM PC compatible computer and that would include an environment for testing and debugging a linguistic description. The PC-KIMMO program is actually a shell program that serves as an interactive user interface to the primitive PC-KIMMO functions. These functions are available as a source code library that can be included in a program written by the user.

The coding has been done in Microsoft C by David Smith and Stephen McConnel under the direction of Gary Simons and under the auspices of the Summer Institute of Linguistics. Every effort has been made to maintain portability. Both the PC-KIMMO shell and the program modules will run on any hardware using MS-DOS or PC-DOS version 2.0 or higher. It can be run with as little as 256KB of memory, but will use up to 640KB. PC-KIMMO has also been compiled and tested for UNIX System V (SCO UNIX V/386 and A/UX) and for 4.2 BSD UNIX.

We have also ported PC-KIMMO to the Macintosh, though it retains its command-line interface rather than using the graphical user interface one expects from Macintosh programs. Also, a few commands are not available in the Macintosh version; see the README file on the Macintosh version of the PC-KIMMO release diskette for detailed information.

There are two versions of the PC-KIMMO release diskette, one for IBM PC compatibles and one for the Macintosh. Each contains the executable PC-KIMMO program, examples of language descriptions, and the source code library for the primitive PC-KIMMO functions. The PC-KIMMO executable program and the source code library are copyrighted but are made freely available to the general public under the condition that they not be resold or used for commercial purposes.

For those who wish to compile PC-KIMMO for their UNIX system, the complete source code for both the user shell and the primitive functions is available for the cost of the media and shipping from Academic Computing Department, Summer Institute of Linguistics, 7500 W. Camp Wisdom Road, Dallas, TX 75236.

The English description referred to in this chapter is based on Karttunen and Wittenburg 1983 as modified by Steve Echerd and Evan

Antworth; see appendix A for a detailed exposition of the English description. The English files are found in the ENGLISH subdirectory on the PC-KIMMO release diskette.

7.2 Installing PC-KIMMO

The following instructions apply to installing the IBM PC version of PC-KIMMO. Most of the information is also consistent with the UNIX version. For information on installing and running the Macintosh version, see the README file on the Macintosh version of the PC-KIMMO release diskette.

If your computer has floppy disks only, make a working copy of the PC-KIMMO release diskette that came with this book. Store the original in a safe place. Insert your working copy of the PC-KIMMO diskette in drive A of your machine.

If your computer has a hard disk, use the INSTALL.BAT procedure on the PC-KIMMO diskette to install the system on your hard disk. To do this, insert the PC-KIMMO diskette in one of your disk drives. Type *A:* (or whatever the name of the drive is) in order to log control to that disk. Now type *install* followed by the name of the hard disk on which you want to install PC-KIMMO (for instance, *install C:*). This will create a subdirectory called PCKIMMO on your hard disk and copy the contents of the release diskette (with all its subdirectories) into it.

Whether you are using a floppy or hard disk system, the operating system's PATH variable must be set to include the directory where the PC-KIMMO program is found. The AUTOEXEC.BAT file on your boot disk should contain a path statement that specifies all the disks and directories that contain programs. On a floppy disk system, the path statement should include as a minimum the root directory of drive A, for instance, PATH=A:\. On a hard disk system, add ;C:\PCKIMMO to the end of the path statement. For the path statement to become effective, you must reboot the computer. (If you want to change the path variable without changing the AUTOEXEC.BAT file and rebooting, enter a path command directly at the operating system prompt.)

In order to use PC-KIMMO's *edit* command, you must set the operating system environment variable EDITOR to the name of your text editing program. This is done by including in the AUTOEXEC.BAT file a line of this form:

SET EDITOR=*filespec*

where *filespec* specifies the path and full file name of your editing program. For example, if your editor's file name is EMACS.EXE and is found in the UTIL subdirectory directly under the root directory, include this line:

    SET EDITOR=\UTIL\EMACS.EXE

7.3 Starting PC-KIMMO

Be sure that DOS is logged onto the drive where PC-KIMMO is located. To change to the subdirectory that contains the English example, enter *cd \english* on a floppy disk system, or *cd \pckimmo\english* on a hard disk system. Now type *pckimmo* (if your PATH variable is not correctly set to include the PC-KIMMO subdirectory, type *..\pckimmo*). When PC-KIMMO has successfully started up, you will see a version message and the PC-KIMMO command line prompt.

PC-KIMMO can also be started with optional command line arguments. The format of the command line is:

    pckimmo [-c *char*] [-r *rulefile*] [-l *lexfile*] [-t *cmdfile*]

The options are used as follows:

- The -c option changes the character used to delimit comments in files used by PC-KIMMO. The argument *char* is a single character. If this option is not specified, the semicolon (;) will be used as the comment delimiter. This option is equivalent to issuing the *set comment* command from the program prompt.

- The -r option specifies a rules file to be loaded. It is equivalent to issuing the *load rules* command from the program prompt.

- The -l option specifies a lexicon file to be loaded. It is equivalent to issuing the *load lexicon* command from the program prompt. It must be used with the -r option.

- The -t option specifies a command file from which PC-KIMMO reads and executes commands. It is equivalent to issuing the *take* command from the program prompt.

7.4 Entering commands and getting on-line help

The user interacts with PC-KIMMO by entering commands at the command line prompt, in much the same way that one enters commands at the operating system prompt. Case is ignored for all command keywords.

Keywords can be shortened to any unambiguous form. For instance, *load rules*, *load rul*, *load r*, and *loa r* are all acceptable. Typing just *l* is ambiguous for the commands *load*, *log*, and *list*. However, because *load* is such a frequently used command, it takes special precedence over the other commands beginning with *l*, which means that typing just *l* will execute only the *load* command.

PC-KIMMO can be used with a TSR (Terminate and Stay Resident) command line editor such as CED or NDOSEDIT. This allows the user to recall and edit several previous command lines. The list of previous PC-KIMMO command lines is kept separate from the list of previous operating system command lines. If you exit PC-KIMMO and then run it again, the set of command lines from your previous PC-KIMMO session is still available. Neither of the command line editors remembers a command shorter than three characters. It should be noted that CED uses the ^ character as a kind of "virtual carriage return." This means that forms containing ^ as an alphabetic character cannot be entered from the keyboard with the *generate* and *recognize* commands, though of course such words can be read from a file.

Screen scrolling can be halted by pressing *Ctrl-S* (that is, hold down the *Ctrl* (Control) key and press *S*); any key will resume scrolling.

Processing can be interrupted by pressing *Ctrl-C*. Note that this action does not abort PC-KIMMO, but returns it to the program prompt. It is useful for stopping a long screen display (such as a trace) or a file processing command.

Pressing *Ctrl-P* causes screen output to be echoed to the printer. Pressing *Ctrl-P* again stops printer echoing.

There are several ways to get on-line help:

- To get a list of the available commands, type *?*.

- To get information on what these commands do, type *help*.

- To get the specific syntax and use for a command, type *help* plus a specific command name.

- To get a list of the keywords that can go with a particular command, type the command name followed by *?*. Note however that if the command does not take a keyword it will be executed; for instance typing *new ?* will execute the *new* command.

7.5 Command reference by function

The following subsections document each command, arranged by function, of the PC-KIMMO system. Square brackets in the command line summaries indicate optional elements. The notation {x | y} means either *x* or *y* (but not both). Command keywords and arguments in boldface are typed literally; for instance, the command summary **set tracing** {**on | off**} means to type either *set tracing on* or *set tracing off*. Command arguments in italics are replaced by elements of the specified type; for instance, the command summary **set comment** *char* means to replace *char* with a single character, such as *set comment ;* .

7.5.1 Get help

?

Displays a list of command names.

help [*command-name*]

Issuing the *help* command with no argument displays a list of commands with a brief description of their function. Issuing the *help* command with the name of a specific command displays a usage summary for the command.

command-name **?**

Typing a command name followed by *?*, instead of a keyword, displays a message listing the keywords expected for that command.

7.5.2 Load rules and lexicon

The *load* command is used to load either rules or a lexicon from a file.

load rules [*filespec*]

The *load rules* loads a set of rules from the file specified on the command line. The *filespec* can contain a path, for example, B:\ENGLISH\ENGLISH.RUL. The default file name extension is .RUL; thus, the command *load rules english* will load the file ENGLISH.RUL. If no file name is given, the default file name RULES.RUL is used. The rules file must be in the format described later in this chapter (see section 7.7.1).

An error in the format of the rules file will cause the program to stop loading the file, erase the rules already loaded, and report an error message with the line number where the error was encountered. Refer to section 7.10 on error messages for more details.

The rules file must be loaded before the lexicon and before performing any generation or recognition operations.

The *load rules* command can also be invoked by using the *-r* command line option when starting up PC-KIMMO (see section 7.3).

load lexicon [*filespec*]

The *load lexicon* command loads a lexicon from the file specified in the command line. The *filespec* can contain a path, for example, B:\ENGLISH\ENGLISH.RUL. The default file name extension is .LEX; thus, the command *load lexicon english* will load the file ENGLISH.LEX. If no file name is given, the default file name LEXICON.LEX is used. The lexicon file must be in the format described later in this chapter (see section 7.7.2).

An error in the format of the lexicon file will cause the program to stop loading the file, erase the parts of the lexicon already loaded, and report an error message with the line number where the error was encountered. Refer to section 7.10 on error messages for more details.

The rules file must be loaded before the lexicon. The lexicon file must be loaded before performing any recognition operations. A generation operation can be performed without loading the lexicon.

The *load lexicon* command can also be invoked by using the *-l* command line option when starting up PC-KIMMO (see section 7.3).

7.5.3 Select new language

new

The *new* command clears the rules and lexicon currently loaded. Strictly speaking it is not needed, since the *load rules* command erases all existing rules and the *load lexicon* command erases any existing lexicon.

7.5.4 Take commands from a file

take [*filespec*]

The *take* command causes PC-KIMMO to read and execute commands from a file. The *filespec* can contain a path, for example, B:\KIMMO\ENGLISH.TAK. The *take* command recognizes the default file name PCKIMMO.TAK and the default file extension .TAK. The command file can itself issue the *take* command to call another command file down to a depth of three files. That is, the user can specify a command file <file1> that contains the command *take* <file2>, that itself contains the command *take* <file3>. It would be an error for <file3> to contain a *take* command.

A command file can also be specified by using the *-t* command line option when starting up PC-KIMMO (see section 7.3). Note that a command file cannot submit forms to the special generator and recognizer prompts (see sections 7.5.10 and 7.5.11).

7.5.5 List rule names, feasible pairs, or sublexicon names

The *list* command is used to display either rule names, feasible pairs, or sublexicon names.

list pairs

The *list pairs* command displays on the screen the set of feasible pairs specified by the set of rules currently turned on.

list rules

The *list rules* command displays on the screen the current state of the rules that are loaded. The display consists of each rule by number, an indication of whether the rule is on or off, and the rule name from the header lines of its state table in the rules file.

list lexicon

The *list lexicon* command displays on the screen the names of the sublexicons of the lexicon currently in use.

7.5.6 Set system parameters

The *set* command is used to turn tracing on or off, to turn on or off certain rules, to turn on or off various processing flags, and to change the comment delimiter character.

set tracing {on I off I *level*}

The *set tracing* command allows you turn the tracing mechanism on or off. When tracing is on, details of the analysis of a form are displayed on the screen during generation or recognition operations. If logging (see section 7.5.7) is on, the trace will also be written to the log file. Tracing is operative for these commands: *generate, recognize, file compare generate, file compare recognize, file compare pairs, file generate,* and *file recognize.*

The amount of detail shown in the trace display is set by the tracing level. The *level* argument to the *set tracing* command can range from 0 to 3, where 0 is no tracing at all and 3 is the most detailed level of tracing. Issuing the command *set tracing off* sets tracing to level 0. Issuing the command *set tracing on* sets tracing to level 2. At level 1, no information is given as to which feasible pair is being tried or the condition of the rules (that is, what state each automaton is in). Both the generator and recognizer report each RESULT line, with all NULL symbols being explicitly printed. The recognizer also displays lexicon information; that is, it reports which sublexicon is being entered or backed out of. At level 2, the feasible pairs being tried and the state of each rule (automaton) is displayed. The recognizer displays lexicon information as it does at level 1. At level 3, more detailed information is given on which feasible pairs are being tried and the state of each rule. For more information on the format of the trace display, see section 7.8 on trace formats.

set rules {on | off} {*list-of-numbers* | all}

The *set rules* command allows you to turn selected rules on or off for testing or debugging purposes. When a rule is turned off, it is completely ignored in the recognition or generation of forms. One effect of this is to cause the recalculation of feasible pairs, considering only the rules which remain on. Use the *list pairs* command to see the set of feasible pairs currently in use.

On the command line, you can specify the action *on* or *off* followed by a list of rule numbers or the keyword *all* (in which case all rules are turned on or off). Specific rules are turned on or off by listing their rule numbers (shown by the *list rules* command), each separated by a space.

set comment *char*

The *set comment* command changes the comment delimiter character (see section 7.7). The default is semicolon (;). The comment delimiter can also be set with the -c command line option when starting up PC-KIMMO (see section 7.3).

set limit {on | off}

The *set limit* command limits the result of a generation or recognition function to one form. That is, if limit is set off, then PC-KIMMO backtracks after finding a correct result so that it can find every possible result. With limit set on, after finding one correct result form PC-KIMMO does not backtrack to try to find more results.

set timing {on | off}

The *set timing* command uses the computer's system clock to time the execution of generation and recognition operations. It displays the result as the number of seconds the operation lasted. It applies to these commands: *generate, recognize, file compare generate, file compare recognize, file compare pairs, file generate,* and *file recognize.*

set verbose {on | off}

The *set verbose* command affects the amount of information displayed on the screen during a file comparison operation (either generate, recognize, or pairs, see section 7.5.12). If verbose is set off, a file comparison operation displays only a dot for each form correctly analyzed, though any exceptional results will cause the complete form and warning messages to be displayed. If verbose is set on, a file comparison operation displays the complete contents of the file (minus comments) plus confirmation and warning messages.

7.5.7 Turn logging on or off

The *log* and *close* commands are used to turn logging on and off.

log [*filespec*]

The *log* command turns the logging mechanism on. When logging is on, the information displayed on the screen during execution of generation or recognition operations is also written to a disk file whose name is specified in the command line. The *filespec* can contain a path, for example, B:\ENGLISH\ENGLISH.LOG. If no file name is given, a log file named PCKIMMO.LOG is written to the default directory. If a *log* command is given when a log file is already open, then the open log file is closed before the new log file is created. Logging records the processing of these commands: *generate, recognize, file compare generate, file compare recognize, file compare pairs, file generate*, and *file recognize*. Tracing displays are also recorded in a log file.

close

The *close* command turns logging off and closes the log file.

7.5.8 Show system status

The *status* command is used to display on the screen the status of various system parameters.

status

The *status* command displays the names of the rules and lexicon files currently loaded, the name of the log file (if logging is on), the comment delimiter character, and the status of the limit, timing, tracing and verbose flags. It can also be invoked with the synonyms *show status* or *show*.

7.5.9 Show rule or sublexicon

show rule *rule-number*

The *show rule* command first displays the number, on/off status, and name of the rule (similar to the *list rules* command). If the rule is turned on, it then displays each column header of the state table for that rule with the set of feasible pairs that it specifies. This command is used primarily for debugging purposes.

show lexicon *sublexicon-name*

The *show lexicon* command displays the contents of a sublexicon. It shows each lexical item, its gloss, and its continuation class. If the continuation class of a lexical entry names an alternation, the alternation is expanded into a list of sublexicon names. Note that this command displays the parts of the lexical entry in the following order (rather than the order in which they appear in the lexicon file): *lexical item, gloss, continuation class.*

7.5.10 Generate surface forms from a lexical form

generate [*lexical-form*]

The *generate* command accepts as input a lexical form and returns one or more surface forms. If no lexical form argument is given, PC-KIMMO supplies a special generator prompt where forms can be typed in directly without the *generate* keyword. Entering a blank line at the generator prompt returns the program to the main command line prompt.

7.5.11 Recognize lexical forms from a surface form

recognize [*surface-form*]

The *recognize* command accepts as input a surface form and returns one or more lexical forms. If no surface form argument is given, PC-KIMMO supplies a special recognizer prompt where forms can be typed in directly without the *recognize* keyword. Entering a blank line at the recognizer prompt returns the program to the main command line prompt.

7.5.12 Compare data from a file

The *compare* commands compare data prepared by the user to the results of data processed by PC-KIMMO. The data are contained in files whose formats are described in section 7.7.

[file] compare generate [*filespec*]

The *compare generate* command reads lexical forms from a file, submits them to the generator for analysis, and compares the resulting surface form(s) with the expected results listed in the file. The *filespec* can contain a path, for example, B:\ENGLISH\ENGLISH.GEN. A generation comparison file has the default extension .GEN and the default file name DATA.GEN. The format of the generation comparison file is described in section 7.7.3.

Results of the comparison are reported according to the setting of the verbosity flag (see the *set verbose* command described in section 7.5.6). If verbosity is set off, only exceptions (that is, actual results from the generator that are different from the expected results as specified in the file) are reported. A dot is displayed on the screen as each input (lexical) form is processed. If verbosity is set on, each group of lexical and surface forms in the file is displayed, either with an error message for wrong comparisons or the message OK if the actual and expected results match exactly.

[file] compare recognize [*filespec*]

The *compare recognize* command reads surface forms from a file, submits them to the recognizer for analysis, and compares the resulting lexical form(s) with the expected results specified in the file. The *filespec* can contain a path, for example, B:\ENGLISH\ENGLISH.REC. A recognition comparison file has the default extension .REC and the default file name DATA.REC. The format of the recognition comparison file is described in section 7.7.4.

Results of the comparison are reported according to the setting of the verbosity flag (see the *set verbose* command described in section 7.5.6). If verbosity is set off, only exceptions (that is, actual results from the recognizer that are different from the expected results as specified in the file) are reported. A dot is displayed on the screen as each input (surface) form is processed. If verbosity is set on, each group of surface and lexical forms in the file is displayed, either with an error message for wrong comparisons or the message OK if the actual and expected results compared identically.

[file] compare pairs [*filespec*]

The *compare pairs* command allows lexical:surface pairs of forms listed in the file specified on the command line to be compared in both directions. The *filespec* can contain a path, for example, B:\ENGLISH\ENGLISH.PAI. A pairs comparison file has the default extension .PAI and the default file name DATA.PAI. The format of the pairs comparison file is described in section 7.7.5.

PC-KIMMO considers each pair of forms (a lexical form followed by its surface form). The lexical form is input to the generator to produce one or more surface forms. The surface form listed in the file is compared with the generated surface forms to see if there is a successful match. The surface form listed in the file is then input to the recognizer to produce one or more lexical forms. The lexical form listed in the file is compared with the recognized lexical forms to see if there is a successful match.

Results of the comparison are reported according to the setting of the verbosity flag (see the *set verbose* command described in section 7.5.6). If verbosity is set off, only exceptions (that is, one of the comparisons failed) are reported. A dot is displayed on the screen as each pair of forms is processed. If verbosity is set on, each pair of lexical and surface forms in the file is displayed, either with an error message for wrong comparisons or the message OK if the forms match exactly.

7.5.13 Generate forms from a file

file generate *input-filespec* [*output-filespec*]

The *file generate* command reads lexical forms from a file, submits them to the generator for analysis, and returns each lexical form followed by the resulting surface form(s). The format of the generation input file is described in section 7.7.6.

If an *output-filespec* argument is specified, the results are written to that file; otherwise, the results are displayed on the screen. The format of the output file created by this command is identical to a comparison generation file. The *filespec* of either file can contain a path, for example, B:\ENGLISH\ENGLISH.LST. The command does not recognize any default file names or extensions. The verbosity flag (see the *set verbose* command described in section 7.5.6) has no effect on the *file generate* command.

7.5.14 Recognize forms from a file

file recognize *input-filespec* [*output-filespec*]

The *file recognize* command reads surface forms from a file, submits them to the recognizer for analysis, and returns each surface form followed by the resulting lexical form(s). The format of the recognition input file is described in section 7.7.7. If an *output-filespec* argument is specified, the results are written to that file; otherwise the results are displayed on the screen. The format of the output file created by this command is identical to a comparison recognition file. The *filespec* of either file can contain a path, for example, B:\ENGLISH\ENGLISH.LST. The command does not recognize any default file names or extensions. The verbosity flag (see the *set verbose* command described in section 7.5.6) has no effect on the *file recognize* command.

For details on the format of the recognition input file, see section 7.7.7.

7.5.15 Execute an operating system command

system [*system-command*]

The *system* command allows you to execute an operating system command from within PC-KIMMO. For example, on an IBM PC-compatible computer, the command *system dir* will execute the DOS directory command. If no command argument is given, then PC-KIMMO is pushed into the background and a new system command processor shell is started. While you are in the shell, you can execute any commands or programs. To leave the shell and return to PC-KIMMO, type *exit*. On an IBM PC-compatible computer, the *system* command will not work unless a copy of the DOS system file COMMAND.COM is available. Note that if you are running PC-KIMMO under MS-DOS version 2, issuing the *system* command with no argument will *not* invoke a new processor shell. To get a new shell you must enter the *system command*. This will directly execute COMMAND.COM. Type *exit* to return to PC-KIMMO.

The system command has the alias *!* (exclamation point), which does not require a space between it and the following command. For example, *!dir* performs the DOS directory command.

7.5.16 Edit a file

edit *filespec*

The *edit* command attempts to edit a file using the editing program specified by the operating system environment variable EDITOR. If this environment variable is not defined, then the command will try to use EDLIN (on a DOS machine) or vi (on a UNIX machine) to edit the file. To set the environment variable, include a line such as this in your AUTOEXEC.BAT file:

SET EDITOR=*filespec*

where *filespec* specifies the path and full file name of your editing program, for example, \UTIL\EMACS.EXE.

You can use the *edit* command, for example, to invoke your text editor and modify the rules or lexicon files. After saving the files and leaving the editor, you must *load* the files again in order for PC-KIMMO to utilize the changes.

7.5.17 Halt the program

exit

The *exit* command causes PC-KIMMO to exit back to the operating system.

quit

The command *quit* is the same as *exit*.

7.6 Alphabetic list of commands

This section documents each command, arranged alphabetically, of the PC-KIMMO system. Square brackets in the command line summaries indicate optional elements. The notation {*x* | *y*} means either *x* or *y* (but not both). Command keywords and arguments in boldface are typed literally; for instance, the command summary **set tracing** {**on** | **off**} means to type either *set tracing on* or *set tracing off*. Command arguments in italics are replaced by elements of the specified type; for instance, the command summary **set comment** *char* means to replace *char* with a single character, such as *set comment ; .*

! [*system-command*]

Executes an operating system command or invoke a new command processor shell (same as *system*).

?

Displays a list of command names.

close

Turns logging off and closes the log file.

edit *filespec*

Edits *filespec* using the editing program specified by the operating system environment variable EDITOR.

exit

Exits PC-KIMMO and returns to the operating system.

[file] compare generate [*filespec*]

Reads lexical forms from *filespec*, submits them to the generator, and compares the resulting surface form(s) with the expected results listed in *filespec*.

[file] compare recognize [*filespec*]

Reads surface forms from *filespec*, submits them to the recognizer, and compares the resulting lexical form(s) with the expected results listed in *filespec*.

[file] compare pairs [*filespec*]

Reads pairs of lexical and surface forms from *filespec* and analyzes them to see if the surface form can generated from the lexical form and the lexical form can be recognized from the surface form.

file generate *input-filespec* [*output- filespec*]

Reads a list of lexical forms from *input-filespec*, submits them to the generator, and returns each lexical form followed by the resulting surface form(s).

file recognize *input-filespec* [*output- filespec*]

Reads a list of surface forms from *input-filespec*, submits them to the recognizer, and returns each surface form followed by the resulting lexical form(s).

generate [*lexical-form*]

Accepts as input a lexical form and returns one or more surface forms.

help [*command-name*]

Without a command name argument, displays a list of commands with a brief explanation of each. With a command name argument, displays a usage summary for the command.

list lexicon

Displays on the screen the names of the sublexicons of the lexicon currently in use.

list pairs

Displays the set of feasible pairs specified by the set of rules currently turned on.

list rules

Displays the current state of the rules that are loaded.

load lexicon [*filespec*]

Loads the lexicon from *filespec*.

load rules [*filespec*]

Loads rules from *filespec*.

log [*filespec*]

Turns the logging mechanism on.

new

Clears the rules and lexicon currently loaded.

quit

Same as *exit*.

recognize [*surface-form*]

Accepts as input a surface form and returns one or more lexical forms.

set comment *char*

Changes the comment delimiter character. The default is semicolon (;).

set limit {**on** I **off**}

Limits the result of a generation or recognition function to one form.

set rules {**on** I **off**} {*list of numbers* I **all**}

Turns selected rules on or off.

set timing {on | off}

Times the execution of generation and recognition functions and displays the result.

set tracing {on | off | *level*}

Turns the tracing mechanism on or off.

set verbose {on | off}

Determines the amount of information shown on the screen during a file comparison operation.

show [status]

Same as *status*.

show lexicon *sublexicon-name*

Displays the contents of the named sublexicon. For each lexical entry it shows the lexical form, gloss, and continuation class.

show rule *rule-number*

Displays the number, on/off status, and name of the rule (similar to the list rules command). If the rule is turned on, it then displays each column header of the state table for that rule with the set of feasible pairs that it specifies.

status

Displays the names of the rules and lexicon files currently loaded, the name of the log file (if logging is on), the comment delimiter character, and the status of the limit, timing, tracing, and verbose flags. Obeys the synonyms *show status* and *show*.

system [*system-command*]

Executes an operating system command or invokes a new command processor shell. See also *!*.

take [*filespec*]

Reads and executes commands from *filespec*.

7.7 File formats

This section describes the formats for the files that are used as input to PC-KIMMO. In any of the files, comments can be added to any line by preceding the comment with the comment delimiter character. This character is normally a semicolon (;), but can be changed either on the PC-KIMMO command line with the *-c* option (see section 7.3) or with the *set comment* command (see section 7.5.6). Anything following a comment delimiter (until the end of the line) is considered part of the comment and is ignored by PC-KIMMO.

In the descriptions below, reference to the use of a space character implies any whitespace character (that is, any character treated like a space character). The following control characters when used in a file are whitespace characters: ^I (ASCII 9, tab), ^J (ASCII 10, line feed), ^K (ASCII 11, vertical tab), ^L (ASCII 12, form feed), and ^M (ASCII 13, carriage return).

The control character ^Z (ASCII 26) cannot be used because MS-DOS interprets it as marking the end of a file. Also the control character ^@ (ASCII 0, null) cannot be used.

Examples of each of the following file types are found on the release diskette as part of the English description.

7.7.1 Rules file

The general structure of the rules file is a list of declarations composed of a keyword followed by data. The set of valid keywords is ALPHABET, NULL, ANY, BOUNDARY, SUBSET, RULE, and END. Only the SUBSET and RULE keywords can appear more than once. The ALPHABET declaration must appear first in the file. The other declarations can appear in any order. The NULL, ANY, BOUNDARY, and SUBSET declarations can even be interspersed among the rules. However, these declarations must appear before any rule that uses them or an error will result.

Figure 7.1 shows the structure of a rules file. The order of the keyword declarations is according to common style. Note that the notation {x | y} means either *x* or *y* (but not both). The following specifications apply to the rules file.

- Extra spaces, blank lines, and comment lines are ignored.

- The first line of the file (excluding comment lines) must contain the keyword ALPHABET.

- <alphabet character list> is a list of single characters that make up the combined alphabet of all the characters used in both lexical and surface representations. Each character must be separated from the others by at least one space. The list can span multiple lines, but ends with the next valid keyword. All alphanumeric characters (such as *a*, *B*, and *2*), symbols (such as *$* and *+*), and punctuation characters (such as . and *?*) are available as alphabet members. The characters in the IBM extended character set (above ASCII 127)

Figure 7.1 Structure of the rules file

```
ALPHABET <alphabet character list>
NULL <null symbol>
ANY <"wildcard" symbol>
BOUNDARY <word boundary symbol>
SUBSET <subset name> <subset character list>
. (more subsets)
.
.
RULE <rule name> <number of states> <number of columns>
    <lexical element list>
    <surface element list>
<state number>{: | .} <state number list>
    . (more states)
    .
    .
. (more rules)
.
.
END
```

are also available. Control characters (below ASCII 32) can also be used, with the exception of whitespace characters (see above), ˆZ (end of file), and ˆ@ (null). The alphabet can contain a maximum of 255 characters.

- After the ALPHABET declaration, the NULL, ANY, BOUNDARY, SUBSET, and RULE declarations can occur in any order.

- The BOUNDARY declaration is obligatory, even if the rules do not use a BOUNDARY symbol. This is because the lexicon file requires a BOUNDARY symbol. The NULL, ANY, and SUBSET declarations are not obligatory if the rules do not use a NULL symbol, an ANY symbol, or subsets.

- The keyword NULL is followed by a <null symbol>, a single character that represents a null (empty, zero) element. The NULL symbol is considered to be an alphabetic character, but cannot also be listed in the ALPHABET declaration. The NULL symbol declared in the rules file is also used in the lexicon file to represent a null lexical entry.

- The keyword ANY is followed by a <"wildcard" symbol>, a single character that represents a match of any character in the alphabet. The ANY symbol is not considered to be an alphabetic character, though it is used in the column headers of state tables. It cannot be listed in the ALPHABET declaration. It is not used in the lexicon file.

- The keyword BOUNDARY is followed by a <word boundary symbol>, a single character that represents an initial or final word boundary. The BOUNDARY symbol is considered to be an alphabetic character, but cannot also be listed in the ALPHABET declaration. When used in the column header of a state table, it can only appear as the pair #:# (where, for instance, # has been declared as the BOUNDARY symbol). The BOUNDARY symbol is also used in the lexicon file in the continuation class field of a lexical entry to indicate the end of a word (that is, no continuation class).

- The keyword SUBSET is followed by the <subset name> and <subset character list>. <subset name> is a single word (one or more characters) that names the list of characters that follows it. The subset name must be unique (that is, if it is a single character it cannot also be in the alphabet or be any other declared symbol). It can be composed of any characters (except space); that is, it is not limited to the characters declared in the ALPHABET section. It must not be identical to any keyword used in the rules file. The subset name is used in rules to represent all members of the subset of the alphabet that it defines. Note that SUBSET declarations can be interspersed among the rules. This allows subsets to be placed near the rule that uses them if such a style is desired. However, a subset must be declared before a rule that uses it.

- <subset character list> is a list of single characters, each of which is separated by at least one space. The list can span multiple lines. Each character in the list must be a member of the previously defined ALPHABET with the exception of the NULL symbol, which can appear in a subset list but is not included in the ALPHABET declaration. Neither the ANY symbol nor the BOUNDARY symbol can appear in a subset character list.

- The keyword RULE signals that a state table immediately follows.

- <rule name> is the name or description of the rule which the state table encodes. It functions as an annotation to the state table and has no effect on the computational operation of the table. It is displayed by the *list rules* and *show rule* commands and is also displayed in traces. The rule name must be surrounded by a pair of identical delimiter characters. Any material can be used between the delimiters of the rule name with the exception of the current comment delimiter character and of course the rule name delimiter character of the rule itself. Each rule in the file can use a different pair of delimiters. The rule name must be all on one line, but it does not have to be on the same line as the RULE keyword.

- <number of states> is the number of states (rows in the table) that will be defined for this table. The states must begin at 1 and go in sequence through the number defined here (that is, gaps in state numbers are not allowed).

- <number of columns> is the number of state transitions (columns in the table) that will be defined for each state.

- <lexical character list> is a list of elements separated by one or more spaces. Each element represents the lexical half of a lexical:surface correspondence which, when matched, defines a state transition. Each element in the list must be either a member of the alphabet, a subset name, the NULL symbol, the ANY symbol, or the BOUNDARY symbol (in which case the corresponding surface character must also be the BOUNDARY symbol). The list can span multiple lines, but the number of elements in the list must be equal to the number of columns defined for the rule.

- <surface character list> is a list of elements separated by one or more spaces. Each element represents the surface half of a lexical:surface correspondence which, when matched, defines a state transition. Each element in the list must be either a member of the alphabet, a subset name, the NULL symbol, the ANY symbol, or the BOUNDARY symbol (in which case the corresponding lexical character must also be the BOUNDARY symbol). The list can span multiple lines, but the number of characters in the list must be equal to the number of columns defined for the rule.

- <state number> is the number of the state or row of the table. The first state number must be 1, and subsequent state numbers must follow in numerical sequence without any gaps.

- {: | .} is the final or nonfinal state indicator. This should be a colon (:) if the state is a final state and a period (.) if it is a nonfinal state. It must follow the <state number> with no intervening space.

- <state number list> is a list of state transition numbers for a particular state. Each number must be between 1 and the number of states (inclusive) declared for the table. The list can span multiple lines, but the number of elements in the list must be equal to the number of columns declared for this rule.

- The keyword END follows all rules and indicates the end of the rules file. Any material in the file thereafter is ignored by PC-KIMMO. The END keyword is optional; the physical end of the file also terminates the rules file.

7.7.2 Lexicon file

The general structure of the lexicon file is a list of declarations composed of a keyword followed by data. The set of valid keywords is ALTERNATION, LEXICON, INCLUDE, and END. The only required declaration is LEXICON INITIAL; that is, a lexicon file must minimally be composed of one sublexicon named INITIAL. The declarations can appear in any order with the exception that an alternation name used in the continuation class field of a lexical entry (including a lexical entry in an INCLUDE file) must first be declared with the ALTERNATION keyword.

Figure 7.2 shows the structure of a lexicon file. The order of the keyword declarations is according to common style. Note that the notation $\{x \mid y\}$ means either x or y (but not both). The following specifications apply to the lexicon file.

- Extra spaces, blank lines, and comment lines are ignored.

- The keyword ALTERNATION is followed by an <alternation name> and an <alternation list>.

- <alternation name> is a name associated with the following <alternation list>. It is a word composed of one or more characters, not limited to the ALPHABET characters declared in the rules file. An alternation name can be any word other than a keyword used in the lexicon file. The program does not check to see if an alternation name is actually used in the lexicon file.

- <alternation list> is a list of sublexicon names. It can span multiple lines until the next valid keyword is encountered. Each sublexicon name in the list must be declared at some point in the file with the LEXICON keyword. Although it is not enforced at the time the lexicon file is loaded, an undeclared sublexicon named in an alternation list will cause an error when a recognition function tries to use it.

- The keyword LEXICON is followed by a <sublexicon name> and a list of lexical entries.

Figure 7.2 Structure of the lexicon file

ALTERNATION <alternation name> <alternation list>
. (more alternations)
.
.

LEXICON INITIAL
<lexical item>   {<alternation name> | <BOUNDARY symbol>}
<gloss>
. (more lexical entries)
.
.

INCLUDE <filespec>
. (more include files)
.
.

LEXICON <sublexicon name>
<lexical item>   {<alternation name> | <BOUNDARY symbol>}
<gloss>
. (more lexical entries)
.
.

. (more sublexicons)
.
.

END

- <sublexicon name> is the name associated with a sublexicon. It is a word composed of one or more characters, not limited to the alphabetic characters declared in the rules file. A sublexicon name can be any word other than a keyword used in the lexicon file.

- In each sublexicon section are lexical entries, each of which is composed of three parts or fields separated by one or more spaces. Each lexical entry must all be on one line. The three parts are the lexical item, the continuation class, and the gloss.

- <lexical item> is one or more characters that represent an element (typically a morpheme or word) of the lexicon. Each character must be in the alphabet defined for the language. The lexical item uses only the lexical subset of the alphabet.

- {<alternation name> | <BOUNDARY symbol>} fills the continuation class field of a lexical entry. It must be either an alternation name or the BOUNDARY symbol declared in the rules file.

- <gloss> is a string of text surrounded by a pair of identical delimiter characters. Whenever the lexical item in the lexical entry is matched, everything between the delimiters is appended to the result. If there is no gloss associated with the lexical item, the gloss field must contain a pair of delimiters with nothing in between (for example, ""). Any material can be used between the delimiters of the gloss with the exception of the current comment delimiter character and of course the gloss delimiter character of the entry itself. Each lexical entry in the file can use a different pair of delimiters. The gloss must be all on one line with the rest of the lexical entry.

- The INCLUDE keyword is followed by a <filespec> that names a file containing another lexicon file. This included lexicon file has the same structure and specifications as the main lexicon file with the exception that it cannot contain an INCLUDE declaration; that is, INCLUDE files cannot be nested. Alternation names and sublexicon names in INCLUDE files must be unique; that is, not used anywhere else in the lexicon. The END keyword (or the physical end of the file) will terminate reading of the included file and return to reading the main lexicon file.

- The keyword END follows all lexical information and indicates the end of the lexicon file. Any material in the file thereafter is ignored by PC-KIMMO. See also the use of the END keyword in an included file. The END keyword is optional; the physical end of the file also terminates the lexicon file.

7.7.3 Generation comparison file

The generation comparison file serves as input to the *compare generate* command (see section 7.5.12). It consists of groupings of a lexical form followed by one or more surface forms that are expected to be generated from the lexical form. The following specifications apply to the generation comparison file.

- Each form must be on a separate line.
- Leading spaces are ignored.
- A blank line (or end of file) indicates the end of a grouping. Extra blank lines are ignored.
- The first form in each grouping is the lexical form to be input to the generator. Its gloss does not have to be included, since the generator

does not use the lexicon; however, including a gloss with the lexical form does no harm—it is simply ignored.

- Succeeding forms in each grouping are surface forms that are the expected output of the generator.

7.7.4 Recognition comparison file

The recognition comparison file serves as input to the *compare recognize* command (see section 7.5.12). It consists of groupings of a surface form followed by one or more lexical forms that are expected to be recognized from the surface form. The following specifications apply to the recognition comparison file.

- Each form must be on a separate line.

- Leading spaces are ignored.

- A blank line (or end of file) indicates the end of a grouping. Extra blank lines are ignored.

- The first form in each grouping is the surface form to be input to the recognizer.

- Succeeding forms in each grouping are lexical forms that are the expected output of the recognizer. The gloss of a form follows it on the same line, separated by one or more spaces. The gloss must match exactly (including spaces) the way it is output from the recognizer.

7.7.5 Pairs comparison file

The pairs comparison file serves as input to the *compare pairs* command (see section 7.5.12). It consists of pairs of lexical and surface forms; that is, a lexical form followed by exactly one surface form. It is expected that the surface form will be recognized from the lexical form and that the lexical form will be generated from the surface form. Glosses do not have to be included with lexical forms, since the generator does not use the lexicon; however, including a gloss with the lexical form does no harm—it is simply ignored. When recognizing a surface form, the lexicon is used to identify the constituent morphemes and verify that they occur in the correct order, but the gloss part of a lexical entry is not used. The following specifications apply to the pairs comparison file.

- Each form must be on a separate line.

- Leading spaces are ignored.

- A blank line (or end of file) indicates the end of a grouping. Extra blank lines are ignored.

- The first form of a pair is the lexical form, which is input to the generator. It is the expected output on inputting the second (surface) form to the recognizer. The gloss is not included with the lexical form.

- The second form of a pair is the surface form, which is input to the recognizer. It is the expected output on inputting the first (lexical) form to the generator.

7.7.6 Generation file

The generation file consists of a list of lexical forms. It serves as input to the *file generate* command (see section 7.5.13), which returns a file (or screen display) whose format is identical to the generation comparison file. The following specifications apply to the generation file.

- Each form must be on a separate line.

- Extra white space, blank lines, and comment lines are ignored.

- Each form is assumed to be a lexical form. If a gloss is included, it is ignored.

7.7.7 Recognition file

The recognition file consists of a list of surface forms. It serves as input to the *file recognize* command (see section 7.5.14), which returns a file (or screen display) whose format is identical to the recognition comparison file. The following specifications apply to the recognition file.

- Each form must be on a separate line.

- Extra spaces, blank lines, and comment lines are ignored.

- Each form is assumed to be a surface form.

7.7.8 Summary of default file names and extensions

Figure 7.3 summarizes the default file names and extensions assumed by PC-KIMMO. Two entries are given for the different kinds of files. The first is the name PC-KIMMO will assume if no file name at all is given to a command that expects that kind of file. The second entry (with the *) shows what extension PC-KIMMO will add if a file name without an extension is given.

Figure 7.3 Default file names and extensions

Rules file:	RULES.RUL
	*.RUL
Lexicon file:	LEXICON.LEX
	*.LEX
Generation comparison file:	DATA.GEN
	*.GEN
Recognition comparison file:	DATA.REC
	*.REC
Pairs comparison file:	DATA.PAI
	*.PAI
Take file:	PCKIMMO.TAK
	*.TAK
Log file:	PCKIMMO.LOG

7.8 Trace formats

This section explains how to read the output of the generator and recognizer traces. Traces are produced by the *set tracing* command described in section 7.5.6. The amount of detail shown in the trace display is set by the tracing level. The *level* argument to the *set tracing* command can range from 0 to 3, where 0 is no tracing at all and 3 is the most detailed level of tracing.

7.8.1 Generator trace

The purpose of the generator trace is to allow the user to see how a lexical form is processed through multiple recursive calls to the generator. The generator algorithm used to process the form is described in section 7.9.1.

Figure 7.4 Level 1 generator trace

```
'fox+s

    RESULT = 0fox0es

foxes
```

There are three levels of tracing differing in the amount of detail they display: Level 1 gives the least amount of detail, level 2 (the default) gives a moderate amount of detail, and level 3 gives the most detail. Figure 7.4

is a level 1 generator trace of the lexical form '*fox+s* (taken from the English example). The only difference from no tracing at all is that the RESULT line is displayed. This line differs from the normal result that is returned because it prints all NULL symbols in the output surface form.

Figure 7.5 is from a level 2 generator trace for the form '*fox+s*. To limit the size of the trace, the Gemination rules (14 and 15) were turned off. Line numbers and column numbers are printed here for reference in the description that follows. Each description refers to an element beginning at the line and column indicated.

- Line 1: Input line. Lexical form input to the generator function.

- Line 19: RESULT line. Surface form produced by the generator function. At the point where the input lexical form is empty and each automaton is in a final state, the trace shows that the generator has recorded a result. The generator continues looking for additional results (lines 21 and following).

- Column 1: Level number (all lines except 1, 19, and 42). This represents the level of recursion. Level 0 represents the initial invocation of the generator. Notice that the number coincides with the number of characters in the result string so far.

- Column 1: Backtracking indicator (lines 10, 11, 13). The symbol − indicates that the generator is blocked at that level. The symbol < indicates that the generator is backtracking (that is, returning to a lower level to try another path).

- Column 2: Input pair (lines 2–9, 12, 14–16). This is the lexical:surface pair (from the set of feasible pairs) that is currently being considered by the generator (for example, *f:f* on line 4). The rest of the line shows the results of stepping the automata with the pair as input. The results are indicated by either a new state configuration (for example, line 5) or a BLOCKED BY RULE message (for example, line 10).

- Lines 10, 13: BLOCKED BY RULE message. Indicates that a feasible pair input to the function that steps the automata caused a rule to fail. Gives the number and name of the rule (from the header line of the state table) that failed.

- Columns 3–17: State configuration (lines 2–9, 11–12, 14–17). These are the current states of each of the rules. The leftmost number is the state of rule 1, the second is rule 2, and so on.

- Column 18: Result (lines 4–9, 11–12, 14–17). This is the current value of the result string.

Figure 7.5 Level 2 generator trace

	1	2	3	4	5	6	7	8	9	10	11	12	13	14	15	16	17	18
1	'fox+s																	
2	0	#:#	1	1	1	1	1	1	1	1	1	1	1	1	1	1	1	
3	0	':0	1	1	1	1	1	1	1	1	1	1	1	1	1	1	1	
4	1	f:f	1	1	1	1	1	1	1	2	2	1	1	1	1	1	1	0
5	2	o:o	1	1	1	1	2	2	1	3	3	1	1	1	1	1	1	0f
6	3	x:x	1	1	1	1	1	1	1	7	4	2	1	1	1	1	1	0fo
7	4	+:0	1	1	3	3	2	2	1	4	4	1	1	1	1	1	1	0fox
8	5	s:s	1	1	5	5	1	1	2	4	4	1	1	1	1	1	1	0fox0
9	6	#:#	1	1	6	2	2	2	3	3	4	1	1	1	1	1	1	0fox0s
10	6-	BLOCKED BY RULE 3: Epenthesis, 0:0 /⇐ [S|ch|sh|y:i] +:0 ___ s[+:0|#]																
11	5<		1	1	5	5	1	1	2	4	4	1	1	1	1	1	1	0fox0
12	5	s:0	1	1	5	5	1	1	2	4	4	1	1	1	1	1	1	0fox0
13	5-	BLOCKED BY RULE 7: S-deletion, s:0 ⇔ +:0 (0:e) s +:0 ' ___																
14	5	0:e	1	1	5	5	1	1	2	4	4	1	1	1	1	1	1	0fox0
15	6	s:s	1	1	1	6	1	1	2	4	4	1	1	1	1	1	1	0fox0e
16	7	#:#	1	1	4	7	2	2	3	3	4	1	1	1	1	1	1	0fox0es
17	7		1	1	1	1	1	1	1	3	4	1	1	1	1	1	1	0fox0es
18																		
19		RESULT = 0fox0es																
20																		
21	6<		1	1	1	6	1	1	2	4	4	1	1	1	1	1	1	0fox0e
22	6	s:0	1	1	1	6	1	1	2	4	4	1	1	1	1	1	1	0fox0e
23	6-	BLOCKED BY RULE 4: Epenthesis, 0:e ⇒ [S|ch|sh|y:i] +:0 ___ s[+:0|#]																
24	6	0:e	1	1	1	6	1	1	2	4	4	1	1	1	1	1	1	0fox0e
25	6-	BLOCKED BY RULE 4: Epenthesis, 0:e ⇒ [S|ch|sh|y:i] +:0 ___ s[+:0|#]																
26	5<		1	1	5	5	1	1	2	4	4	1	1	1	1	1	1	0fox0
27	4<		1	1	3	3	2	2	1	4	4	1	1	1	1	1	1	0fox
28	4	0:e	1	1	3	3	2	2	1	4	4	1	1	1	1	1	1	0fox
29	4-	BLOCKED BY RULE 4: Epenthesis, 0:e ⇒ [S|ch|sh|y:i] +:0 ___ s[+:0|#]																
	...																	
39	0<		1	1	1	1	1	1	1	1	1	1	1	1	1	1	1	
40	0	0:e	1	1	1	1	1	1	1	1	1	1	1	1	1	1	1	
41	0-	BLOCKED BY RULE 4: Epenthesis, 0:e ⇒ [S|ch|sh|y:i] +:0 ___ s[+:0|#]																
42	foxes																	

- Lines 21–41: The generator continues to backtrack, looking for other possible paths to a result, until finding no other path it returns to its initial state.

There is one other tracing message not exemplified in the above display. This is the END OF INPUT message. It indicates that the end of the input form has been reached but the generator function has failed on the rule specified because it was not in a final state. For example,

END OF INPUT, FAILED RULE 4: Palatalization

would indicate that when the end of the input form was reached, rule 4 was not left in a final state.

Figure 7.6 is part of a level 3 trace for the same form. The level 3 trace differs from the level 2 trace in how it displays rule failures that block the generator. Compare line 10 in the level 2 trace with lines 10 and 11 of the level 3 trace. The level 3 trace explicitly shows what state the automata are in after stepping them. In line 10 of the level 3 trace we can see that the proposed input pair puts rule 3 in state 0, which means that it

Figure 7.6 Level 3 generator trace

	1	2	3	4	5	6	7	8	9	10	11	12	13	14	15	16	17	18
1	'fox+s																	
2	0	#:#	1	1	1	1	1	1	1	1	1	1	1	1	1	1	1	
3	0	':0	1	1	1	1	1	1	1	1	1	1	1	1	1	1		
4	1	f:f	1	1	1	1	1	1	1	2	2	1	1	1	1	1	1	0
5	2	o:o	1	1	1	1	2	2	1	3	3	1	1	1	1	1	1	0f
6	3	x:x	1	1	1	1	1	1	1	7	4	2	1	1	1	1	1	0fo
7	4	+:0	1	1	3	3	2	2	1	4	4	1	1	1	1	1	1	0fox
8	5	s:s	1	1	5	5	1	1	2	4	4	1	1	1	1	1	1	0fox0
9	6	#:#	1	1	6	2	2	2	3	3	4	1	1	1	1	1	1	0fox0s
10	6-		1	1	0	?	?	?	?	?	?	?	?	?	?	?	?	0fox0s
11		BLOCKED BY RULE 3: Epenthesis, 0:0 /⇐ [Slchlshly:i] +:0 ___ s[+:0l#]																	
12	5<		1	1	5	5	1	1	2	4	4	1	1	1	1	1	1	0fox0
13	5	s:0	1	1	5	5	1	1	2	4	4	1	1	1	1	1	1	0fox0
14	5-		1	1	1	1	1	1	0	?	?	?	?	?	?	?	?	0fox0
15		BLOCKED BY RULE 7: S-deletion, s:0 ⇔ +:0 (0:e) s +:0 ' ___																	
16	5	0:e	1	1	5	5	1	1	2	4	4	1	1	1	1	1	1	0fox0
17	6	s:s	1	1	1	6	1	1	2	4	4	1	1	1	1	1	1	0fox0e
18	7	#:#	1	1	4	7	2	2	3	3	4	1	1	1	1	1	1	0fox0es
19	7		1	1	1	1	1	1	1	3	4	1	1	1	1	1	1	0fox0es
20																			
21		RESULT = 0fox0es																	
22																			
23	foxes																		

fails. Notice that the rest of the state array is filled with question marks. This is because if one rule fails the whole configuration fails, so the rest of the rules are not even tried. (This shows that even though conceptually the automata operate in parallel they must still be stepped one at a time).

7.8.2 Recognizer trace

The purpose of the recognizer trace is to allow the user to see how a surface form is processed through multiple recursive calls to the recognizer. The recognizer algorithm used to process the form is described in section 7.9.2.

There are three levels of tracing differing in the amount of detail they display: level 1 gives the least amount of detail, level 2 (the default) gives a moderate amount of detail, and level 3 gives the most detail.

Figure 7.7 is a level 1 recognizer trace of the surface form *foxes* (taken from the English example). Like the level 1 generator trace, the level 1 recognizer trace displays the RESULT line but does not show the feasible

Figure 7.7 Level 1 recognizer trace

```
foxes
     ENTERING LEXICON INITIAL
     ENTERING LEXICON N_ROOT
     ENTERING LEXICON NUMBER
     ENTERING LEXICON GENITIVE
     ENTERING LEXICON End

 RESULT = 'fox+0s [ N(fox)+PL ]

     BACKING UP FROM LEXICON End TO LEXICON GENITIVE
     BACKING UP FROM LEXICON GENITIVE TO LEXICON NUMBER
     ENTERING LEXICON GENITIVE
     ENTERING LEXICON End
     BACKING UP FROM LEXICON End TO LEXICON GENITIVE
     BACKING UP FROM LEXICON GENITIVE TO LEXICON NUMBER
     BACKING UP FROM LEXICON NUMBER TO LEXICON N_ROOT
     BACKING UP FROM LEXICON N_ROOT TO LEXICON INITIAL
     ENTERING LEXICON ADJ_PREFIX
 ...
     BACKING UP FROM LEXICON V_ROOT_NEG TO LEXICON V_PREFIX
     BACKING UP FROM LEXICON V_PREFIX TO LEXICON INITIAL
 'fox+s [ N(fox)+PL ]
```

pairs as they are tried or the states of the rules. However, it does display a record of how the recognizer moves through the lexicon, either with an ENTERING or a BACKING UP message.

Figure 7.8 is from a level 2 recognizer trace of the form *foxes*. To limit the size of the trace, the Gemination rules (14 and 15) were turned off. Line numbers and column numbers are printed here for reference in the description that follows. Each description refers to an element beginning at the line and column indicated.

- Line 1: Input line. Surface form input to the recognizer function.

- Line 30: RESULT line. At the point where there are no lexicons in the continuation class of an entry, the input surface form is empty, and each automaton is in a final state, the trace shows that the recognizer has recorded a result. The recognizer continues looking for additional results (lines 32 and following).

- Column 1: Level number (lines 2, 6–11, 13–19, 21–23, 27–28). This represents the level of recursion. Level 0 represents the initial invocation of the recognizer. Notice that the number coincides with the number of characters in the result string so far.

- Column 1: Backtracking indicator (lines 8, 15, 18, 22–23). The symbol − indicates that the recognizer is blocked at that level. The symbol < indicates that the recognizer is backtracking (that is, returning to a lower level to try another path).

- Column 2: Input pair (lines 2, 6–7, 9–11, and so on). This is the lexical:surface pair (from the set of feasible pairs) that is currently being considered by the recognizer (for example, *f:f* on line 9). The results of stepping the automata with the pair as input are indicated by either a new state configuration (for example, line 10) or a BLOCKED BY RULE message (for example, line 15).

- Lines 3, 5, 12, 20, 25: ENTERING LEXICON message. This is the name of the sublexicon that the recognizer is about to search.

- Lines 4, 24, 26: ACCEPTING NULL ENTRY message. Indicates that a null lexical entry (that is, an entry whose lexical item is the NULL symbol) has been accepted.

- Line 22: BLOCKED IN LEXICON message. Indicates that no lexical entry could be found in the current lexicon that continues with the input pair under consideration. The remaining part of the input form is displayed on the line (in line 22 it happens that nothing is left of the input form).

Figure 7.8 Level 2 recognizer trace

```
     1  2  3  4  5  6  7  8  9 10 11 12 13 14 15 16 17    18
  1|foxes
  2|0  #:#  1  1  1  1  1  1  1  1  1  1  1  1  1  1  1
  3|       ENTERING LEXICON INITIAL
  4|       ACCEPTING NULL ENTRY
  5|       ENTERING LEXICON N_ROOT
  6|0  ':0  1  1  1  1  1  1  1  1  1  1  1  1  1  1  1      [
  7|1  s:0  1  1  1  1  1  1  1  2  2  1  1  1  1  1  1    ' [
  8|1-     BLOCKED BY RULE 7: S-deletion, s:0 ⇔ +:0 (0:e) s +:0 ' ___
  9|1  f:f  1  1  1  1  1  1  1  2  2  1  1  1  1  1  1    ' [
 10|2  o:o  1  1  1  2  2  1  3  3  1  1  1  1  1  1       'f [
 11|3  x:x  1  1  1  1  1  1  7  4  2  1  1  1  1  1       'fo [
 12|       ENTERING LEXICON NUMBER
 13|4  +:0  1  1  3  3  2  2  1  4  4  1  1  1  1  1  1    'fox [ N(fox)
 14|5  s:0  1  1  5  5  1  1  2  4  4  1  1  1  1  1  1    'fox+ [ N(fox)
 15|5-     BLOCKED BY RULE 7: S-deletion, s:0 ⇔ +:0 (0:e) s +:0 ' ___
 16|5  0:e  1  1  5  5  1  1  2  4  4  1  1  1  1  1  1    'fox+ [ N(fox)
 17|6  s:0  1  1  1  6  1  1  2  4  4  1  1  1  1  1  1    'fox+0 [ N(fox)
 18|6-     BLOCKED BY RULE 4: Epenthesis, 0:e ⇒ [S|ch|sh|y:i] +:0 ___ s[+:0|#]
 19|6  s:s  1  1  1  6  1  1  2  4  4  1  1  1  1  1  1    'fox+0 [ N(fox)
 20|       ENTERING LEXICON GENITIVE
 21|7  +:0  1  1  4  7  2  2  3  3  4  1  1  1  1  1  1    'fox+0s [ N(fox)+PL
 22|8-     BLOCKED IN LEXICON GENITIVE, INPUT =
 23|7<      1  1  4  7  2  2  3  3  4  1  1  1  1  1  1    'fox+0s [ N(fox)+PL
 24|       ACCEPTING NULL ENTRY
 25|       ENTERING LEXICON End
 26|       ACCEPTING NULL ENTRY
 27|7  #:#  1  1  4  7  2  2  3  3  4  1  1  1  1  1  1    'fox+0s [ N(fox)+PL
 28|7       1  1  1  1  1  1  1  3  4  1  1  1  1  1  1    'fox+0s [ N(fox)+PL
 29|
 30|   RESULT = 'fox+0s [ N(fox)+PL ]
    |...
108|       BACKING UP FROM LEXICON V_ROOT_NEG TO LEXICON V_PREFIX
109|0<      1  1  1  1  1  1  1  1  1  1  1  1  1  1  1      [
110|       BACKING UP FROM LEXICON V_PREFIX TO LEXICON INITIAL
111|0<      1  1  1  1  1  1  1  1  1  1  1  1  1  1  1
112|'fox+s [ N(fox)+PL ]
```

- Lines 108, 110: BACKING UP message. Indicates that there were no further sublexicons left in the continuation class, so the recognizer must back up to the previous lexicon branch.

- Lines 8, 15, 18: BLOCKED BY RULE message. Indicates that a feasible pair input to the function that steps the automata caused a rule to fail. Gives the number and name of the rule (from the header line of the state table) that failed.

- Columns 3–17: State configuration (lines 2, 6–7, 9–11, and so on). These are the current states of each of the rules. The leftmost number is the state of rule 1, the second is rule 2, and so on.

- Column 18: Result (lines 6–7 and so on). This is the current value of the result string.

- Lines 108–111: The recognizer continues to backtrack, looking for other possible paths to a result, until finding no other path it returns to its initial state.

The END OF INPUT message may also occur in a recognizer trace. See section 7.8.1 on the generator trace for an explanation of it.

Figure 7.9 is part of a level 3 trace for the same form. Like level 3 of the generator trace, level 3 of the recognizer trace explicitly shows the state array when a rule fails. Compare line 8 of the level 2 trace with lines 18 and 19 of the level 3 trace. In addition, the level 3 recognizer trace shows pairs that are weeded out by the lexicon even before they are tried with the rules. Compare lines 3–4 of the level 2 trace with lines 3–10 of the level 3 trace. In lines 4–9 the level 3 trace shows explicitly several pairs that are tried but immediately fail. Since the recognizer is at the beginning of the input form, the only possible feasible pairs to try are those whose surface character is *0* (the NULL symbol) or *f* (the first character of the input form *foxes*). Rather than trying each of these pairs with the rules, the recognizer first looks to see if the lexical character of each pair matches any lexical character available in the sublexicon it is currently searching. In each case the match fails, indicated by the message LEXICAL CHARACTER NOT MATCHED. After trying all the pairs, the lexicon accepts the null entry and enters a new sublexicon. This exhaustive process takes place at each point in the recognition process where the recognizer is trying a new pair.

Figure 7.9 Level 3 recognizer trace

	1	2	3	4	5	6	7	8	9	10	11	12	13	14	15	16	17	18

```
 1 foxes
 2 0  #:# 1  1  1  1  1  1  1  1  1  1  1  1  1  1  1
 3          ENTERING LEXICON INITIAL
 4 0-  -:0 LEXICAL CHARACTER NOT MATCHED
 5 0-  ':0 LEXICAL CHARACTER NOT MATCHED
 6 0-  +:0 LEXICAL CHARACTER NOT MATCHED
 7 0-  s:0 LEXICAL CHARACTER NOT MATCHED
 8 0-  e:0 LEXICAL CHARACTER NOT MATCHED
 9 0-  f:f LEXICAL CHARACTER NOT MATCHED
10          ACCEPTING NULL ENTRY
11          ENTERING LEXICON N_ROOT
12 0-  -:0 LEXICAL CHARACTER NOT MATCHED
13 0  ':0 1  1  1  1  1  1  1  1  1  1  1  1  1  1  1    [
14 1-  -:0 LEXICAL CHARACTER NOT MATCHED
15 1-  ':0 LEXICAL CHARACTER NOT MATCHED
16 1-  +:0 LEXICAL CHARACTER NOT MATCHED
17 1  s:0 1  1  1  1  1  1  1  2  2  1  1  1  1  1  1    ' [
18 1-      1  1  1  1  1  1  0  ?  ?  ?  ?  ?  ?  ?  ?    ' [
19          BLOCKED BY RULE 7: S-deletion, s:0 ⇔ +:0 (0:e) s +:0 '___
   ...
75          ACCEPTING NULL ENTRY
76 7  #:# 1  1  4  7  2  2  3  3  4  1  1  1  1  1  1    'fox+0s [ N(fox)+PL
77 7      1  1  1  1  1  1  1  3  4  1  1  1  1  1  1    'fox+0s [ N(fox)+PL
78
79    RESULT = 'fox+0s [ N(fox)+PL ]
80
81 'fox+s [ N(fox)+PL ]
```

7.9 Algorithms

The algorithms used by PC-KIMMO to generate surface forms and recognize lexical forms are based on descriptions in Karttunen 1983.

7.9.1 Generating surface forms

The generator function recursively computes surface forms from a lexical form using a set of two-level rules expressed as finite state automata. The generator function does not make use of the lexicon. This means that it will accept input forms that are not found in the lexicon or that even violate the lexicon's constraints on morpheme order, and will still apply the phonological rules to them. To produce a surface form from a lexical form, the generator processes the input form one character at a time, left to right. For each lexical character, it tries every surface character that has been declared as corresponding to it in a feasible pair sanctioned by the description. The generator function has these inputs:

Lexical form: Initially the input form, this string contains whatever is left to process. As the function is recursively called, this string gets shorter as the result string gets longer.

Result: Initially empty, this string contains the results of the generator up to the point of the current function call.

Rules: This is the set of active finite state automata defined for this language.

Configuration: This is an array representing the current state of all rules (automata). Initially, all states are set to 1.

The generator function also uses a list of *feasible pairs* sanctioned by the set of rules; these are all the lexical:surface pairs of alphabetic characters that appear as column headers in the state tables. The *input pair* is a feasible pair selected by the generator as a possible next lexical:surface pair in the process of computing a **surface form** that corresponds to the given **lexical form**. Each time the generator is called it iteratively goes through the list of feasible pairs, selecting one as the input pair.

The generator algorithm works as follows:

1. If the **lexical form** is empty (that is, there are no more characters in it to process), do the following steps:

    (a) If any of the state tables contains a word boundary column header, step the automata using an input pair consisting of the BOUNDARY symbol as both the lexical and surface character.

If this fails, then the **result** is rejected and the function returns to the previous level.

(b) Check that the **configuration** array contains a valid final state for each of the **rules**. If so, then the **result** is accepted and added to the output list. Otherwise, it is rejected. In either case, the function returns to the previous level.

Otherwise, if the lexical form is not empty (that is, it contains more characters to process), do steps 2 and 3.

2. For each input pair containing the first character in the **lexical form** as the lexical character, do the following steps:

(a) Step the automata using the input pair and the input **configuration** array, producing a new **configuration**.

(b) If this succeeds, recursively call the generator function with these inputs:

Lexical form: This is the input lexical form with the first character removed.

Result: This is the input result string with the surface character from the current input pair appended.

Configuration: This is the state array produced by stepping the automata.

(c) If this fails, choose another input pair from the list of feasible pairs and do either step 2 or step 3.

3. For each input pair containing the NULL symbol as the lexical character, do the following steps:

(a) Step the automata using the input pair and the input **configuration** array to produce a new **configuration**.

(b) If this succeeds, recursively call the generator function with these inputs:

Lexical form: This is the input lexical form with no character removed (since the lexical character posited was NULL).

Result: This is the input result string with the surface character from the current input pair appended.

Configuration: This is the state array produced by stepping the automata.

(c) If this fails, choose another input pair from the list of feasible pairs and do either step 2 or step 3.

7.9.2 Recognizing lexical forms

The recognizer function recursively computes lexical forms from a surface form using a lexicon and a set of two-level rules expressed as finite state automata. The recognizer function operates in a way similar to the generator, only in a surface to lexical direction. The recognizer processes the surface input form one character at a time, left to right. For each surface character, it tries every lexical character that has been declared as corresponding to it in a feasible pair sanctioned by the description.

The recognizer also consults the lexicon. The lexical items recorded in the lexicon are structured as a letter tree. When the recognizer tries a lexical character, it moves down the branch of the letter tree that has that character as its head node. If there is no branch starting with that letter, the lexicon blocks further progress and forces the recognizer to backtrack and try a different lexical character. For example, figure 7.10 is a letter tree for the lexical items *spiel*, *spit*, *spy*, and *sty*.

Figure 7.10 A lexical letter tree

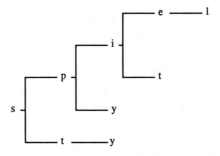

Besides applying the phonological rules and identifying morphemes, the recognizer also must enforce morpheme order constraints. The PC-KIMMO lexicon is divided into classes of lexical items that behave alike with respect to order constraints. These lexical classes are called *sublexicons*. The entry for each lexical item specifies the name of the sublexicon that can follow it. This following sublexicon is called a *continuation class*. Lexical items that occur only at the end of a word have no continuation class, indicated by the BOUNDARY symbol.

The names of the sublexicons that make up the entire lexicon are used as nodes at the head of branches of the letter tree. The piece of a letter tree shown in figure 7.10 may actually be under a branch node called Noun. When the recognizer successfully finds a lexical item in the letter tree, it looks at its specified continuation class and jumps to the branch of the lexicon it names.

It is often the case that at a given point in a word, more than one continuation is possible. Sets of alternative continuing sublexicons are called *alternations*. Thus the continuation class field of a lexical entry may contain the name of an alternation that specifies a list of the sublexicons that can follow it.

When the recognizer successfully recognizes a lexical item (word or morpheme), it reads its gloss from its lexical entry and appends it to the **gloss** string being built up for the entire word.

The recognizer function has these inputs:

Surface form: Initially the input form, this string contains whatever is left to process. As the function is recursively called, this string gets shorter as the result string gets longer.

Result: Initially empty, this string contains the results of the recognizer up to the point of the current function call.

Gloss: Initially empty, this string contains glosses for the lexical items contained in the **result** string.

Rules: This is the set of active finite state automata defined for this language.

Configuration: This is an array representing the current state of all rules (automata). Initially, all states are set to 1.

Lexicon: Initially, this is the entire lexicon defined for the language. During the process of recognition it is restricted to a branch of the lexicon.

Like the generator, the recognizer function uses a list of *feasible pairs* sanctioned by the set of rules; these are all the lexical:surface pairs of alphabetic characters that appear as column headers in the state tables. The *input pair* is a feasible pair selected by the recognizer as a possible next lexical:surface pair in the process of computing a **lexical form** that corresponds to the given **surface form**. Each time the recognizer is called it iteratively goes through the list of feasible pairs, selecting one as the input pair.

When a complete lexical item has been recognized, the lexicon is at a *terminal node* of the letter tree. Terminal nodes have glosses and continuation classes attached to them. The recognizer algorithm is initialized as though it has successfully recognized a lexical item and the lexicon is at a terminal node pointing to a continuation class consisting of the INITIAL sublexicon. It then proceeds as follows:

1. If the input **lexicon** is at a terminal node, then for each sublexicon in the continuation class of that item, recursively call the recognizer function with these inputs:

   Surface form: This string contains whatever is left to process.

   Result: This string contains the results of the recognizer up to the point of the current function call.

   Gloss: This is the input gloss string with the gloss of the current lexical entry appended.

   Rules: This is the input set of rules.

   Configuration: This is the input configuration.

   Lexicon: This is the current continuation sublexicon.

   If the continuation class of the lexical entry is empty (that is, the lexical item can only be followed by word boundary) and the input **surface form** is empty, do the following steps:

   (a) If any of the state tables contains a word boundary column header, step the automata using an input pair consisting of the BOUNDARY symbol as both the lexical and surface character. If this fails, then the **result** is rejected and the function returns to the previous level.

   (b) Check that the **configuration** array contains a valid final state for each of the **rules**. If so, then the **result** is accepted, the gloss of the lexical entry is appended to the **gloss**, and both the **result** and the **gloss** are added to the output list. Otherwise, the **result** is rejected. In either case, the function returns to the previous level.

   If the continuation class of the lexical entry is empty but the **surface form** is not empty, the **result** is rejected and the function returns to the previous level.

2. For each input pair that has the head of a branch in the lexicon as the lexical character and the first character of the **surface form** as the surface character, do the following steps:

   (a) Step the automata using the input pair and the input **configuration** array to produce a new **configuration**.

   (b) If this succeeds, recursively call the recognizer function with these inputs:

   Surface form: This is the input surface form with the first character removed.

Result: This is the input result string with the lexical character from the current input pair appended.

Gloss: This is the input gloss string.

Rules: This is the input set of rules.

Configuration: This is the state array produced by stepping the automata.

Lexicon: This is the branch of the lexicon corresponding to the lexical character from the current input pair.

3. For each input pair that has the head of a branch in the lexicon as the lexical character and has the NULL symbol as the surface character, do the following steps:

   (a) Step the automata using the input pair and the input **configuration** array to produce a new **configuration**.

   (b) If this succeeds, recursively call the recognizer function with these inputs:

      Surface form: This is the input surface form.

      Result: This is the input result string with the lexical character from the current input pair appended.

      Gloss: This is the input gloss string.

      Rules: This is the input set of rules.

      Configuration: This is the state array produced by stepping the automata.

      Lexicon: This is the branch of the lexicon corresponding to the lexical character from the current input pair.

4. If the NULL symbol is the head of a branch of the lexicon (that is, a null lexical entry), recursively call the recognizer function with these inputs:

   Surface form: This is the input surface form.

   Result: This is the input result string.

   Gloss: This is the input gloss string.

   Rules: This is the input set of rules.

   Configuration: This is the input state array.

   Lexicon: This is the branch of the lexicon which has the NULL symbol as its head.

7.10 Error messages

This section lists the various error and warning messages you may en-counter. They are listed in numerical sequence and are generally grouped according to the type of error or warning. A warning means that the oper-ation in progress has successfully completed, but an anomalous condition may have resulted. An error means that the operation in progress could not be successfully completed and was therefore prematurely terminated. Only in the case of a memory error is the PC-KIMMO program aborted and control returned to the operating system. Note that in the following error messages the words printed in italics are not literal but are cover terms for a set of items of the type suggested by the term. For instance, when the error message "Missing keyword in *command-name* command" actually appears on the computer screen, the term *command-name* will be replaced by a specific command name, such as *load* or *set*.

7.10.1 Errors related to reading and parsing commands

WARNING 100 Input line too long – ignoring after first *number* characters

ERROR 101 Ambiguous command: *command-name*

> *command-name* did not specify a unique command. Type more of the command name to insure that it is not ambiguous.

ERROR 102 Invalid command: *command-name*

> *command-name* is not a valid command. Type *?* or *help* for a list of valid commands.

ERROR 103 Missing keyword in *command-name* command

> Expected a keyword to be used with the command. Type the com-mand name followed by *?* for a list of valid keywords.

ERROR 104 Missing argument in *command-name* command

> Expected an argument to complete the command. Type *help* fol-lowed by the command name for an explanation of what arguments the command needs.

ERROR 105 Ambiguous keyword in *command-name* command: *keyword*

> *keyword* did not specify a unique keyword. Type more of the key-word to insure that it is not ambiguous.

ERROR 106 Invalid keyword in *command-name* command: *keyword*

> *keyword* is not a valid keyword. Type the command name followed by *?* for a list of valid keywords for that command.

ERROR 107 Invalid argument in *command-name* command: *argument*

argument was not valid for the command. Type *help* followed by the command name for an explanation of what arguments the command needs.

ERROR 108 Missing input file argument in *command-name* command

Expected a file name with the command.

ERROR 109 Cannot open input file *filename* in *command-name* command

Cannot find the file *filename*. Check to see if the file is in the current directory or the path you specified in the command. The command may also be expecting a different default file name or extension.

ERROR 110 Cannot open output file *filename* in *command-name* command

Check to see if the file is in the current directory or in the path you specified in the command. The command may also be expecting a different default file name or extension.

ERROR 111 Must load rules before loading lexicon

The rules file must be loaded before the lexicon in order to verify the lexical forms in the lexicon against the alphabet defined in the rules file.

ERROR 112 TAKE files nested too deeply

TAKE files can only be nested three deep.

ERROR 113 TAKE file aborted due to invalid command: *command-name*

command-name is not a valid command. Type *?* or *help* for a list of valid commands.

ERROR 114 No log file was open

Result of issuing the CLOSE command when no log file has been opened.

WARNING 115 Closing the existing log file *filename*

Occurs when the LOG command is issued when a log file is already open.

ERROR 116 Missing file name for EDIT command

EDIT command must specify a file to be edited.

7.10.2 Errors related to reading the rules file

ERROR 200 Rules file could not be opened: *filename*

> Check to see if the file is in the current directory or in the path you specified in the command. The command may also be expecting a different default file name or extension.

ERROR 201 Unexpected end of rules file: *filename*

> The rules file is incomplete. Check to see if the last table in the file has fewer states than expected.

ERROR 202 Expected ALPHABET keyword

> The first declaration in a rules file must be the ALPHABET declaration.

ERROR 203 Alphabet contains no members

> The ALPHABET keyword does not have any characters listed after it.

WARNING 204 Too many characters in the alphabet

> The alphabet can contain a maximum of 255 characters.

WARNING 205 Character is already in the alphabet: *character*

> A character has been repeated in the ALPHABET declaration.

ERROR 206 No value given for NULL keyword

> A single character must appear after the NULL keyword.

ERROR 207 Value given for NULL symbol was already declared as alphabetic: *character*

> The character specified for NULL may not also be declared in the ALPHABET.

ERROR 208 The NULL symbol has already been defined

> There is more than one NULL declaration.

ERROR 209 Value given for NULL symbol was already declared for ANY

ERROR 210 Value given for NULL symbol was already declared for BOUNDARY

ERROR 211 No value given for ANY keyword

> A single character must appear after the ANY keyword.

ERROR 212 Value given for ANY symbol was already declared as alphabetic: *character*

The character specified for ANY may not also be declared in the ALPHABET.

ERROR 213 The ANY symbol has already been defined

There is more than one ANY declaration.

ERROR 214 Value given for ANY symbol was already declared NULL

ERROR 215 Value given for ANY symbol was already declared for BOUNDARY

ERROR 216 No value given for BOUNDARY keyword

A single character must appear after the BOUNDARY keyword.

ERROR 217 Value given for BOUNDARY symbol was already declared as alphabetic: *character*

The character specified for BOUNDARY may not also be declared in the ALPHABET.

ERROR 218 The BOUNDARY symbol has already been defined

There is more than one BOUNDARY declaration.

ERROR 219 Value given for BOUNDARY symbol was already declared for NULL

ERROR 220 Value given for BOUNDARY symbol was already declared for ANY

ERROR 221 Subset name not given

Occurs if there is a SUBSET keyword with nothing after it until the next keyword.

ERROR 222 Subset name *subset-name* is not unique

A subset name, if it is a single character, cannot be the same as one of the characters specified in the ALPHABET, NULL, ANY, or BOUNDARY declarations. If the subset name is more than one character, then it is a duplicate of another subset name already declared.

ERROR 223 Subset *subset-name* contains no members

ERROR 224 Subset *subset-name* contains a nonalphabetic character: *character*

All characters used in subsets must be listed in the ALPHABET declaration, with the exception of the NULL symbol, which can appear in a subset but is not included in the ALPHABET list.

WARNING 225 Subset *subset-name* already contains *character*

A character has been repeated.

ERROR 226 Invalid keyword: *keyword*

The only valid keywords in a rules file are ALPHABET, NULL, ANY, BOUNDARY, SUBSET, and RULE.

WARNING 227 ANY symbol not defined

Are you sure the rules do not use an ANY symbol?

WARNING 228 NULL symbol not defined

Are you sure the rules do not use a NULL symbol?

WARNING 229 BOUNDARY symbol not defined

The BOUNDARY declaration is obligatory. Even if the BOUNDARY symbol is not used in the rules file, it must be used in the lexicon file.

WARNING 230 Missing closing delimiter for the name of a rule: *rule-name*

The first nonspace character after the RULE keyword is the opening delimiter of the rule name. A matching delimiter (identical character) was not found in the same line; thus PC-KIMMO will use everything up to the end of the line as the rule name. This is because the rule name must be contained in one line.

ERROR 231 Invalid number of rows: *number*

Must be a number greater than zero.

ERROR 232 Invalid number of columns: *number*

Must be a number greater than zero.

ERROR 233 Invalid state number: *number*

State (row) numbers must start with 1 and ascend consecutively.

ERROR 234 Expected final (:) or nonfinal (.) state indicator: *character*

A state (row) number must be followed by colon (:) or period (.) with no intervening space.

ERROR 235 State table entry out of range: *number*

number must not be greater than the specified number of states for the table.

ERROR 236 Lexical character not in alphabet: *character*

A character in a table's lexical character list is not a member of the alphabet declared earlier in the rules file.

ERROR 237 Surface character not in alphabet: *character*

A character in a table's surface character list is not a member of the alphabet declared earlier in the rules file.

ERROR 238 Nonnumeric character in state table: *character*

Expected a numeric state table entry but found a nonnumeric character.

ERROR 239 Rule number *number*, column *number* pairs a BOUNDARY symbol with something else: *column-header*

Occurs if a column header consists of a BOUNDARY symbol is paired with anything but another BOUNDARY symbol; only *#:#* is allowed.

WARNING 240 No feasible pairs for this set of rules

Either there are no rules in the file or the rules contain only subset correspondences. In the latter case, simple rules listing all the default correspondences are needed.

WARNING 241 RULE *number* (*rule-name*) – *char*:*char* specified by both columns *number* (*char*:*char*) and *number* (*char*:*char*)

There is an overlap between two columns of the state table. Issue a *show rule* command for the rule causing the warning and examine the set of pairs specified by each column header.

WARNING 242 RULE *number* (*rule name*) – *char*:*char* not specified by any column

The entire set of feasible pairs must be specified by each table. The table is probably missing an ANY:ANY column.

ERROR 243 Rule number *number*, column *number* pairs two NULL symbols: *column-header*

NULL:NULL is not a legal column header, since it cannot be a feasible pair.

7.10.3 Errors related to reading the lexicon file

ERROR 300 Lexicon file could not be opened: *filename*

Check to see if the file is in the current directory or in the path you specified in the command. The command may also be expecting a different default file name or extension.

ERROR 301 No data in lexicon file *filename*

ERROR 302 Missing alternation name

The ALTERNATION keyword must be followed by an alternation name.

WARNING 303 Empty alternation definition: *alternation-name*

An ALTERNATION keyword was found with no following alternation name or list of lexicon names.

WARNING 304 Adding to existing alternation: *alternation-name*

ERROR 305 No lexicon sections in lexicon file *filename*

A lexicon file must contain sublexicons.

ERROR 306 Missing lexicon name

The keyword LEXICON must be followed by a sublexicon name.

WARNING 307 Lexicon section *sublexicon-name* is not listed as a member of any alternations

This will not necessarily result in a processing error if this is what you intended to do.

ERROR 308 Expected continuation class or BOUNDARY symbol for *entry*

A lexical entry is missing its continuation class element.

ERROR 309 Invalid continuation class *name* for *entry*

A name appearing in the continuation class field of a lexical entry must be the name of an ALTERNATION that has already been declared.

ERROR 310 Expected gloss element for *entry*

Each lexical entry must have a gloss element.

ERROR 311 Invalid gloss element *gloss* for *entry*

The gloss element must be bracketed by matching delimiters (identical characters).

ERROR 312 Form contains character not in alphabet: *character*

Each character used in lexical items must be listed in the ALPHABET declaration of the rules file.

ERROR 313 INITIAL lexicon not found

A lexicon file must as a minimum have a sublexicon named INITIAL.

ERROR 314 Cannot nest lexicon INCLUDE files

An INCLUDE file cannot call another INCLUDE file.

ERROR 315 Missing INCLUDE file name
An INCLUDE keyword must be followed by a file name.

ERROR 316 Lexicon INCLUDE file could not be opened: *filename*

ERROR 317 Invalid lexicon file keyword: *word*
The only valid keywords in a lexicon file are ALTERNATION, LEX-ICON, INCLUDE, and END.

7.10.4 Errors related to recognizing or generating a form

WARNING 400 Surface form not found in comparison pairs file
A lexical:surface pair in a pairs comparison file is missing the surface form.

ERROR 800 Form [*form*] contains character not in alphabet: *character*
An input form contains a character that was not listed in the AL-PHABET declaration in the rules file.

ERROR 801 RULE *number* is invalid—input *char* :*char* is not specified by any column
Could happen if a table does not have an ANY:ANY column.

ERROR 802 Invalid lexicon for recognizer
Probably will never occur!

ERROR 803 Lexicon section *sublexicon-name* is empty
There are no lexical entries in the named sublexicon.

ERROR 804 Cannot recognize forms without a lexicon
The lexicon is not loaded.

7.10.5 Errors that abort program execution

ERROR 900 Out of memory
The rules and lexicon are too large to fit in memory.

Runtime error – stack overflow
Occurs when the generator or recognizer gets into an infinite loop due to an incorrectly written rule or lexicon continuation.

A

DEVELOPING A DESCRIPTION OF ENGLISH

The purpose of this appendix is to demonstrate how to develop a PC-KIMMO description of some language data. The focus is on the set of phonological rules, with only a brief look at the lexicon. The general approach is inductive. First, a small set of data is given that exemplifies a certain phonological alternation and rules to account for it are constructed. Then the data set is expanded to include exceptional cases, forcing revision of the rules. Finally, as more rules are added to account for other alternations, interactions with previously written rules may require that the rules be revised in order to operate together correctly.

The data used in this description are English words written in standard orthography rather than actual phonological transcriptions. The rules account for alternate spellings of certain morphemes in specific environments. For example, the plural suffix for nouns has the alternants *s* and *es* as in *cats* versus *foxes*. To account for this, the lexicon contains a lexical entry for the plural suffix that has the form *+s* (where + symbolizes a morpheme boundary) and the rule set contains a rule that inserts an *e* in the environment after a stem-final *s*, *x*, *z*, *sh*, or *ch* and before the plural suffix *+s* (precisely, between the + and the *s*). Thus the lexical form *fox+s* will produce the surface form *foxes*. Notice that the rules required for describing orthographic alternations do not differ in form from phonological rules.

The description of English in this appendix is based on the analysis in Karttunen and Wittenburg 1983. Our description differs from Karttunen and Wittenburg's in several ways. First, their description performs the insertion of a surface character by pairing it with a lexical morpheme boundary; for instance, the lexical form *fox+s* is related to the surface form *foxes* by means of a rule that allows the correspondence *+:e*. This trick is possible because PC-KIMMO treats boundary symbols the same as any other character. Linguistically, however, a morpheme boundary is not a phonological segment and never has a surface realization. In our description, morpheme boundaries are always deleted; insertions are done by pairing a surface character with a lexical NULL symbol, for instance, *0:e*.

Second, Karttunen and Wittenburg's description posits two lexical entries for the possessive suffix: *+'s* for the singular possessive and *+'* for the plural possessive. In our description, there is only one lexical entry for the possessive suffix, namely *+'s*, and an *s*-deletion rule that accounts for the loss of the *s* in plural forms.

Third, where Karttunen and Wittenburg's description represents each rule with only one ⇔ state table, we have in most cases written separate state tables for the ⇐ and ⇒ parts of each rule (and for the Elision rule there is also a /⇐ table). This is done to make the tables simpler and more understandable to the PC-KIMMO learner.

The rules file, lexicon file, and test files for this English example are found in the ENGLISH subdirectory on the PC-KIMMO release diskette.

A.1 Alphabet and default correspondences

First, we declare the alphabet, special symbols, and subsets. Stress is marked in lexical forms with the symbol ', which is distinct from the orthographic apostrophe (') used in possessive forms. When English words are cited below, stress is marked only where it is germane to the rule being developed. Plus sign (+) indicates a morpheme boundary, and hyphen (-) is the orthographic hyphen as in *re-do*.

```
ALPHABET
   a b c d e f g h i j k l m n o p q r s t u v w x y z ' - ' +
NULL 0
ANY @
BOUNDARY #
SUBSET C      b c d f g h j k l m n p q r s t v w x y z  ; consonants
SUBSET Csib  s x z            ; sibilants
SUBSET Cpal  c g             ; soft palatals
SUBSET V      a e i o u       ; vowels
SUBSET Vbk   a o u           ; back vowels
```

Next we declare the default correspondences. Notice that the morpheme boundary symbol plus (+) corresponds to zero; that is, it is deleted by default unless specified otherwise. Stress (') is also always deleted. The hyphen corresponds to either hyphen or zero, reflecting the fact that a hyphen is often optional in English spelling. (Tables 1 and 2 could be combined into one table.)

T1   "Consonant defaults" 1 22

```
    |b c d f g h j k l m n p q r s t v w x y z @
    |b c d f g h j k l m n p q r s t v w x y z @
 1: |1 1 1 1 1 1 1 1 1 1 1 1 1 1 1 1 1 1 1 1 1 1
```

T2   "Vowels and other defaults" 1 11

```
    |a e i o u ' - - ' + @
    |a e i o u ' - 0 0 @
 1: |1 1 1 1 1 1 1 1 1 1 1
```

A.2 Epenthesis

The following data show that the plural suffix for nouns has two surface alternants, *s* and *es*. The plural suffix is given the lexical representation *+s*.

LR: cat+s   fox+0s   kiss+0s
SR: cat0s   fox0es   kiss0es

The two-level rule below expresses these correspondences by inserting *e* after a member of the *Csib* subset, which contains *s*, *x*, and *z* (precisely, the insertion is between the *+* and the *s* of the plural suffix).

Epenthesis
R3   0:e ⇔ Csib +:0 ___ s#

While the two-level Epenthesis rule is written as a ⇔ rule, we have compiled it into separate ⇒ and ⇐ state tables. (For more on writing insertion rules, see section 3.3.7.)

Epenthesis
T3   "0:e ⇒ Csib +:0 ___ s#" 5 6

	s	Csib	+	0	#	@
	s	Csib	0	e	#	@
1:	2	2	1	0	1	1
2:	2	2	3	0	1	1
3:	2	2	1	4	1	1
4:	5	0	0	0	0	0
5:	0	0	0	0	1	0

Epenthesis
T4   "0:0 ⇐ Csib +:0 ___ s#" 4 5

	s	Csib	+	#	@
	s	Csib	0	#	@
1:	2	2	1	1	1
2:	2	2	3	1	1
3:	4	2	1	1	1
4:	2	2	1	0	1

The state tables above include both the column headers *s:s* and *Csib:Csib*. This is necessary because *s* occurs both as part of the environment (as a member of the *Csib* subset) and as the plural suffix. Notice that in state 4 of table 3 the *s* (as the plural suffix) must be distinguished from the rest of subset *Csib* (*x* and *z*). In effect, by including *s:s* as a column header, *Csib:Csib* specifies only the pairs *x:x* and *z:z*. This can be seen by using the *show rule* command when running PC-KIMMO (see section 7.5.9). Note also that the tables encode a word-final boundary after the plural suffix (see section 3.3.10 on word boundaries in state tables).

The following data show that Epenthesis also occurs following *ch* or *sh.*

LR: church+0s   lash+0s
SR: church0es   lash0es

Since digraphs such as *ch* and *sh* cannot be included in subsets (only single characters are allowed), they must be individually included in the rule environment. In the state table, columns for *c, h,* and *s* must be included. The Epenthesis rule and tables are thus revised as follows.

Epenthesis
R3a   0:e ⇔ [Csib | ch | sh] +:0 ___ s#

Epenthesis
T3a   "0:e ⇒ [Csib | ch | sh] +:0 ___ s#" 7 8

	c	h	s	Csib	+	0	#	@
	c	h	s	Csib	0	e	#	@
1:	2	1	4	3	1	0	1	1
2:	2	3	3	3	1	0	1	1
3:	2	1	3	3	5	0	1	1
4:	2	3	3	3	5	0	1	1
5:	2	1	2	2	1	6	1	1
6.	0	0	7	0	0	0	0	0
7.	0	0	0	0	0	0	1	0

Epenthesis
T4a   "0:0 ⇐ [Csib | ch | sh] +:0 ___ s#" 6 7

	c	h	s	Csib	+	#	@
	c	h	s	Csib	0	#	@
1:	2	1	4	3	1	1	1
2:	2	3	3	3	1	1	1
3:	2	1	3	3	5	1	1
4:	2	3	3	3	5	1	1
5:	2	1	6	3	1	1	1
6:	2	3	4	3	1	0	1

A.3 *y:i*-spelling

The following data show that a lexical *y* is realized as a surface *i* after a consonant and before a suffix.

LR: boy+s   spy+0s   spy+ed   happy+ly   spot0+y+ness
SR: boy0s   spi0es   spi0ed   happi0ly   spott0i0ness

Notice that in the word *spottiness*, *y:i*-spelling occurs after a consonant that is inserted by the Gemination rule (see section A.7 below). This means that *y:i*-spelling applies after a surface consonant, expressed as @:C. The rule and tables for *y:i*-spelling are as follows.

y:i-spelling

R5   y:i ⇔ :C___+:0

y:i-spelling

T5   "y:i ⇐ :C___+:0" 3 5

	@	y	y	+	@
	C	i	@	0	@
1:	2	1	1	1	1
2:	2	1	3	2	1
3:	2	1	1	0	1

y:i-spelling

T6   "y:i ⇒ :C___+:0" 3 4

	@	y	+	@
	C	i	0	@
1:	2	0	1	1
2:	2	3	2	1
3.	0	0	1	0

Since Epenthesis applies after *y:i* (as in *spies*), the Epenthesis rule must be changed to include *y:i*.

Epenthesis

R3b   0:e ⇔ [Csib | ch | sh | y:i] +:0___s#

Epenthesis

T3b   "0:e ⇒ [Csib | ch | sh | y:i] +:0___s#" 7 9

	c	h	s	Csib	y	+	0	#	@
	c	h	s	Csib	i	0	e	#	@
1:	2	1	4	3	3	1	0	1	1
2:	2	3	3	3	3	1	0	1	1
3:	2	1	3	3	3	5	0	1	1
4:	2	3	3	3	3	5	0	1	1
5:	2	1	2	2	2	1	6	1	1
6.	0	0	7	0	0	0	0	0	0
7.	0	0	0	0	0	0	0	1	0

Epenthesis

T4b   "0:0 ⇐ [Csib | ch | sh | y:i] +:0 ___ s#" 6 8

	c	h	s	Csib	y	+	#	@
	c	h	s	Csib	i	0	#	@
1:	2	1	4	3	3	1	1	1
2:	2	3	3	3	3	1	1	1
3:	2	1	3	3	3	5	1	1
4:	2	3	3	3	3	5	1	1
5:	2	1	6	3	3	1	1	1
6:	2	3	4	3	3	1	0	1

The following verbs show that *y:i*-spelling does not occur before a suffix beginning with *i* or ' (see below on the possessive suffix).

LR: spy+ed   spy+ing   spy+'s   try+ed   try+ing
SR: spi 0ed   spy0ing   spy0's   tri 0ed   try0ing

One strategy to account for these exceptional forms might be to amend the *y:i*-spelling rule by adding a ⇐ table that prohibits *y:i* before *i* and '.

y:i-spelling

"y:i ⇐ ___ +:0 [i | ']" 3 5

	y	+	i	'	@
	i	0	i	'	@
1:	2	1	1	1	1
2:	2	3	1	1	1
3:	0	1	0	0	1

However, this ⇐ table conflicts with table 5, the ⇐ rule for *y:i*-spelling. Notice that the environment of the ⇐ table is subsumed by the environment of table 5; that is, any input form that matches the environment of the ⇐ table will also match the environment of table 5. The tables conflict in that table 5 says that a lexical *y* in its environment must be realized as a surface *i*, but the ⇐ table says that a lexical *y* must *not* be realized as a surface *i* in its environment. This is called a ⇐ conflict and is discussed in section 3.3.13. To resolve the conflict, table 5 must be revised so that it does not always force *y* to be realized as *i*; it must allow a form that matches the expression *C y:y +:0 [i | ']* to pass through. Notice that this is expressed in the two-level rule formalism as rule 5a, where ~[i | '] means neither *i* nor '.

y:i-spelling

R5a   y:i ⇐ :C ___ +: ~[i | ']

See now table 5a, to which the columns *i:i* and ':' and state 4 have been added.

y:i-spelling

T5a   "y:i ⇐ :C___+:0 ~[i | ']" 4 7

	@	y	y	+	i	'	@
	C	i	@	0	i	'	@
1:	2	1	1	1	1	1	1
2:	2	1	3	2	1	1	1
3:	2	1	1	4	1	1	1
4:	0	0	0	0	1	1	0

Now, by adding ~[i | '] to the environment of the ⇒ rule for *y:i*-spelling (table 6), it can be made to subsume the ⇐ table, which is no longer included in the description:

y:i-spelling

T6a   "y:i ⇒ :C___+:0 ~[i | ']" 4 6

	@	y	+	i	'	@
	C	i	0	i	'	@
1:	2	0	1	1	1	1
2:	2	3	2	1	1	1
3.	0	0	4	0	0	0
4.	2	1	1	0	0	1

A.4 *s*-deletion

The following data exemplify nouns with the possessive suffix, which is given the lexical representation +'s. The forms are all accounted for by the rules that have been developed thus far.

    LR: cat+'s fox+'s church+'s boy+'s spy+'s
    SR: cat0's fox0's church0's boy0's spy0's

The following data are possessive forms of plural nouns.

    LR: cat+s+'s   fox+0s+'s   church+0s+'s   boy+s+'s   spy+s+'s
    SR: cat0s0'0   fox0es0'0   church0es0'0   boy0s0'0   spies0'0

These forms show a deletion of the *s* of the possessive suffix when it follows the plural suffix. The following *s*-deletion rule, a ⇔ rule, has been compiled into a single state table combining both the ⇐ and ⇒ parts of the rule. Note that the *s:@* column in table 7 serves as both the *s:~0* header that is expected in a ⇐ table and as the header that recognizes an *s* in the left context.

s-deletion

R7   s:0 ⇔ +:0 (0:e) s +:0 '___

s-deletion

T7   "s:0 ⇔ +:0 (0:e) s +:0 '___" 5 6

	+	0	s	'	s	@
	0	e	@	'	0	@
1:	2	1	1	1	0	1
2:	2	2	3	1	0	1
3:	4	1	1	1	0	1
4:	2	1	3	5	0	1
5:	2	1	0	1	1	1

Table 7 works for *cat+s+'s* and *boy+s+'s*, but *fox+s+'s* comes out as *foxs'* and *spy+s+'s* as *spis'*. The Epenthesis rule must be revised to allow it to operate before a plural suffix that is followed either by word boundary or a morpheme boundary.

Epenthesis

R3c   0:e ⇔ [Csib | ch | sh | y:i]___s [+:0 | #]

Epenthesis

T3c   "0:e ⇒ [Csib | ch | sh | y:i] +:0___s [+:0 | #]" 7 9

	c	h	s	Csib	y	+	#	0	@
	c	h	s	Csib	i	0	#	e	@
1:	2	1	4	3	3	1	1	0	1
2:	2	3	3	3	3	1	1	0	1
3:	2	1	3	3	3	5	1	0	1
4:	2	3	3	3	3	5	1	0	1
5:	2	1	2	2	2	1	1	6	1
6.	0	0	7	0	0	0	0	0	0
7.	0	0	0	0	0	1	1	0	0

Epenthesis

T4c   "0:0 ⇐ [Csib | ch | sh | y:i] +:0___s [+:0 | #]" 6 8

	c	h	s	Csib	y	+	#	@
	c	h	s	Csib	i	0	#	@
1:	2	1	4	3	3	1	1	1
2:	2	3	3	3	3	1	1	1
3:	2	1	3	3	3	5	1	1
4:	2	3	3	3	3	5	1	1
5:	2	1	6	3	3	1	1	1
6:	2	3	4	3	3	0	0	1

A.5 Elision

In English orthography, a silent *e* is found in any word that matches the expression *[C | V | ']*VCC*e#*. In other words, a silent *e* is an unstressed *e* that occurs finally in a lexical stem following a vowel plus at least one consonant. For instance, silent *e*'s occur at the end of the words *move, seize,* and *parse.* The following data show that a silent *e* is deleted (elided) before a vowel-initial suffix.

LR:	move+ed	move+ing	move+able	seize+ure	desire+ous
SR:	mov00ed	mov00ing	mov00able	seiz00ure	desir00ous

The rule and $\Leftarrow$ table for Elision are as follows.

Elision

R8   e:0 $\Leftrightarrow$ VCC* ___ +:0 V

Elision

T8   "e:0 $\Leftarrow$ VCC* ___ +:0 V" 5 6

	C	e	e	+	V	@
	C	0	@	0	V	@
1:	1	1	2	1	2	1
2:	3	1	2	1	2	1
3:	3	1	4	1	2	1
4:	1	1	2	5	2	1
5:	1	1	0	1	0	1

The following data show that Elision does not apply to a silent *e* when it follows either of the soft palatal consonants *c* and *g* and precedes a suffix that begins with a vowel other than *i* or *e.*

LR:	trace+ing	trace+ed	trace+able	change+able	courage+ous
SR:	trac00ing	trac00ed	trace0able	change0able	courage0ous

These restrictions can be encoded as a $\nLeftarrow$ table that prohibits *e:0* in the environment described above. In the following table, note that subset *Cpal* contains *c* and *g* and subset *Vbk* contains *a, o,* and *u* (that is, all vowels except *i* and *e*).

Elision

T9   "e:0 $\nLeftarrow$ VC*Cpal ___ +:0 Vbk" 5 7

	V	C	Cpal	e	+	Vbk	@
	V	C	Cpal	0	0	Vbk	@
1:	2	1	1	1	1	2	1
2:	2	2	3	1	1	2	1
3:	2	1	1	4	1	2	1
4:	2	1	1	1	5	2	1
5:	2	1	1	1	1	0	1

However, table 9 conflicts with table 8. Notice that the environment of table 9 is subsumed by the environment of table 8; that is, any input form that matches the environment of table 9 will also match the environment of table 8. The tables conflict in that table 8 says that a lexical e in its environment must be realized as a surface 0, but table 9 says that a lexical e must *not* be realized as a surface 0 in the same environment. This is called a $\Leftarrow$ conflict and is discussed in section 3.3.13. To resolve the conflict, table 8 must be revised so that it does not always elide a silent e; it must allow a form that matches the expression $VC^*Cpal\ e{:}e\ +{:}0\ Vbk$ to pass through. This is handled in table 8a, to which the columns $Cpal{:}Cpal$ and $Vbk{:}Vbk$ have been added.

Elision

T8a   "e:0 $\Leftarrow$ VCC*___+:0 V (except in Cpal___+:0 Vbk)" 8 8

	C	Cpal	e	e	+	V	Vbk	@
	C	Cpal	0	@	0	V	Vbk	@
1:	1	1	1	2	1	2	2	1
2:	3	6	1	2	1	2	2	1
3:	3	6	1	4	1	2	2	1
4:	1	1	1	2	5	2	2	1
5:	1	1	1	0	1	0	0	1
6:	1	1	1	7	1	2	2	1
7:	1	1	1	2	8	2	2	1
8:	1	1	1	0	1	0	1	1

There is another environment in which a silent e occurs, namely $CVe\#$; that is, stem-finally following a single vowel. The following data show that a silent e in this environment is elided before a vowel-initial suffix, but only if the vowel is e.

LR: agree+ed   agree+ing   agree+able   hoe+ed   hoe+ing
SR: agre00ed   agree0ing   agree0able   ho00ed   hoe0ing

In addition, the following data show that the letter preceding the silent e can be either a vowel (as above) or a y:

LR: dye+ed   dye+ing   dye+able
SR: dy00ed   dye0ing   dye0able

The following $\Leftarrow$ table expresses Elision in these environments. Note that the column header $e{:}@$ serves as both the $e{:}{\sim}0$ header that is expected in a $\Leftarrow$ table and as the header that recognizes an e in the right context.

Elision

T10   "e:0 ⇐ C[V | y]___+:0 e" 5 8

	C	V	y	e	e	+	'	@
	C	V	y	0	@	0	0	@
1:	2	1	1	1	1	1	1	1
2:	2	3	3	1	3	1	2	1
3:	2	1	1	1	4	1	3	1
4:	2	1	1	1	1	5	4	1
5:	2	1	1	1	0	1	5	1

The following data show Elision in a very similar environment, namely following CV and preceding a vowel-initial suffix. But in these words, if the vowel preceding the silent e is u, then Elision occurs regardless of what vowel follows.

LR: argue+ed   argue+ing   argue+able
SR: argu00ed   argu00ing   argu00able

Table 11 expresses Elision is this environment.

Elision

T11   "e:0 ⇐ Cu___+:0 V" 5 7

	C	u	e	e	+	V	@
	C	u	0	@	0	V	@
1:	2	1	1	1	1	1	1
2:	2	3	1	1	1	1	1
3:	2	1	1	4	1	1	1
4:	2	1	1	1	5	1	1
5:	2	0	1	0	1	0	1

At this point all that remains to be done to finish the Elision rule is to write a ⇒ or clean-up table that matches the three ⇐ tables developed above, namely tables 8a, 10, and 11 (see section 3.3.14 on clean-up tables). The purpose of this table is to restrict the application of Elision to a lexical e found only in the environments of the ⇐ tables. Table 12 has three disjunctive environments. The environment corresponding to table 8a is found in rows 1–5; the environment corresponding to table 10 is found in rows 1 and 6–9; and the environment corresponding to table 11 is found in rows 1, 6, and 10–12. (Note that the rule name is printed on multiple lines; in the actual rules file it must be all on a single line.)

Elision

T12   "e:0 ⇒ VCC*___+:0 V *or*
        C[V | y]___+:0 e *or*
        Cu___+:0 V" 12 9

	C	e	+	y	V	e	u	'	@
	C	0	0	y	V	e	u	0	@
1:	6	0	1	6	2	2	2	1	1
2:	3	0	1	3	2	2	2	2	1
3:	3	4	1	3	7	7	10	3	1
4.	0	0	5	0	0	0	0	4	0
5.	0	0	0	0	1	1	1	5	0
6:	6	0	1	7	7	7	10	6	1
7:	3	8	1	1	2	2	2	7	1
8.	0	0	9	0	0	0	0	8	0
9.	0	0	0	0	0	1	0	9	0
10:	6	11	1	6	1	1	1	10	1
11.	0	0	12	0	0	0	0	11	0
12.	0	0	0	0	1	1	1	12	0

A.6 *i:y*-spelling

The following data show that a lexical *i* is realized as a surface *y* before an elided *e* that is followed by a suffix beginning with *i*. This could be viewed as dissimilation; that is, where Elision would result in an *ii* sequence, *i:y*-spelling changes it to the sequence *yi*.

LR: tie+ed   tie+ing   die+ed   die+ing
SR: ti00ed   ty00ing   di00ed   dy00ing

The *i:y*-spelling rule and tables are as follows.

i:y-spelling
R13   i:y ⇔ ___e: +:0 i

i:y-spelling
T13   "i:y ⇐ ___e: +:0 i" 4 5

	i	e	+	i	@
	y	@	0	i	@
1:	1	1	1	2	1
2:	1	3	1	2	1
3:	1	1	4	2	1
4:	1	1	1	0	1

i:y-spelling

T14   "i:y $\Rightarrow$ ___ e: +:0 i" 4 5

	i	e	+	i	@
	y	0	0	i	@
1:	2	1	1	1	1
2.	0	3	0	0	0
3.	0	0	4	0	0
4.	0	0	0	1	0

Because *i:y*-spelling occurs in the environment of Elision, table 13 has the implicit effect of adding another Elision rule to the description, specifically *e:0* $\Leftarrow$ *i:y* ___ *+:0 i*. We could even explicitly add the following table that expresses this new Elision rule:

Elision

"e:0 $\Leftarrow$ i:y ___ +:0 i" 4 6

	i	e	e	+	i	@
	y	0	@	0	i	@
1:	2	1	1	1	1	1
2:	2	1	3	1	1	1
3:	2	1	1	4	1	1
4:	2	1	1	1	0	1

Since table 13 already expresses this rule, it will not be added to the description. However, this new Elision rule does mean that the $\Rightarrow$ table for Elision must be modified to include its environment. This is handled in table 12a, to which has been added a column for *i:y*.

Elision

T12a "e:0 ⇒ VCC*___+:0 V *or*
      C[V | y]___+:0 e *or*
      Cu___+:0 V *or*
      i:y___+:0 i" 12 10

	C	e	+	i	y	V	e	u	'	@
	C	0	0	y	y	V	e	u	0	@
1:	6	0	1	10	6	2	2	2	1	1
2:	3	0	1	10	3	2	2	2	2	1
3:	3	4	1	10	3	7	7	10	3	1
4.	0	0	5	0	0	0	0	0	4	0
5.	0	0	0	0	0	1	1	1	5	0
6:	6	0	1	10	7	7	7	10	6	1
7:	3	8	1	10	1	2	2	2	7	1
8.	0	0	9	0	0	0	0	0	8	0
9.	0	0	0	0	0	1	0	9	0	
10:	6	11	1	10	6	1	1	1	10	1
11.	0	0	12	0	0	0	0	0	11	0
12.	0	0	0	0	0	1	1	1	12	0

Notice also that table 13 contains the column header *e:@* rather than the expected *e:0.* This is necessary to force Elision to apply in the environment of *i:y.* Using *e:0* overspecifies the environment and results in overgeneration (see section 3.3.12).

A.7 Gemination

The following data show that certain word-final consonants are geminated (doubled) when they occur in a stressed syllable and preceding a suffix beginning with a vowel.

    LR: re'fer0+ed   re'fer0+ing   'travel+ed   'travel+ing
    SR: re0ferr0ed   re0ferr0ing   0travel0ed   0travel0ing

To be more precise as to what qualifies as a final consonant, notice that gemination does not apply to a consonant that is part of a consonant cluster (for instance, *tested*) or to a consonant that is followed by a silent *e* (for instance, *taping* from *tape* but *tapping* from *tap*). Notice also that gemination occurs only when the consonant is preceded by not more than one vowel:

    LR: 'slip0+ing   'sleep+ing
    SR: 0slipp0ing   0sleep0ing

The following words show that Gemination also applies before the suffix *y*, which makes adjectives from nouns. Notice that the *y:i*-spelling rule can apply to the *y* suffix.

LR: 'spot0+y   'spot0+y+ness
SR: 0spott 0y   0spott 0 i 0ness

We will start by developing a rule that accounts for the consonants *l*, *p*, and *r*. Gemination will be handled by inserting a consonant identical to the preceding one. This is done by including columns for each consonant that can be geminated. See also section 6.4.2 on gemination. Following the procedure in section 3.3.7 for writing insertion rules, we construct the ⇒ table for Gemination first.

Gemination

R15   0:{l,p,r} ⇔ ':0 C* V {l,p,r} ___ +:0 [V ǀ y:]

Gemination

T15   "0:{l,p,r} ⇒ ':0 C* V {l,p,r} ___ +:0 [V ǀ y:]" 8 11

	'	V	y	l	p	r	0	0	0	+	@
	0	V	@	l	p	r	l	p	r	0	@
1:	2	1	1	1	1	1	0	0	0	1	1
2:	2	5	1	2	2	2	0	0	0	1	2
3.	0	0	0	0	0	0	0	0	0	4	0
4.	0	1	1	0	0	0	0	0	0	0	0
5:	2	1	1	6	7	8	0	0	0	1	1
6:	2	5	1	1	1	1	0	0	0	1	1
7:	2	5	1	1	1	1	0	0	0	1	1
8:	2	5	1	1	1	1	0	0	0	1	1

The following ⇐ rule will make Gemination obligatory in a stressed syllable.

Gemination

T16   "0:0 ⇐ ':0 C* V {l,p,r} ___ +:0 [V ǀ y:]" 5 8

	'	V	y	l	p	r	+	@
	0	V	@	l	p	r	0	@
1:	2	1	1	1	1	1	1	1
2:	2	4	2	2	2	2	1	2
3:	2	0	0	1	1	1	1	1
4:	2	1	1	5	5	5	1	1
5:	2	1	1	1	1	1	3	1

The following are the same tables, but with all the relevant consonants added (specifically, {C} in the two-level rule notation stands for {b, d, f, g, l, m, n, p, r, s, t}).

Gemination

T15a   "0:{C} ⇒ ':0 C* V {C}___+:0 [V | y:]" 16 27

	'	V	y	b	d	f	g	l	m	n	p	r	s	t	0	0	0	0	0	0	0	0	0	0	0	+	@
	0	V	@	b	d	f	g	l	m	n	p	r	s	t	b	d	f	g	l	m	n	p	r	s	t	0	@
1:	2	1	1	1	1	1	1	1	1	1	1	1	1	1	0	0	0	0	0	0	0	0	0	0	0	1	1
2:	2	5	1	2	2	2	2	2	2	2	2	2	2	2	0	0	0	0	0	0	0	0	0	0	0	1	2
3.	0	0	0	0	0	0	0	0	0	0	0	0	0	0	0	0	0	0	0	0	0	0	0	4	0
4.	0	1	1	0	0	0	0	0	0	0	0	0	0	0	0	0	0	0	0	0	0	0	0	0	0
5:	2	1	1	6	7	8	9	10	11	12	13	14	15	16	0	0	0	0	0	0	0	0	0	0	0	1	1
6:	2	5	1	1	1	1	1	1	1	1	1	1	1	1	3	0	0	0	0	0	0	0	0	0	0	1	1
7:	2	5	1	1	1	1	1	1	1	1	1	1	1	1	0	3	0	0	0	0	0	0	0	0	0	1	1
8:	2	5	1	1	1	1	1	1	1	1	1	1	1	1	0	0	3	0	0	0	0	0	0	0	0	1	1
9:	2	5	1	1	1	1	1	1	1	1	1	1	1	1	0	0	0	3	0	0	0	0	0	0	0	1	1
10:	2	5	1	1	1	1	1	1	1	1	1	1	1	1	0	0	0	0	3	0	0	0	0	0	0	1	1
11:	2	5	1	1	1	1	1	1	1	1	1	1	1	1	0	0	0	0	0	3	0	0	0	0	0	1	1
12:	2	5	1	1	1	1	1	1	1	1	1	1	1	1	0	0	0	0	0	0	3	0	0	0	0	1	1
13:	2	5	1	1	1	1	1	1	1	1	1	1	1	1	0	0	0	0	0	0	0	3	0	0	0	1	1
14:	2	5	1	1	1	1	1	1	1	1	1	1	1	1	0	0	0	0	0	0	0	0	3	0	0	1	1
15:	2	5	1	1	1	1	1	1	1	1	1	1	1	1	0	0	0	0	0	0	0	0	0	3	0	1	1
16:	2	5	1	1	1	1	1	1	1	1	1	1	1	1	0	0	0	0	0	0	0	0	0	0	3	1	1

Gemination

T16a   "0:0 ⇐ ':0 C* V {C}___+:0 [V | y:]" 5 16

		V	y	b	d	f	g	l	m	n	p	r	s	t	+	@
	0	V	@	b	d	f	g	l	m	n	p	r	s	t	0	@
1:	2	1	1	1	1	1	1	1	1	1	1	1	1	1	1	1
2:	2	4	2	2	2	2	2	2	2	2	2	2	2	2	1	2
3:	2	0	0	1	1	1	1	1	1	1	1	1	1	1	1	1
4:	2	1	1	5	5	5	5	5	5	5	5	5	5	5	1	1
5:	2	1	1	1	1	1	1	1	1	1	1	1	1	1	3	1

A.8   The lexicon

The lexicon file for the English description contains sublexicons for only three major classes of roots: nouns, adjectives, and verbs. The sublexicons for noun roots and verb roots are actually contained in separate files that are read in by the main lexicon file by means of INCLUDE declarations (see section 7.7.2).

The ALTERNATIONS section of the main lexicon file expresses the morphotactic constraints encoded in the lexicon. Alternation names have been chosen that suggest a particular state in the morphotactic finite state machine; the list of sublexicon names that follow specify all the allowable continuations from that state. For example, the alternation Adj_Prefix2 is declared as follows:

ALTERNATION Adj_Prefix2   ADJ_ROOT1 ADJ_ROOT2

This alternation means that if during the recognition of a word we are at the state called Adj_Prefix2, then only lexical items from the sublexicons ADJ_ROOT1 and ADJ_ROOT2 can follow. Notice that alternation names are capitalized while sublexicon names are all uppercase.

For nouns, the lexicon has affix entries for the inflectional suffixes for the plural number suffix +s and the possessive (genitive) ending +'s:

+s	"+PL"
+'s	"+GEN"

Irregular plurals such as *cacti* and *mice* are included as lexical entries. The continuations specified for mass nouns such as *ice* prevent them from being pluralized, but allow them to be possessed. Lexical entries for three derivational suffixes, which all change nouns into adjectives, are also included:

+ish	"+ADJR1"
+ly	"+ADJR2"
+y	"+ADJR3"

For adjectives, the lexicon has affix entries for the negative prefix *un+*, the adverbializing suffix *+ly*, the comparative and superlative suffixes *+er* and *+est*, and the nominalizing suffix *+ness*. For a detailed discussion of morphotactic constraints in English adjectives, see section 4.2.

un+	"NEG1+"
+ly	"+ADVR"
+er	"+COMP"
+est	"+SUPER"
+ness	"+NOMR"

For verbs, the lexicon has affix entries for the prefixes *re-+* (glossed 'repetitive'), *un+* (glossed 'reversive'), and *dis+* (glossed 'negative'); for the inflectional suffixes *+ing* (glossed 'progressive'), *+ed* (glossed 'past'), *+ed* (glossed 'past participle'), and *+s* (glossed 'third person, singular, present'); and for the derivational suffixes *+able* (glossed 'adjectivalizer') and *+er* (glossed 'agentive').

re-+	"REP+"
un+	"REV+"
dis+	"NEG2+"
+ing	"+PROG"
+ed	"+PAST"
+ed	"+PAST.PRTC"
+s	"+3sg.PRES"
+able	"+ADJR"
+er	"+AGENT"

Verb roots have different continuation classes depending on which sublexicons of suffixes can follow them. Some verb roots, such as *am* and *go*, do not take any suffixes because their inflected forms are suppletive and thus require their own entries. Other verb roots, such as *be* and *have*, have irregular past and third person, singular, present forms that require their own entries. And other verb roots, such as *sleep* and *bite*, have irregular past forms that require their own entries.

Appendix

B

OTHER APPLICATIONS OF THE TWO-LEVEL PROCESSOR

by Gary F. Simons

The opening chapter of this book (section 1.3) observed that the two-level model is more a general-purpose tool than a theory of phonology. Nevertheless, the book focuses on applying the two-level processor to implementing the phonological component of a morphological recognizer or generator. This appendix demonstrates how the two-level processor can be applied as a general tool in situations where the nature of the problem is that of mapping between symbols in two levels of representation. The particular applications illustrated are analyzing phonotactic structure, simulating historical sound change, and solving a logic problem. Building on the method for phonotactic analysis, a minimum lexicon parser is also illustrated in which the lexicon lists all known affixes, but no roots; it uses phonotactic patterns to guess at the roots.

B.1 Analyzing phonotactic structure

The first application is a phonotactic analyzer. In this application of the two-level processor, the upper level represents the syllable structure of a word and the lower level gives its segmental representation. In recognizer mode, this application takes a word in phonemic orthography and returns an analysis of its syllable structure. In generator mode, it generates all word forms that correspond to a given syllable structure analysis.

A sample implementation of a phonotactic analyzer for the To'aba'ita language of the Solomon Islands is given in the CVCV subdirectory on the PC-KIMMO release diskette. In the To'aba'ita example, the alphabet of the upper level contains only three symbols: C (for consonant), V (for vowel), and . (period, for syllable boundary). (A more complex application might add other factors like stress, or more refined phoneme classes such as L (for laryngeals) to handle syllable positions with restricted fillers.) The following table of default correspondences maps each of the lower-level symbols for the segmental phonemes onto the corresponding upper-level symbol (C or V). Also, syllable break is defined to correspond to 0 on the lower level (that is, it is deleted).

"Default correspondences" 1 20

V	C	C	V	C	C	V	C	C	C	C	V	C	C	C	V	C	C	.	@
a	b	d	e	f	g	i	k	l	m	n	o	r	s	t	u	w	'	0	@
1: 1	1	1	1	1	1	1	1	1	1	1	1	1	1	1	1	1	1	1	1

The To'aba'ita orthography represents four phonemes as digraphs. For instance, *ng* represents the velar nasal. Note that *n* and *g* by themselves also represent single phonemes. However, they cannot occur in sequence; thus *ng* unambiguously represents a single consonant. The two-level representation of *ng* is thus taken to be *C:n 0:g*. To prevent the incorrect analysis

of *ng* as two consonants, the following rule expresses the constraint that
0:g occurs always and only following *C:n*. Similar rules handle the other
digraphs.

```
"2 ng" 2 4
    | C  0  C  @
    | n  g  g  @
1: | 2  0  1  1
2: | 2  1  0  1
```

In a phonotactic analyzer, the role of the lexicon is to express the constraints on possible syllable (and even word) structures. Each sublexicon
represents a slot in the structure of a syllable; the sublexicon elements are
the phoneme class symbols (like C and V) of the upper-level alphabets;
and the continuation classes express constraints on the ordering of the
phoneme classes in the structural slots. (Constraints on the cooccurrence
of phoneme classes could be expressed either through continuation classes
or through rules. Cooccurrence restrictions involving individual phonemes
would be expressed through rules.) The following is the complete lexicon
for the To'aba'ita phonotactic analyzer:

ALTERNATION C		Consonant	
ALTERNATION V		Vowel	
ALTERNATION Break		Break	
LEXICON INITIAL			
0	C		""
LEXICON Consonant			
C	V		""
0	V		""
LEXICON Vowel			
V	Break		""
V	#		""
LEXICON Break			
	C		""
END			

This lexicon contains four sublexicons. These express the following facts
about To'aba'ita phonotactics, respectively:

1. The first thing in a word structure is a consonant slot.

2. The consonant slot may be filled by C or nothing; the next thing is
   always the vowel slot.

3. The vowel slot is always filled by V; the next thing may be a syllable break or the end of the word.

4. A syllable break is realized as a period and is always followed by the consonant slot.

In other words, there are only two syllable patterns, CV and V.

When this description is run in the recognizer mode, it takes To'aba'ita words as input, and produces the corresponding syllable structure analysis. For instance,

```
recognizer>>ano
   V.CV

recognizer>>ngata
   CV.CV
```

In the generator mode, this description takes a syllable structure and generates all the possible word forms with that structure. For instance,

```
generator>>CV.V
   baa
   bae
   bai
   bao
   bau
   bea
   bee
   bei
   ...
   buo
   buu
   daa
   dae
   dai
   dao
   ...
```

This result happens to be the very same thing a program called a "blank word list generator" would generate. Special-purpose programs of this nature have been used in the past by linguists working on dictionaries. A native speaker can review the output from such a program to point out meaningful roots that the linguist may not have discovered yet. Another use of such output is to test the correctness of the phonotactic description; if the list contains unpronounceable forms, stricter constraints are needed in the description.

B.2 Parsing with a minimum lexicon

Some of the methods used in implementing a phonotactic analyzer can be employed to implement a minimum lexicon morphological parser. The lexicon used by such a parser has a full inventory of the affixes of the language, but has no entries for the roots. Instead, it uses a phonotactic description to recognize the part of a word that is the probable root. Such a parser has the advantage over a typical parser that it should be able to handle any word of the language; it will not fail when given a word with a root that has not yet been entered into the lexicon. This is offset by the disadvantage that there are often multiple parses, most of which would be constrained away if the class of the root were known.

A sample implementation of a minimum lexicon parser for the To'aba'ita language of the Solomon Islands is given in the MINLEX sub-directory on the PC-KIMMO release diskette. The upper and lower levels are the same as for a conventional morphological analyzer. The rules component gives a complete phonological description as normal. The difference lies in the lexicon. It includes normal lexical entries for all of the affixes in the language, but has no entries for the open-ended root classes. Instead, the lexicon encodes the phonotactic structure of a root in terms of allowed patterns of consonants and vowels.

Since the upper level is underlying phonemes in this application (rather than C and V), the coding of phonotactics is done a bit differently. The vowel and consonant sublexicons list all of the phonemes in that class as the "morphemes" of the class. In To'aba'ita, a root must have at least two syllables. Note in the lexicon that this constraint is encoded by having two consonant classes and two vowel classes with identical members, but with different continuations. The first vowel class continues to the second consonant class which continues to the second vowel class; this insures that a root has two vowels. The second vowel class then continues to the suffix classes or back to the second consonant class, which thus allows roots of two or more syllables.

The following sample run demonstrates the output of the minimum lexicon parser. It also exercises the three phonological processes coded in the rules component of the description:

```
recognizer>>suila
  suli+na      [ Root+3sg.POSS ]
  suli+na      [ Root+ORD ]
  suila      [ Root ]

recognizer>>memela
  RE+mela      [ REDUP+Root ]
  memela      [ Root ]
```

The parser recognizes *suila* as a root in itself, or as the root *suli* plus the third person singular possessive suffix or the ordinal-forming suffix. (A full lexicon would be able disambiguate between the latter two depending on whether the root were a noun or a number.) This form illustrates the elision of *l* between *u* and a high vowel, with the compensatory assimilation of the *n* of the suffix. The second form illustrates the recognition of the initial syllable as being a possible reduplication.

B.3 Simulating historical sound change

It is not particularly surprising that the two-level processor could be applied to simulating historical sound change. Indeed, synchronic morphophonemic alternations often reflect historical sound changes. In this application, the upper level represents the phonemes of the parent language. The lower level represents the phonemes of the daughter language. The default correspondences in the rules file represent the regular reflexes of the protophonemes. Rules are used to encode the context-sensitive sound changes.

A sample implementation of a sound change simulator is given in the PROTO subdirectory on the PC-KIMMO release diskette. This example, too, is drawn from the Solomon Islands; the daughter language is 'Are'are from the south tip of Malaita and the parent language is Proto-Cristobal-Malaitan. One fact about 'Are'are that the simulator encodes is the fact that it has undergone the merger of Proto-Cristobal-Malaitan *r*, *l*, and *th* to *r*.

The following sample runs show the effect of the simulator. In the generator mode, it applies the sound changes to a protoform to generate all the possible daughter forms that it could change into. For instance,

```
generator>>*thathu
  raru

generator>>*ralu
  raru
```

In the recognizer mode, it takes a daughter form and runs all the sound changes in reverse to produce all of the possible protoforms from which it could have descended. For instance,

```
recognizer>>raru
  *lalu
  *laru
  *lathu
  *ralu
  *raru
  *rathu
  *thalu
  *tharu
  *thathu
```

B.4 Solving a logic problem

The final application shows how the two-level processor can be used to solve a logic problem. The problem is of the variety in which a single set of people is independently identified by two sets of labels and enough clues are given to pair the labels.

Consider, for instance, the following example,[1] in which there are four people referred to by four names and four occupations. The task is to link each name with the proper occupation.

> Boronoff, Pavlow, Revitsky, and Sukarek are four talented creative artists, one a dancer, one a painter, one a singer, and one a writer (though not necessarily respectively).
>
> 1. Boronoff and Revitsky were in the audience the night the singer made his debut on the concert stage.
> 2. Both Pavlow and the writer have sat for portraits by the painter.

---

[1]From *101 Puzzles in Thought and Logic,* by C. R. Wylie, Jr., New York: Dover Publications, 1957, page 2.

3. The writer, whose biography of Sukarek was a best-seller, is planning to write a biography of Boronoff.

4. Boronoff has never heard of Revitsky.

What is each man's artistic field?

In programming this problem for the two-level processor, the upper level represents the names and the lower level represents the occupations. The rules file encodes the facts about the cooccurrence of names with occupations that the clues give us; these amount to constraints on the relationships between symbols in the two levels.

The two-level implementation of this logic problem is given in the LOGIC subdirectory on the PC-KIMMO release diskette. The rules file in that sample does essentially four things. First, it declares the alphabet of symbols used to represent the entities in the problem. The four capital letters *B, P, R,* and *S* are the first letters of the four names and are used as the upper level alphabet; the four lowercase letters *d, p, s,* and *w* are the first letters of the four occupations and are used as the lower level alphabet.

ALPHABET   B P R S d p s w

Second, an initial rule must declare all the possible associations of names with occupations; that is,

```
"1 All possible combinations" 1 16
   |B  B  B  B  P  P  P  P  R  R  R  R  S  S  S  S
   |d  p  s  w  d  p  s  w  d  p  s  w  d  p  s  w
  1:|1  1  1  1  1  1  1  1  1  1  1  1  1  1  1  1
```

Third, there are rules which express the constraints given in the clues of the problem. For instance, the first clue tells us that neither Boronoff nor Revitsky is the singer. This translates into the following (trivial) rule:

```
"2 B:s /⇐ ___ , R:s /⇐ ___ " 1 3
   |B  R  @
   |s  s  @
  1:|0  0  1
```

The second and third clues add constraints which are coded in similar rules. Considering the fourth clue with the second tells us that if Boronoff is the painter then Revitsky can't be the writer. (We already know from clue three that the reverse situation in which Boronoff would be the writer is not possible.) This constraint is coded in the following rule:

"5 B:p $\Longleftarrow$ ___@* R:w, R:w $\Longleftarrow$ ___@* B:p" 3 3

	B R @		
	p w @		
1:	2	3	1
2:	2	0	2
3:	0	3	3

Fourth, there are eight rules (one for each name and occupation) to encode the implicit constraints that there can only be one instance of each name and of each profession in any given solution. For instance,

"6 There can be only one B" 2 2

	B @	
	@ @	
1:	2	1
2:	0	2

Finally, if the problem solver is to be run in the recognizer mode, a lexicon file is needed as well. The needed lexicon has only one class which sanctions the occurrence of the four upper level symbols in any order; that is,

ALTERNATION INITIAL	INITIAL	
LEXICON INITIAL		
B	INITIAL	""
P	INITIAL	""
R	INITIAL	""
S	INITIAL	""
0	#	""
END		

When this statement of the facts of the problem is run in the generator mode, it takes a string of four name symbols (in any order) and produces the corresponding string of occupation symbols. In the recognizer mode it does the reverse. (If you want to check your answer, go to the LOGIC subdirectory of the PC-KIMMO release diskette and run ..*pckimmo -t logic*.) Though this application has little more than curiosity value, it does serve to demonstrate that the two-level processor can be applied to a wide variety of problems that involve the mapping of elements between two levels of representation.

C

USING THE PC-KIMMO FUNCTIONS IN A C PROGRAM

by Stephen R. McConnel

The functions used by the PC-KIMMO program to implement the two-level recognizer and generator are written in the C programming language. They have been written in such a way as to facilitate their reuse in other programs. This appendix describes how this is done by first explaining the calling protocols for each of the functions and then illustrating their use in two sample programs. The discussion assumes that the reader is familiar with the C language.

C.1 An overview of the PC-KIMMO function library

The PC-KIMMO function library is made available in source code form. The library consists of two data structures and five functions that are packaged in six source code files. The files and a summary of their contents are shown in figure C.1. The following sections discuss each of the data structures and functions in turn.

Figure C.1 Contents of the PC-KIMMO function library

file	*contents*
pckimmo.h	LANGUAGE and RESULT data structures
rules.c	*load_rules* function
lexicon.c	*load_lexicons* function
generate.c	*generator* function
recogniz.c	*recognizer* function
pckfuncs.c	*free_result* function and other utility functions

C.2 The LANGUAGE data structure

The LANGUAGE structure, defined in figure C.2, stores the language data provided by the rules file (as well as the data provided by the lexicon file for word recognition). In general, the application program must provide storage for at least one copy of this structure. Its internal detail need not concern us since the *load_rules*, *generator*, and *recognizer* functions do all the work of storing and using the information.

C.3 The RESULT data structure

The RESULT structure, defined in figure C.3, is used to build a linked list of results from the *generator* and *recognizer* functions. Generally, the only fields relevant to the *generator* function are the *link* and *str* fields. The recognizer function uses the *feat* field as well. The *okay* field is provided for complex functions such as the *file compare* commands of PC-KIMMO.

Figure C.2 The LANGUAGE data structure

```
typedef struct
    {
    /*
     *  data loaded (or derived) from the rules file
     */
    unsigned char *alphabet;      /* alphabet */
    unsigned char null;           /* null character */
    unsigned char any;            /* wild card character */
    unsigned char boundary;       /* word boundary character */
    SUBSET *subsets;              /* alphabet subsets */
    int numsubsets;               /* number of alphabet subsets */
    RULE *automata;               /* array of automata (RULEs) */
    int num_rules;                /* number of rules in automata */
    unsigned char *lex_pair;      /* lex half of feasible pairs */
    unsigned char *surf_pair;     /* surface half of feasible pairs */
    int num_pairs;                /* number of feasible pairs */
    /*
     *  data loaded from the lexicon file
     */
    ALTERNATION *alterns;         /* array of alternations */
    int num_alterns;              /* number of alternations */
    LEXICON *lex_sections;        /* array of lexicon sections */
    LEXICON *initial_lex;         /* first ("INITIAL") section */
    int num_lex_sections;         /* number of lexicon sections */
    } LANGUAGE;
```

Figure C.3 The RESULT data structure

```
typedef struct s_result
    {
    struct s_result *link;
    unsigned char *str;      /* primary result string */
    unsigned char *feat;     /* feature string for result */
    short okay;              /* flag that this result is okay */
    } RESULT;
```

The following lines of C code illustrate the use of the RESULT structure in connection with the *generator* function.

```
RESULT *resp, *rp, *generator();
...
resp = generator( word, &Lang, 0, 0, (FILE *)NULL);
if (resp == (RESULT *)NULL) printf("Invalid lexical form\n");
else
    {                                       /* write the results */
    for ( rp = resp ; rp ; rp = rp->link )
        printf("    %s\n", resp->str);
    free_result(resp);
    }
```

Note the idiomatic C code for traversing a linked list of structures.

C.4 The *load_rules* function

The *load_rules* function handles the job of loading the two-level rules file; its calling protocol is given in figure C.4. The function converts the rules file written by the user (in the format described in sections 3.4 and 7.7.1) into the LANGUAGE data structure stored in memory.

Figure C.4 Calling protocol for the *load_rules* function

```
int load_rules(rulefile, lang, comment)
unsigned char *rulefile;      /* name of a PC-KIMMO rules file */
LANGUAGE *lang;               /* pointer to a LANGUAGE structure */
unsigned char comment;        /* comment character in rules file */
```

The function is controlled entirely by its three arguments. There are no global variables hidden behind the scenes to influence its behavior. The three arguments of the *load_rules* function are defined as follows:

rulefile is the address of a NUL-terminated array of characters (a *string* in C terminology) that provides the function with the name of the input rules file. On computers with hierarchical file systems, this name may include a directory path as well as the name of the file itself.

lang is the address of a LANGUAGE structure that will store the data loaded from the input rules file.

comment is the character value used in the input rules file to initiate comments.

The *load_rules* function returns a value of zero (0) if it succeeds, or a value of negative one (-1) if there is an error in the input rules file. In the case of an error, the function prints on the screen one of the error messages listed in section 7.10 before returning.

C.5   The *load_lexicons* function

The *load_lexicons* function handles the job of loading the lexicon file; its calling protocol is given in figure C.5. The function converts the lexicon file written by the user (in the format described in sections 4.3 and 7.7.2) into the LANGUAGE data structure stored in memory.

Figure C.5 Calling protocol for the *load_lexicons* function

```
int load_lexicons(lexiconfile,lang,comment)
unsigned char *lexiconfile;    /* name of the lexicon file */
LANGUAGE *lang;                /* pointer to a LANGUAGE data */
unsigned char comment;         /* comment character for input file */
```

The function is controlled entirely by its three arguments. There are no global variables hidden behind the scenes to influence its behavior. The three arguments of the *load_lexicons* function are defined as follows:

lexiconfile is the address of a NUL-terminated array of characters (a *string* in C terminology) that provides the function with the name of the input lexicon file. On computers with hierarchical file systems, this name may include a directory path as well as the name of the file itself.

lang is the address of a LANGUAGE structure that stores the data loaded from the input lexicon file.

comment is the character value used in the input lexicon file to initiate comments.

The *load_lexicons* function returns a value of zero (0) if it succeeds, or a value of negative one (-1) if there is an error in the input lexicon file. In the case of an error, the function prints on the screen one of the error messages listed in section 7.10 before returning.

C.6   The *generator* function

The calling protocol for the *generator* function is defined in figure C.6. It applies the supplied rules to a single lexical form to produce a linked list of surface forms stored in RESULT structures.

Figure C.6 Calling protocol for the *generator* function

```
RESULT *generator(lexform,lang,limit,trace,logfp)
unsigned char *lexform;  /* pointer to lexical form string */
LANGUAGE *lang;          /* data for the current language */
int limit;               /* flag for limit on/off */
int trace;               /* flag for tracing on/off */
FILE *logfp;             /* log FILE pointer */
```

The function is controlled entirely by its five arguments. There are no global variables hidden behind the scenes to influence its behavior. The five arguments of the *generator* function are defined as follows:

lexform is the address of a NUL-terminated array of characters (a *string* in C terminology) that provides the function with the lexical form to generate from. Since it is an array of unsigned characters, the lexical form may contain 8-bit values such as those in the IBM PC extended character set.

lang is the address of a LANGUAGE structure that stores the data loaded from the input rules file.

limit is a flag controlling whether or not the *generator* function stops after the first successful generation. If *limit* is zero, then the *generator* function produces all possible results. Otherwise it produces only one.

trace is a flag controlling whether or not the *generator* produces the tracing output described in section 7.8.1. If *trace* is zero, then the *generator* function works silently. Otherwise, it outputs a step-by-step description, with the amount of detail depending on the exact value of *trace* as described in section 7.5.6.

logfp is a FILE pointer as defined for the C standard I/O library of functions. If *logfp* is NULL, then no logging is performed. Otherwise, the *generator* function writes a copy of all output to the indicated log file as well as to the screen.

The *generator* function returns a pointer to a linked list of RESULT structures, or NULL if no results could be generated from the input lexical form.

C.7 The *recognizer* function

The calling protocol for the *recognizer* function is defined in figure C.7. It applies the supplied rules and lexicon to a single surface form to produce a linked list of surface forms and glosses stored in RESULT structures.

Figure C.7 Calling protocol for the *recognizer* function

```
RESULT *recognizer(surf_form,lang,limit,trace,logfp)
unsigned char *surf_form;      /* pointer to surface form */
LANGUAGE *lang;                /* data for the current language */
int limit;                     /* flag for limit on/off */
int trace;                     /* flag for tracing on/off */
FILE *logfp;                   /* log FILE pointer */
```

The function is controlled entirely by its five arguments. There are no global variables hidden behind the scenes to influence its behavior. The five arguments of the *recognizer* function are defined as follows:

surf_form is the address of a NUL-terminated array of characters (a *string* in C terminology) that provides the function with the surface form to analyze. Since it is an array of unsigned characters, the surface form may contain 8-bit values such as those in the IBM PC extended character set.

lang is the address of a LANGUAGE structure that stores the data loaded from the input rules and lexicon files.

limit is a flag controlling whether or not the *recognizer* function stops after the first successful generation. If *limit* is zero, then the *recognizer* function produces all possible results. Otherwise it produces only one.

trace is a flag controlling whether or not the *recognizer* produces the tracing output described in section 7.8.2. If *trace* is zero, then the *recognizer* function works silently. Otherwise, it outputs a step-by-step description, with the amount of detail depending on the exact value of *trace* as described in section 7.5.6.

logfp is a FILE pointer as defined for the C standard I/O library of functions. If *logfp* is NULL, then no logging is performed. Otherwise, the *recognizer* function writes a copy of all output to the indicated log file as well as to the screen.

The *recognizer* function returns a pointer to a linked list of RESULT structures, or NULL if no results could be generated from the input lexical form.

C.8 The *free_result* function

The calling protocol for the *free_result* function is defined in figure C.8. It releases the memory allocated to the linked list of RESULT structures pointed to by its argument. Dynamic memory allocation is used by the *generator* and *recognizer* functions because the maximum number of different results cannot be predicted. The *free_result* function does not return a value. (It would be called a procedure, rather than a function, in FORTRAN terminology.)

Figure C.8 Calling protocol for the *free_result* function

```
void free_result(resp)
RESULT *resp;    /* pointer to linked list of RESULTs */
```

C.9 Two sample programs

The program shown in figure C.9 illustrates the use of the *generator* function. It has been simplified to a bare minimum. The user interface is also very simple. The user types the name of the rules file after the name of the program in response to the operating system command prompt. After the rules are loaded, the program reads a lexical form typed at the keyboard and applies the rules to produce one or more surface forms; this interaction can be repeated until the user signals the end of the input (usually with *Ctrl-Z* on MS-DOS or *Ctrl-D* on UNIX). For example,

```
A>kgen english.rul
Rules being loaded from english.rul
'ski+s
  skis
'fly+s
  flies
'baby+s
  babies
^Z
A>
```

The program shown in figure C.10 illustrates the use of the *recognizer* function. It also is very simple. The user interface is the same as in the preceding example except that the user types both the name of the rules file and the name of the lexicon file in the command line. After the rules and the lexicon are loaded, the program reads a surface form typed at the keyboard, searches the lexicon, and applies the rules to produce one or more lexical forms; this interaction can be repeated until the user signals the end of the input (usually with *Ctrl-Z* on MS-DOS or *Ctrl-D* on UNIX). For example,

```
A>krec english.rul
Rules being loaded from english.rul
Lexicon being loaded from english.lex
skis
  'ski+s     [ N(ski)+PL ]
  'ski+s     [ V(ski)+3sg.PRES ]
flies
  'fly+s     [ N(fly)+PL ]
  'fly+s     [ V(fly)+3sg.PRES ]
babies
  form not recognized
^Z
A>
```

Figure C.9 Simple word generation program

```c
#include <stdio.h>
#include "pckimmo.h"
extern RESULT *generator();
extern char *strchr();
int main(argc,argv)
int argc;                /* number of command line arguments */
char *argv[];            /* pointer to array of command arguments */
{
LANGUAGE Lang;           /* structure which holds the language data */
RESULT *resp;            /* pointer to linked list of results */
RESULT *rp;              /* pointer to traverse list of results */
char word[400];          /* 400 should be more than ample... */
char *p;
/*
 * load the rules file (given by the command line argument)
 * first check for a plausible number of command arguments
 */
if (argc != 2)
    {
    fprintf(stderr, "usage: %s rulefile <input >output\n", argv[0]);
    exit(1);
    }
if (load_rules(argv[1], &Lang, ';') < 0)
    exit(1);
/*
 * process the data, reading from stdin and writing to stdout
 */
while (gets(word) != (char *)NULL)
    {
    if (!isatty(fileno(stdin)))
        puts(word);
    if ((p = strchr(word,' ')) != (char *)NULL)
        *p = '\0';      /* ignore anything following a space */
    resp = generator( word, &Lang, 0, 0, (FILE *)NULL);
    if (resp == (RESULT *)NULL)
        printf("    invalid lexical form\n");
    else
        {                                /* write the results */
        for ( rp = resp ; rp ; rp = rp->link )
            printf("    %s\n", rp->str);
        free_result(resp);
        }
    }
return(0);       /* signal successful completion of the program */
}
```

Figure C.10 Simple word recognition program

```
#include <stdio.h>
#include "pckimmo.h"
extern RESULT *recognizer();
int main(argc,argv)
int argc;
char *argv[];
{
LANGUAGE Lang;
RESULT *resp;
RESULT *rp;
char word[400];           /* 400 should be more than ample... */
/*
 *  load the rules file and lexicon file
 *  first check for a plausible number of command line arguments
 */
if (argc != 3)
    {
    fprintf(stderr, "usage: %s rulefile lexfile <input >output\n",
              argv[0] );
    exit(1);
    }
if (load_rules(argv[1], &Lang, ';') < 0)
    exit(1);
if (load_lexicons(argv[2], &Lang, ';') < 0)
    exit(1);
/*
 *  process the data, reading from stdin and writing to stdout
 */
while (gets(word) != (char *)NULL)
    {
    if (!isatty(fileno(stdin)))
        puts(word);
    resp = recognizer( word, &Lang, 0, 0, (FILE *)NULL);
    if (resp == (RESULT *)NULL)
        printf("    form not recognized\n");
    else
        {
        for ( rp = resp ; rp ; rp = rp->link )
            printf("    %s    %s\n", rp->str, rp->feat );
        free_result(resp);
        }
    }
return(0);
}
```

REFERENCES

Aho, Alfred V., and Jeffrey D. Ullman. 1972. *The theory of parsing, translation, and compiling.* Englewood Cliffs, NJ: Prentice-Hall.

Alam, Yukiko Sasaki. 1983. A two-level morphological analysis of Japanese. *Texas Linguistic Forum* 22:229–252.

Anderson, Stephen R. 1988. Morphology as a parsing problem. In Wallace 1988, 4–21.

Barton, G. Edward, Robert C. Berwick, and Eric Sven Ristad. 1987. *Computational complexity and natural language.* Cambridge, MA: The MIT Press. (Especially chapter 5, "The complexity of two-level morphology," and chapter 6, "Constraint propagation in KIMMO systems.")

Bear, John. 1986. A morphological recognizer with syntactic and phonological rules. In *Proceedings of Coling '86*, 272–276. Association for Computational Linguistics.

———. 1988. Morphology with two-level rules and negative rule features. In *Proceedings of Coling '88*, 28–31. Association for Computational Linguistics.

Beesley, Kenneth R. 1989. Computer analysis of Arabic morphology: a two-level approach with detours. Cannot determine source.

Blåberg, Olli. 1985. A two-level description of Swedish. In Karlsson 1985, 43–62.

Black, Alan W., Graeme D. Ritchie, Stephen G. Pulman, and Graham J. Russell. 1987. Formalisms for morphographemic description. In *ACL Proceedings, Third European Conference*, 11–18. Association for Computational Linguistics.

Boisen, Sean. 1988. Pro-KIMMO: a Prolog implementation of two-level morphology. In Wallace 1988, 31–53.

Carden, Guy. 1983. The non-finite-state-ness of the word formation component. *Linguistic Inquiry* 14:537–541.

Carson, Julie. 1988. Unification and transduction in computational phonology. In *Proceedings of Coling '88*, 106–111. Association for Computational Linguistics.

Chomsky, Noam. 1957. *Syntactic structures.* The Hague: Mouton.

———. 1964. *Current issues in linguistic theory.* The Hague: Mouton.

———. 1965. On certain formal properties of grammars. In R. D. Luce, R. R. Bush, and E. Galanter, eds., *Readings in mathematical psychology*, Vol. II, 323–418. New York: John Wiley and Sons. First published in 1959.

—, and Morris Halle. 1968. *The sound pattern of English*. New York: Harper and Row.

Church, Kenneth W. 1983. A finite-state parser for use in speech recognition. In *ACL Proceedings, 21st Annual Meeting*, 91–97. Association for Computational Linguistics.

Dalrymple, Mary, R. Kaplan, L. Karttunen, M. Kay, A. Kornai, K. Koskenniemi, S. Shaio, and M. Wescoat. 1987. *DKIMMO/TWOL: a development environment for morphological analysis*. Stanford, CA: Xerox Palo Alto Research Center and Center for the Study of Language and Information.

Dell, François. 1980. *Generative phonology*. Cambridge University Press.

Gajek, O., H. Beck, D. Elder, and G. Whitmore. 1983. KIMMO: LISP implementation. *Texas Linguistic Forum* 22:187–202.

Gazdar, Gerald. 1985. Finite state morphology: a review of Koskenniemi (1983). Technical Report No. CSLI-85-32, Center for the Study of Language and Information. Also in *Linguistics* 23:597–607.

—, and Christopher Mellish. 1989. Finite-state techniques. In *Natural language processing in LISP: an introduction to computational linguistics*, chapter 2, 21–62. Reading, MA: Addison-Wesley Publishing Company.

—, and Geoffrey K. Pullum. 1985. Computationally relevant properties of natural languages and their grammars. *New Generation Computing* 3:273–306.

Gibbon, Dafydd. 1987. Finite state processing of tone systems. In *ACL Proceedings, Third European Conference*, 291–297. Association for Computational Linguistics.

Goldsmith, John. 1976. *Autosegmental phonology*. Bloomington, IN: Indiana University Linguistics Club. Also published by Garland Press, New York, 1979.

Görz, Günther, and Dietrich Paulus. 1988. A finite state approach to german verb morphology. In *Proceedings of Coling '88*, 212–215. Association for Computational Linguistics.

Grimes, Joseph E. 1983. *Affix positions and cooccurrences: the PARADIGM program*. Summer Institute of Linguistics Publications in Linguistics No. 69. Dallas: Summer Institute of Linguistics and University of Texas at Arlington.

Halle, Morris, and G. N. Clements. 1983. *Problem book in phonology*. Cambridge, MA: The MIT Press.

258   References

Hankamer, Jorge. 1986. Finite state morphology and left to right phonology. In Mary Dalrymple, Jeffrey Goldberg, Kristin Hanson, Michael Inman, Chris Pinon, and Stephen Wechsler, eds., *Proceedings of the Fifth West Coast Conference on Formal Linguistics*, 29–34, Stanford, CA. Stanford Linguistics Association, Stanford University.

Hooper, Joan. 1976. *An introduction to natural generative phonology.* New York: Academic Press.

Hopcroft, John E., and Jeffrey D. Ullman. 1979. *Introduction to automata theory, languages, and computation.* Reading, MA: Addison-Wesley Publishing Company.

Jäppinen, H., A. Lehtola, E. Nelimarkka, J. Niemisto, and M. Ylilammi, eds. 1986a. *Morphological analysis of Finnish word forms.* Publications of the Kielikone project, series A, report No. 1.

Jäppinen, H., A. Lehtola, E. Nelimarkka, and M. Ylilammi. 1986b. Knowledge engineering approach to morphological analysis. In Jäppinen and others 1986a.

Jäppinen, H., and M. Ylilammi. 1986. Associative model of morphological analysis: an empirical inquiry. In Jäppinen and others 1986a. Also in *Computational Linguistics* 12(4):257–272.

Johnson, C. Douglas. 1972. *Formal aspects of phonological description.* The Hague: Mouton.

Kaplan, Ronald M., and Martin Kay. 1981. Phonological rules and finite state transducers. Paper presented at the 1981 Winter meeting of the ACL/LSA.

Karlsson, Fred, ed. 1985. *Computational morphosyntax: a report on research 1981–1984.* Publication No. 13. Helsinki: University of Helsinki Department of General Linguistics.

Karlsson, Fred, and Kimmo Koskenniemi. 1985. A process model of morphology and lexicon. *Folia Linguistica* 14:207–231.

Karttunen, Lauri. 1983. KIMMO: a general morphological processor. *Texas Linguistic Forum* 22:163–186.

____, K. Koskenniemi, and R. Kaplan. 1987. *A compiler for two-level phonological rules.* Stanford, CA: Xerox Palo Alto Research Center and Center for the Study of Language and Information.

____, and K. Wittenburg. 1983. A two-level morphological analysis of English. *Texas Linguistic Forum* 22:217–228.

Kasper, Robert, and David Weber. 1986a. *Programmer's reference manual for the C Quechua adaptation program.* Occasional Publications in Academic Computing No. 9. Dallas: Summer Institute of Linguistics.

——— and ———. 1986b. *User's reference manual for the C Quechua adaptation program.* Occasional Publications in Academic Computing No. 8. Dallas: Summer Institute of Linguistics.

Kataja, L., and K. Koskenniemi. 1988. Finite-state description of Semitic morphology: a case study of ancient Akkadian. In *Proceedings of Coling '88,* 313–15. Association for Computational Linguistics.

Kay, Martin. 1983. When meta-rules are not meta-rules. In Karen Sparck Jones and Yorick Wilks, eds., *Automatic natural language parsing,* 94–116. Chichester: Ellis Horwood Ltd. See pages 100–104.

———. 1987. Nonconcatenative finite-state morphology. In *ACL Proceedings, Third European Conference,* 2–10. Association for Computational Linguistics.

Khan, Robert. 1983. A two-level morphological analysis of Rumanian. *Texas Linguistic Forum* 22:253–270.

Khan, Robert, Jocelyn S. Liu, Tatsuo Ito, and Kelly Shuldberg. 1983. KIMMO user's manual. *Texas Linguistic Forum* 22:203–215.

Koskenniemi, Kimmo. 1983a. *Two-level morphology: a general computational model for word-form recognition and production.* Publication No. 11. Helsinki: University of Helsinki Department of General Linguistics.

———. 1983b. Two-level morphology for morphological analysis. In *IJCAI-83,* 683–685. International Joint Conference on Artificial Intelligence.

———. 1984. A general computational model for word-form recognition and production. In *Proceedings of Coling '84,* 178–181. Association for Computational Linguistics.

———. 1985a. An application of the two-level model to Finnish. In Karlsson 1985, 19–42.

———. 1985b. A general two-level computational model for word-form recognition and production. In Karlsson 1985, 1–18.

———, and Kenneth W. Church. 1988. Complexity, two-level morphology and Finnish. In *Proceedings of Coling '88,* 335–340. Association for Computational Linguistics.

Lamb, Sidney M. 1964. On alternation, transformation, realization, and stratification. In *Report of the Fifteenth Annual Round Table Meeting,*

Monograph Series on Languages and Linguistics No. 17, 105–122. Washington, D.C.: Georgetown University Press.

Langendoen, D. Terence. 1975. Finite-state parsing of phrase-structure languages and the status of readjustment rules in the grammar. *Linguistic Inquiry* 6:533–554.

———. 1981. The generative capacity of word-formation components. *Linguistic Inquiry* 12:320–322.

Lindstedt, Jouko. 1984. A two-level description of Old Church Slavonic morphology. *Scando-Slavica* 30:165–189.

Lun, S. 1983. A two-level morphological analysis of French. *Texas Linguistic Forum* 22:271–278.

Merrifield, William, Constance Naish, Calvin Rensch, and Gillian Story. 1987. *Laboratory manual.* Dallas: Summer Institute of Linguistics. 6th edition.

Partee, Barbara, Alice ter Meulen, and Robert Wall. 1987. *Mathematical methods in linguistics.* Kluwer Academic.

Reape, Mike, and Henry S. Thompson. 1988. Parallel intersection and serial composition of finite state transducers. In *Proceedings of Coling '88*, 535–539. Association for Computational Linguistics.

Russell, Graham J., Stephen G. Pulman, Graeme D. Ritchie, and Alan W. Black. 1986. A dictionary and morphological analyser for English. In *Proceedings of Coling '86*, 277–279. Association for Computational Linguistics.

Schane, Sanford A. 1973. *Generative phonology.* Englewood Cliffs, NJ: Prentice-Hall, Inc.

Shieber, Stuart M. 1986. *An introduction to unification-based approaches to grammar.* CSLI Lecture Notes No. 4. Stanford, CA: Center for the Study of Language and Information.

Simons, Gary F. 1988. Studying morphophonemic alternation in annotated text, parts one and two. *Notes on Linguistics* 41:41–46; 42:27–38.

———. 1989. A tool for exploring morphology. *Notes on Linguistics* 44:51–59.

Wallace, Karen, ed. 1988. *Morphology as a computational problem.* UCLA Occasional Paper #7: Working Papers in Morphology. Department of Linguistics, University of California, Los Angeles.

Weber, David J., H. Andrew Black, and Stephen R. McConnel. 1988. *AMPLE: a tool for exploring morphology.* Occasional Publications in Academic Computing No. 12. Dallas: Summer Institute of Linguistics.

——, ——, ——, and Alan Buseman. 1990. *STAMP: a tool for dialect adaptation.* Occasional Publications in Academic Computing No. 15. Dallas: Summer Institute of Linguistics.

——, and William Mann. 1979. *Prospects for computer assisted dialect adaptation. Notes on Linguistics* Special Publication No. 1. Dallas: Summer Institute of Linguistics. Abridged in *American Journal of Computational Linguistics* 7:165–177 (1981).

... ...
... ...
... ...

INDEX

logic problem, 4, 239

M

Mann, William, 7, 164
McConnel, Stephen R., 7, 164
memory, 16, 164, 204, 211
Mende, 140
Merrifield, William, 131
metathesis, 4, 11, 154
modes
    batch processing, 3
    file comparison, 22–26, 119,
      120, 171, 173
    immediate, 22, 119
morpheme, 2, 13, 19, 104, 105,
    112, 185
    boundary, *see* boundary
    zero, 112
morphology, 2
    agglutinative, 5
    computational, 5, 6, 13
    finite state, 11
    nonconcatenative, 4, 11, 152–
    162
morphophonemic alternation, 2, 5
morphophonemics, 118
morphotactics, *see* constraints, mor-
    photactic
MS-DOS, 16, 164

N

nasalization, 4, 135–140
    spreading, 139
natural language processing, 2, 4–
    7, 10, 14
natural phonology, 7
NDOSEDIT, 167
new, 169
nonconcatenative processes, 4, 11,
    152–162
NONE message, 118, 120
NULL keyword, 94, 180, 181

NULL symbol, 31, 49, 53, 73, 96,
    112, 147, 181, 189, 194,
    196, 214

O

obligatory rules, 33, 88, 90, 135
OK message, 173, 174
operating system command, 175
operating systems
    A/UX, 164
    MS-DOS, 16, 164
    PC-DOS, 16, 164
    UNIX, 164
operators
    logical, 32, 33, 46, 47
    rule, 29, 32
    ⇐, 29, 34
    ⇐, 29, 33, 46
    ⇔, 29, 33
    ⇒, 29, 32, 39, 85
    meaning, 29
optional rules, 22, 33, 88
ordered rules, 6, 8, 38, 88, 144
orthography, 2, 16, 214
overgeneration, 89–91, 119, 138,
    155
overrecognition, 89, 119
overspecification, 38, 46, 84, 138

P

pairs comparison file, 22, 25, 187
palatalization, 32, 75, 87, 98
parallel rules, *see* rules, parallel
parentheses, 34, 37, 80
parsing, syntactic, 13
Partee, Barbara, 41
PATH variable, 17, 165
PC-DOS, 16, 164
PC-KIMMO, 2, 5, 7
    calling from user's program, 4
    functional components, 7, 164
    getting help, 3, 18, 167–168
    halting, 176

PC-KIMMO (*continued*)
  implementation, 164
  installing, 16–17, 165–166
  interactive shell, 3, 4, 7, 164
  main components, 3
  portability, 164
  release diskette, 16, 99, 110,
      130, 162, 164, 165, 215,
      234, 237, 238, 240
  source code, 4, 7, 14, 164
  starting, 17–19, 166
    with command line arguments,
      166, 169, 171, 179
  system requirements, 16, 164
  tool vs. theory, 7, 10
  user interface, 3, 7, 164, 166
    command line editor, 167
    echoing to printer, 167
    interrupting processing, 167
    screen scrolling, 167
period in state table, 42, 120, 183
Peru, 5
Philippines, 73, 147
phoneme, 2
phonology, 2
  autosegmental, 12
  generative, 6, 8–10, 28, 30,
      31, 33, 36, 37, 88, 89, 91,
      144
  natural, 7
  nonlinear, 12
  two-level, 2, 8–9
phonotactic analyzer, 234
phonotactics, *see* constraints, phono-
      tactic
positional analysis, 109, 118
pound sign, *see* BOUNDARY sym-
      bol
procedural, 9
prompt, 19, 22, 173
Proto-Cristobal-Malaitan, 238

Q

Quechua, 5
quit, 176

R

realization conflict, *see* rule con-
      flicts
recognition, 2, 3, 41, 164
recognition comparison file, 22,
      24, 187
recognition file, 188
recognize, 21-22, 119, 173
recognizer, 2, 4, 14, 19, 21–22,
      119, 192
  prompt, 22, 173
recognizing forms, 173–175
recursion, 124, 191, 194
reduplication, 4, 11, 157, 158, 160,
      161
regular expression, 7
regular language, 41
representation
  lexical, 19, 29, 89, 104
  nonlinear, 12
  phonological, 8
  surface, 19, 29
  underlying, 2
RESULT line, 189, 190, 194
result string, 105, 191, 196
rule conflicts, 35, 38, 83, 85–88,
      120
  environment or ⇒, 35, 37, 82,
      85–87
  realization or ⇐, 85, 87–88,
      219, 222
RULE declaration, 182
RULE keyword, 94, 97, 180
rule name, 97, 170, 172, 182
rule operator, *see* operator, rule
rules
  bidirectional, 9, 29
  failure-driven, 45, 46

Summer Institute of Linguistics
Occasional Publications in Academic Computing

1. *SIL Software Catalog,* compiled by Robert A. French. 1984. 66 pp. (Out of print.)

2. *A User's Guide to the Manuscripter (PTP Version),* by Gary F. Simons and R. Craig Woods. (Revised for the Osborne-1 by Raymond G. Gordon, Jr.) 1985. 45 pp.

3. *A Programmer's Guide to the Manuscripter (PTP version),* by Gary F. Simons. 1985. 35 pp.

4. *EZTEXT: Integrated Tools for Text Analysis,* by Bryan L. Harmelink. 1985. 58 pp. (Out of print.)

5. *Word List Analysis in the Field with a Notebook Computer,* by Gary F. Simons. 1985. 43 pp.

6. *A Guide to Using KERMIT: Transferring Files Between Computers,* by Stephen R. McConnel. 1985. 58 pp.

7. *Document Preparation Aids for Non-Major Languages,* by Andy Black, Fred Kuhl, Kathy Kuhl, and David Weber. 1987. 44 pp.

8. *User's Reference Manual for the C Quechua Adaptation Program,* by Robert Kasper and David Weber. 1986. 64 pp.

9. *Programmer's Reference Manual for the C Quechua Adaptation Program,* by Robert Kasper and David Weber. 1986. 74 pp.

10. *The RAP Programming Language,* by Richard A. Strangfeld. 1988. 250 pp.

11. *A Common Subroutine Library for RAP Programmers,* by Kirk H. Parker and Gary F. Simons. 1988. 102 pp.

12. *AMPLE: A Tool for Exploring Morphology,* by David J. Weber, H. Andrew Black, and Stephen R. McConnel. 1988. 252 pp.

13. *WORDSURV: A Program for Analyzing Language Survey Word Lists,* by John S. Wimbish. 1989. 108 pp.

14. *Laptop Publishing for the Field Linguist: an Approach Based on Microsoft Word,* edited by Priscilla M. Kew and Gary F. Simons. 1989. 137 pp.

15. *STAMP: A Tool for Dialect Adaptation,* by David J. Weber, Stepen R. McConnel, H. Andrew Black, and Alan Buseman. 1990. 215 pp.

16. *PC-KIMMO: A Two-level Processor for Morphological Analysis,* by Evan L. Antworth. 1990. 273 pp.

Other computer-related publications of the
Summer Institute of Linguistics

Network Grammars, edited by Joseph E. Grimes. 1975. 198 pp.

Affix Positions and Cooccurrences: the PARADIGM Program, by Joseph E. Grimes. 1983. 90 pp.

Powerful Ideas for Text Processing: an Introduction to Computer Programming with the PTP Language, by Gary F. Simons. 1984. 197 pp.

How to Use IT: a Guide to Interlinear Text Processing, by Gary F. Simons and Larry Versaw. Revised edition, 1988. 372 pp.

For further information or a catalog of all S.I.L. publications write to:

International Academic Bookstore
Summer Institute of Linguistics
7500 W. Camp Wisdom Road
Dallas, TX 75236